Misfortunes of Wealth

by
James Oliver Goldsborough

The Local History Company
publishers of history and heritage

Pittsburgh, Pennsylvania, USA

Published by
The Local History Company
112 North Woodland Road
Pittsburgh, PA 15232
www.TheLocalHistoryCompany.com
info@TheLocalHistoryCompany.com

The name "The Local History Company", "Publishers of History and Heritage", and its logo are trademarks of The Local History Company.

Unless otherwise credited, all photos are from the author's personal collection.
Cover photo and title page photo: *Sucasa In Winter, circa 1947.*

ISBN-13: 978-0-9770429-9-9
ISBN-10: 0-9770429-9-5

Library of Congress Cataloging-in-Publication Data

Goldsborough, James Oliver.
Misfortunes of Wealth / by James Oliver Goldsborough.
    p.   cm.
    Includes bibliographical references and index.
    ISBN-13: 978-0-9770429-9-9 (hardcover : alk. paper)
    ISBN-10: 0-9770429-9-5 (hardcover : alk. paper)
    1. Oliver family. 2. Goldsborough, James Oliver—Family. 3. Industrialists—United States—Biography. 4. Landowners—United States—Biography. 5. Politicians—United States—Biography. 6. Wealth—Social aspects—United States—Case studies. 7. East (U.S.)—Biography. 8. Pittsburgh (Pa.)—Biography. 9. Sewickley (Pa.)—Biography. 10. California—Biography. I. Title.

CS71.O47G65 2009
973.931092—dc22
[B]
                            2008034725
Printed in USA   1.0

Mixed Sources
Product group from well-managed forests and other controlled sources
www.fsc.org Cert no. SW-COC-002283
© 1996 Forest Stewardship Council

CONTENTS

For Mother: *If Proust's mother had loved him. . .*

For B.G. Shields: *The soul of Sewickley*

For Kelly: *Always there*

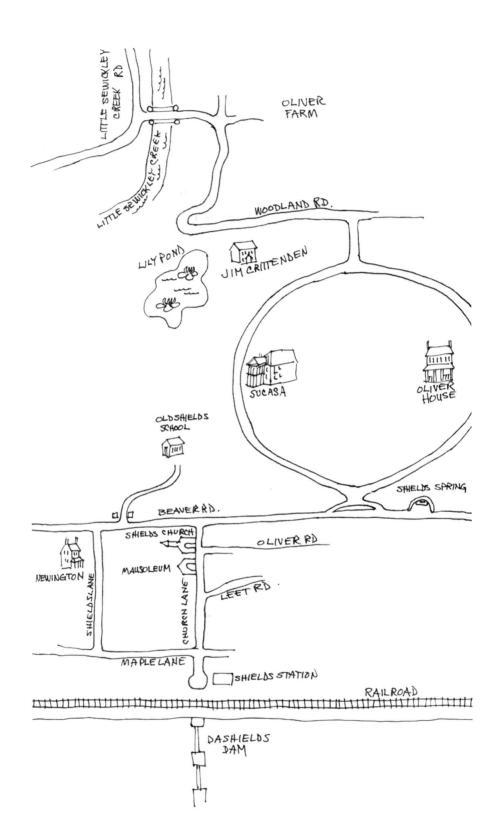

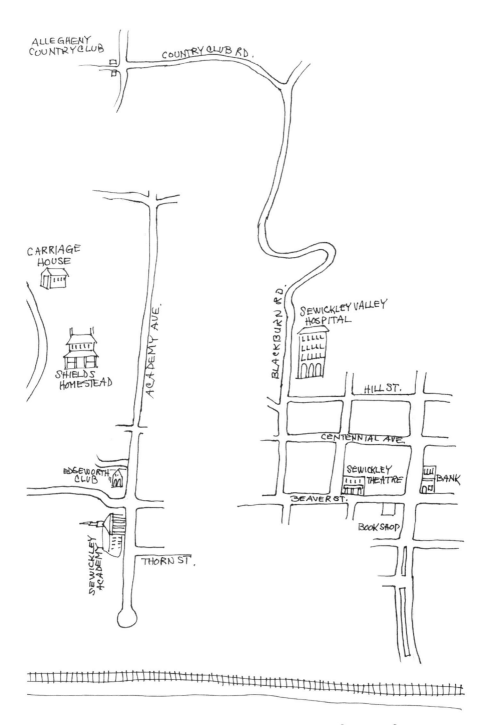

MAP BY RICHARD C. SMITH

Key Members of
the Family Tree

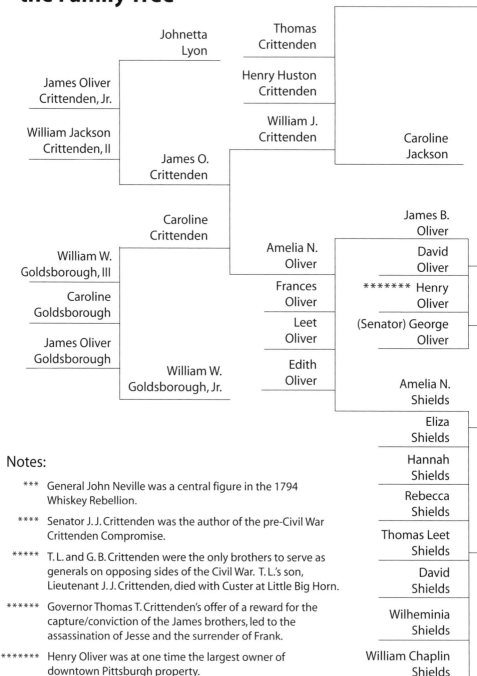

Johnetta Lyon

Thomas Crittenden

James Oliver Crittenden, Jr.

Henry Huston Crittenden

William Jackson Crittenden, II

William J. Crittenden

James O. Crittenden

Caroline Jackson

Caroline Crittenden

James B. Oliver

William W. Goldsborough, III

Amelia N. Oliver

David Oliver

Caroline Goldsborough

Frances Oliver

******* Henry Oliver

Leet Oliver

(Senator) George Oliver

James Oliver Goldsborough

William W. Goldsborough, Jr.

Edith Oliver

Amelia N. Shields

Eliza Shields

Hannah Shields

Rebecca Shields

Thomas Leet Shields

David Shields

Wilheminia Shields

William Chaplin Shields

Notes:

    *** General John Neville was a central figure in the 1794 Whiskey Rebellion.

  **** Senator J. J. Crittenden was the author of the pre-Civil War Crittenden Compromise.

 ***** T. L. and G. B. Crittenden were the only brothers to serve as generals on opposing sides of the Civil War. T. L.'s son, Lieutenant J. J. Crittenden, died with Custer at Little Big Horn.

****** Governor Thomas T. Crittenden's offer of a reward for the capture/conviction of the James brothers, led to the assassination of Jesse and the surrender of Frank.

******* Henry Oliver was at one time the largest owner of downtown Pittsburgh property.

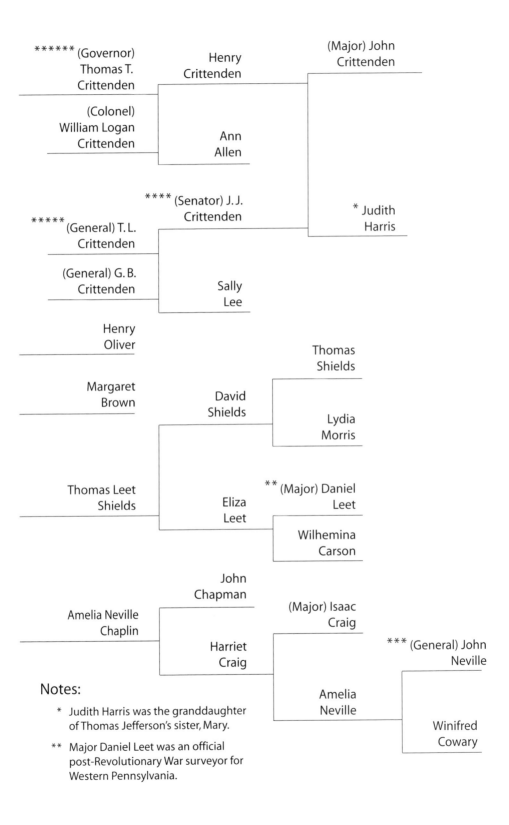

****** (Governor) Thomas T. Crittenden

(Colonel) William Logan Crittenden

Henry Crittenden

Ann Allen

(Major) John Crittenden

**** (Senator) J. J. Crittenden

***** (General) T. L. Crittenden

(General) G. B. Crittenden

Sally Lee

* Judith Harris

Henry Oliver

Margaret Brown

Thomas Leet Shields

David Shields

Eliza Leet

Thomas Shields

Lydia Morris

** (Major) Daniel Leet

Wilhemina Carson

Amelia Neville Chaplin

John Chapman

Harriet Craig

(Major) Isaac Craig

Amelia Neville

*** (General) John Neville

Winifred Cowary

Notes:

* Judith Harris was the granddaughter of Thomas Jefferson's sister, Mary.

** Major Daniel Leet was an official post-Revolutionary War surveyor for Western Pennsylvania.

P R E F A C E

Poverty may be a misfortune to the weaklings who are without courage or ability to overcome it, but it is a blessing to young men of ordinary force of character: it protects them from excesses, withholds unwise pleasures and indulgences, teaches the value of time and of wealth, and the necessity of well doing to better their condition.

Thomas Mellon, *Thomas Mellon and His Times*

With the misfortune of excessive wealth he coped as conscientiously and efficiently as his training and tradition permitted.

Historian Allan Nevins on Andrew Mellon, Thomas' son

Why do people write memoirs?

We know why the rich and famous write them: to set records straight, bear witness, titillate fans, get even, make money, celebrate high and mighty lives. Sometimes such memoirs take on the form of a confession, a genre that follows a time-honored path from Saint Augustine to Jane Fonda, by way of Jean-Jacques Rousseau, Frank Harris and Errol Flynn. The motivations behind such confessions vary from personal redemption to self-promotion to outright scandalization, but the technique is the same: you dramatize, seeking to immortalize, your life by telling all. The main difference between Augustine's *Confessions* and Flynn's *My Wicked, Wicked Ways*, is that Augustine repented his debauchery and found religion; Flynn celebrated his wicked ways. "I intend to live the first half of my life. I don't care about the rest," he wrote. He got his way: He died at fifty of a massive heart attack.

Why would someone less than a celebrity write a memoir? We see it happening more and more today, to the point that memoirs as a literary genre have never been more popular. Unknown writers rise to the top of the best-seller lists with stories of wretched childhoods, self-abuse, and self-discovery. The proliferation of such memoirs—and their success—has led to a controversy over what constitutes a memoir, and just how memoirs differ from fiction and non-fiction. Memoirs seek to be true personal accounts. If the writer makes things up, it is self-invention, not self-revelation; fiction, not fact, thus not a memoir at all. The memoirist is relentless, accepting that his work is a transgression. In his *Confessions*, Rousseau strove to bare his soul and be true to events. "Since my name is fated to live," he wrote, "I must endeavor to transmit with it the memory of that unfortunate man who bore it." He did his job, being so true to people and events that he was forced into exile for a time.

"We all have lives, do we all have to write about them?" asked the *New York Times* in a droll headline over a literary story about memoirs. The answer is no, but if a non-celebrity has led an interesting life or lived through interesting times, why shouldn't the story be told? The interest may be precisely that it *could* have happened to any of us. Thomas Mellon wasn't known beyond Pittsburgh when he penned his autobiography in 1885, printed in only a few dozen copies for friends and family—which the family tried to suppress for revealing more than it wanted revealed. Mellon would have none of it, and today the book is a classic. "The story he unfolds is amazing," writes historian David McCullough in an introduction to the 1994 edition of *Thomas Mellon and his Times*.

This memoir, *Misfortunes of Wealth,* is different for two reasons: First, it is a family and historical memoir, not a personal one. I am fortunate to descend from a long line of interesting and accomplished characters. Many families can surely make that claim, but what makes this particular story worth telling is how these different clans interacted to create more than the sum of their parts. The mixture of history, industry, money, land and politics is not something that happens in every family. Nor perhaps is it quite so easy to trace the effects of these things, especially wealth, on the descendants, who are just as likely to be hindered by it as helped, as was the case of my parents.

The historical part of my story relies to great degree on the following written sources: *The Crittenden Memoirs*, (Putnam, 1936); *Iron Pioneer,* the biography of Henry W. Oliver, (Dutton, 1942); the Oliver family history assembled by Henry Oliver Rea (1959), and the archives of the Sewickley Valley Historical Society. The Historical Society was founded by my cousin, Betty G.Y. Shields, former editor of the *Sewickley Herald,* a kind and inexhaustible fount of Sewickley knowledge. Without B.G. Shields, who carries the name of David Shields,

Philadelphia silversmith at the time of the Revolution, the complete story could not have been told.

As for those parts of the account told to me by others, especially my maternal grandparents, both of whom were great story-tellers, and corroborated when possible, they are as accurate as their memories allowed. That part of the story derived from my own experience is as reliable as my own memory allows. Where I have recreated events and dialogue that took place out of my presence, I have tried to be true to things as I subsequently learned about them. In such a sweeping story there will always be holes unfilled by documents, oral accounts and remembrances. Filling in these holes is a matter of informed extrapolation, inference based on known facts and observations, our imaginations guided by the truth of the life.

The second theme of my story is the East-West connection. My parents moved us to California at the end of 1944, just as World War II was ending. We were an Eastern family up to then, from Pennsylvania, Maryland, Kentucky and Missouri. No one before us had gone west, at least not west of Missouri. California was new to us, as it would be new to so many families after the war, and it was something. It was my father's idea to go west, primarily because he didn't want to return to Wall Street, and in a lifetime of bad decisions, going to California and settling in Playa del Rey was his one good one, though not for him.

Today's forty million or so Californians (because of immigrants, no one knows for sure) cannot imagine the pristine state of 1945, with a few million people scattered over an area larger than Japan. Southern California, stretching from San Diego to Santa Barbara with our little beach town of Playa del Rey dead in the middle, was a paradise of white beaches, tall palms, broad avenues and comfy homes, with good postwar jobs and schools for everyone. The border between San Diego and Tijuana was a sleepy little post with a few guards and a few cars. Mexicans stayed home and drugs didn't exist.

The difference between my immediate family and most others is that we did not pull up our Eastern roots; we maintained and nourished them, returning to the homestead in Pittsburgh and Sewickley constantly, keeping one leg on each side of the continent.

It was a time when you did not cross the continent frivolously, on the spur of the moment or on a weekend jet outing. It was a trek of days by train or car, and with three children in tow, which was the constant fate of my mother, it must have seemed far longer. When we returned to the Sewickley homestead, it was for the whole summer, and, occasionally, the whole winter. As a boy growing up on the beaches around Los Angeles but returning annually to the woods around Sewickley, I had friends in both places who were Pennsylvanians or Californians. I, on the other hand was both, which is another way of saying I was neither.

The historical events I recount in this memoir are true: the "depreciation certificates" that brought the Leets, Shields and others like them into Western Pennsylvania to replace the Indian tribes and led to the populating of the Sewickley Valley; the exchanges between Senator John J. Crittenden of Kentucky and Abraham Lincoln on the eve of the Civil War; the opening up of the Mesabi iron ore range by Henry Oliver, which enabled Andrew Carnegie and Thomas Mellon to turn Pittsburgh into the nation's steel capital; the decree signed by Missouri Governor Thomas Crittenden that led to the murder of Jesse James and the governor's ending up as consul general to Mexico, which resulted in linking Crittendens and Olivers through their collaboration on the Kansas City, Mexico and Orient Railway, today's *Chihuahua al Pacifico* Railway, the famous *El Chepe*.

Finally, there was my father's involvement in Ramsa Airlines, the first California-Mexico airline, through which he hoped to open up the Yucatán peninsula and develop a remote village called Cancún. It was the second family attempt to establish a transport connection to Mexico, one by land, one by air, attempts separated by a half century. These events all fit together in my story, and are enlivened by characters worthy of them.

Central to the story is Mother's father, my grandfather, William Jackson Crittenden, of Kansas City, whose life was changed due to one unfortunate accident, one that changed things for all of us. His house, *Sucasa*, was a mixture of the ante-bellum South and his own notion of what would fit with the spectacular setting along the banks of the Ohio as it sets out from Pittsburgh on its winding journey by Kentucky, Senator Crittenden's home; by Missouri, Governor Crittenden's home, to its ultimate destination of the Mississippi and the Gulf of Mexico. Mexico! Where *Sucasa* would have been built except for that one unfortunate accident.

Will Crittenden performed gracefully under often difficult circumstances, which is the ultimate test.

For a Breath of Fresh Air

*On the origins of the Sewickley Valley, the problem
of the mills, discovery of the baby books, the building
of* Sucasa *and the beginning of our story.*

Beaver Road entrance to Sucasa, 1915.

Like *Gone with the Wind*, this story begins with a house. *Sucasa* was said to be the favorite house of Frederick Russell, of Rutan and Russell, its architects. Russell and his partner, Charles Rutan, were prominent in Pennsylvania at the turn of the twentieth century, known mostly for public buildings such as the old Schenley Hotel, today part of the University of Pittsburgh. But they also built private homes, and so it was that Russell was chosen to build *Sucasa*, my grandparents' home in the Sewickley Valley, thirteen miles down river from Pittsburgh.

The Sewickley Valley, if you don't know it, is a lush area along banks of the Ohio where the titans of industry built their summer homes toward the end of the nineteenth century when the air of Pittsburgh became too foul with the soot of their steel mills to breathe. What educated Pittsburgher hadn't heard of Anthony Trollope's description of the city as "the blackest place I ever saw?" What an extraordinary claim for an Englander! Trollope had to pass through England's "Black Country" on his way to Liverpool to catch the steamer for America, an area described by Dickens as "full of tall chimneys pouring out their plague of smoke, obscuring the light and making foul the already melancholy air." Henry James improved on Dickens by describing the Black Country as a "plunge into darkness lurid with flames; the sense of unknown horror in the weird gloom which never had existed before except in volcanic craters."

Pittsburgh may have been "Hell with the lid off," in Lincoln Steffens' famous description, but the English pot and American kettle were equally black.

And for good reason.

In the last third of the nineteenth century, Pittsburgh became the crucible of Pennsylvania industry, which was the heart of American industry. Pennsylvania sits on one of the richest coal beds on earth, and, in 1859, an unassuming Pennsylvania town called Titusville became the place where oil was first drilled and produced. With coal, iron ore and oil all around them, a generation of Pittsburgh industrialists—a great many of them, like Andrew Carnegie, Thomas Mellon and my own family, the Olivers, of Scotch-Irish, Presbyterian heritage that saw nothing sinful in the accumulation of great wealth—turned the city into a gigantic foul-aired, money-making machine.

Motivated by the inherent energy of new immigrants; drawing on their uniquely rich natural environment; unencumbered by taxes, federal regulation and the rise of labor that soon would alter the balance of power, these men and their families became as rich as anyone since the time of the pharaohs. They became, in Edith Wharton's famous description, "the Lords of Pittsburgh," and played second fiddle to no one, not even the richest New Yorkers. What they did with their wealth is a large part of this story.

The mills provided Pittsburgh's industrialists with the money to build country houses, and as the soot increased and the railroads improved they decamped completely, leaving Pittsburgh to the unfortunates who couldn't afford to leave or to breathe. In the Sewickley Valley they found a verdant region of clear streams and deep woods (Sewickley means "sweet water" in the native Iroquois dialect) where the skies were blue and the air was pure. The region is dotted with former Iroquois nation camping grounds, and as a girl, Granny and her sisters collected arrowheads in the woods around the estate.

Sucasa was one of a kind. It wasn't where Mother was born, for she was born in 1910, four years before its foundation was laid. Both my mother and my uncle were born downtown on Ridge Avenue—known as Pittsburgh's "Park Avenue"—where the moguls first built their mansions to be near the forges, mills and smelters that did the work that made the money. Mother was born four years after the unfortunate accident that brought my grandparents back to Sewickley from their destination in Mexico and gave their home the name it was to have had in Mexico City—*sucasa*, your house, or, more generously, my house is your house. They couldn't have built Frederick Russell's *Sucasa* in Mexico City, for it would have been as out of place as a Lomas hacienda in Sewickley. But for the woodsy hills along the Ohio, *Sucasa* was ideal.

I know a great deal about *Sucasa*. My knowledge comes not just from spending so much time there as a boy, but because all the great houses of Sewickley had thick, portfolio-sized albums done to celebrate their magnificence. I made sure, at Mother's death in the nursing home in Palm Desert in 1999, that the *Sucasa* album she kept in the two-by-two foot beige box under her bed came into my hands. As a boy, I visited many of Sewickley's great houses, many of them owned by cousins, and though some were larger and many were higher up on Sewickley Heights, none was purer than *Sucasa*, the perfect marriage of form, substance and setting. It's easy to understand why *Sucasa* was Russell's favorite.

I turn frequently through the heavy, parchment pages of that 1915 album, revisiting the rooms I knew so well. I didn't grow up at *Sucasa*, of course, but Mother grew up there and so did Uncle Jim. I know the house better than Mother because I loved it, while she hated it. Truth is that she didn't like much anything about Sewickley. Uncle Jim didn't hate it, but it didn't fascinate him like it did me precisely because it is where he grew up. I, on the other hand, was always a visitor to *Sucasa*, though I came to regard it as my own.

I don't need the album to return to *Sucasa*, for every corner of the estate and every inch of the house exist in my mind's eye. I've carried *Sucasa* with me to fifty different lands, roaming through its stately rooms as I lay restless in foreign beds counting sheep and swatting mosquitoes. I know *Sucasa* by heart, including closets, pantries, garages, the basement ballroom and third-floor maid's rooms. The playroom, where I fell in love at almost-twelve with Jane Shape, my baby cousin's nanny, was one of my favorites, as was the "nurse's" room, off Mother's bedroom, with its golden rattan furniture, which became my bedroom most summers and looked directly out on the red beech tree and the fish pond. Another favorite was the linen room—which I could only enter with the upstairs' maids for it was locked. I loved the smells of the linen room—lilac, lavender, rosewater, lily of the valley, aloe—smells I knew before I knew the names.

Grandpa's name was William Jackson Crittenden, and how he came to Sewickley from Mexico City is part of the story. Granny's name was Amelia Neville Oliver, and it was her father's family, the Olivers, who made the money in iron and steel and built their country home on Shields' land—Shields was Granny's mother's family—just down the path from where *Sucasa* would be built thirty years later. The Oliver brothers—Henry Jr. was the smartest—bought up the Mesabi iron range in Minnesota, contracted with John D. Rockefeller to bring the ore on his Great Lakes barges to Pittsburgh and sold it to Andrew Carnegie and others to make steel. They also kept some of it for the Oliver Iron and Steel Works, the Oliver railroads and other Oliver businesses such as wire-making and real estate.

Granny's father, James Brown Oliver, son of an immigrant saddler from Dungannon, Ireland, married Amelia Neville Shields, whose family had come into the Sewickley Valley after the Revolution in the person of Major Daniel Leet, a surveyor who had been with Washington at Valley Forge. When James Oliver married Amelia Shields in 1870, it united industry and land. When Granny married Grandpa a generation later, politics was mixed in, for the Crittendens had been senators, governors and soldiers in Kentucky and Missouri and were the only family to have had generals on both sides in the Civil War. Mixing those three families in the same pot created a potent brew.

If Mother wasn't born at *Sucasa*, she lived there from the day it was completed in 1915 until she married my father, in 1933. I was not introduced to *Sucasa* until 1936, shortly after I was born at Bellevue Hospital in Manhattan and Mother brought me to Sewickley to be baptized. I don't remember that, of course, but starting about 1940, I remember almost everything. Mother never told me anything about the house, for she'd been trying to escape it all her life, which is how we got to California. I learned about *Sucasa* on my own and from my grandparents. What they thought of their house is conveyed on the first page of the *Sucasa* album. In her flowing handwriting, Granny has recorded the date as December 22, 1916. She writes:

> *To my beloved husband—whose genius and untiring energy have been my inspiration in compiling this book of our house, the building of which is itself a monument to that same genius and untiring energy.*

Granny's inscription is penned on the top of that first page. Under it and filling the rest of the nearly two-by-two foot page is the photograph of a fern frond, curved like a scimitar, its delicate leaves reaching out on both sides in perfect parabolic symmetry. A fern frond is a strange thing to see on the first page of such an album, and I've wondered about it. But what else could she put there? Not any part of the house, for that was to come in the book itself; nor any person, for that would detract from the house; nor pictures of newly-planted trees or flowers, for they were too recent. She picked the one thing that, like the house itself, was intricate, harmonious and natural to the place: a frond from the ageless cinnamon fern that faced *Sucasa* across the roundabout.

Sucasa was built in the hills of the Shields-Oliver estate as they rise from the flatlands on the east side of the Ohio River that was once called Sewickley Bottom. On the west side of the river, where Colonel Washington passed on his way downriver to powwow with the Indians when it was still French territory, there are no flatlands, just steep, deep woods marching up the hills. *Sucasa* was two stories of red brick, topped by a third-story, black-slated roof that climbed at sixty degrees and was dotted with five tall chimneys, seven white dormer windows, four facing west, only three facing east because of an L-wing running off the main structure in the rear and housing the kitchen and upstairs children's rooms. The dormers marked the third-story maids' and storage rooms. The house was gabled over four white pillars at each end, the front gable over the driveway porch entrance, which had a large second-floor balcony overlooking the gravel roundabout, and from which Mother, and later my sister, Carol, used the trellises to sneak out at night. The rear gable was over the breakfast room and second-floor sun porch at the rear of the house.

The estate, which covered many square miles, ran from Oliver Road across Beaver and Woodland Roads, high into the hills to Backbone Road. The township was called, naturally enough, Shields, named after David Shields, who married Major Daniel Leet's daughter, Eliza, and built the first Shields house in 1821, called *Newington*, in the flatlands. With its vast farmlands, *Newington* provisioned the wagon trains heading downriver into the Ohio territories. David's father, Thomas, a Philadelphia silversmith, was a Revolutionary War friend of Major Leet, the surveyor, which is how their children met in Philadelphia and eventually married. Leet surreptitiously purchased the lands he had surveyed for the state of Pennsylvania and passed them on to his children.

David and Eliza's son, Thomas Leet Shields, had the bright idea to build in the hills above *Newington*, whose lowlands were subject to flooding, and finished the Shields' house in 1854. When his daughter, Amelia Neville Shields, called Millie, married James Oliver, they built their summer house on those same hills, two hundred yards down the way. When Millie's daughter, Amelia Oliver, my grandmother, married William Jackson Crittenden, of Missouri, they built their house, *Sucasa*, another two hundred yards away. Each house was shielded from the others by great expanses of trees and lawn, and looked down on the flatlands toward the wide river beyond.

Surrounding *Newington* stood acres of fertile cropland, irrigated by plentiful rains and Big and Little Sewickley Creeks. *Newington* stood virtually alone for many years, but late in the nineteenth century, the township of Shields began to fill up, and soon there were new houses and roads, a new school and a church. The church, Shields Presbyterian, was finished in 1869 and gave its name to Church Lane. Church Lane cut from Beaver Road, the main artery heading west, to the river, and was surrounded by Oliver, Shields and Leet Roads, all cozily named after the family.

Sucasa from Beaver Road driveway, 1915.

Church Lane also became the site of the Shields mausoleum, nearly as large as the church. Finished in 1897, the mausoleum was described by church architectural historian James Van Trump as "unique in the country." All the early Leets and Shields but one—Thomas Leet Shields, Jr. and his descendants—are buried there. The unfortunate Thomas Leet Shields, Jr., "young Tom Shields" as he was known, traduced the family and was duly banished from the mausoleum. Church Lane continues on three more blocks to the railroad lines leading to Pittsburgh and, beyond the tracks, to the mighty Ohio. Those railroad lines and the river are also part of the story.

I learned to prowl *Sucasa* on my own. My sister Carol, three years older, didn't do that sort of thing, and my brother, Billy, six years younger, either didn't exist during my prowling years or was too little to accompany me. Mother was never there, and Granny and Grandpa mostly stuck to the main rooms of the house, leaving me to explore attics, basements, closets, maids' rooms, and, above all, the ballroom. My curiosity—nosiness some call it—led to the discovery of secrets that are essential to the story: The correspondence, for example, between Sewickley and Mexico City that explains my grandparents' strange courtship and why they returned to Sewickley just as they'd reached the Mexican border on their honeymoon on the way to a new life. And the three volumes of baby books Granny kept after Mother was born, which throw light on their dysfunctional relationship. These documents filled in large gaps in my knowledge.

The ballroom is where most of these treasures were hidden in boxes under a sea of furniture covers. The ballroom fascinated me because though it was used as storage space in my time, with its lustrous hardwood floor, broad stage, high chandeliers and scarlet stage curtains I could see what it had been. From the gravel driveway, a red brick path wound across the grass to the side doorway leading to the ballroom. A flight of stairs took guests directly down into a large foyer and to a shorter, grand staircase leading to the ballroom. What entrances must have been made in those days! Girls in beaded dresses slinking down the stairs with their beaux as the dancers stomped the Charleston, Shimmy and Black Bottom. They'd held birthday parties and puppet shows in the ballroom when Mother and Jim were little and later had dances and Mother's coming-out party there.

I'd slip alone down the stairway, turn on hallway lights to brighten corridors spooky from disuse and light up the ballroom and stage. Ghosts everywhere. Behind the stage and pulled-back curtains were musty dressing rooms for actors and musicians. Alone on stage, looking out on the undulating sea of furniture covers, I'd imagine how it had been: bands on stage playing for couples twirling to the music while young men, cigarettes dangling, lounged in tuxes waiting for a dance. There'd be a punch bowl somewhere, secretly spiked, for it was Prohibition, and Mother would be ladling some into her glass, for she liked her drinks. Her coming out party would have been in 1928, the height of the "Roaring Twenties," still a year before the "Great Crash", which hurt so many Sewickley families.

I liked to explore deep under the furniture covers where the Oliver belongings—the Oliver house was torn down in 1944—and other treasures were hidden. I would crawl in slowly with a flashlight, aware that other living things might be in there. On one of my forays, I came across boxes containing the baby books and correspondence, going through them perfunctorily, searching for things more interesting to my juvenile tastes. A half century later, rediscovering those same things in mouse-turd covered boxes in the attic of Mother's last house in Playa del Rey, I recognized them immediately. They, too, are part of the story.

Two Caroline Jackson Crittendens, 1914.

There were things under the furniture covers that interested me more. I found toys my mother and uncle had had as children. There were blocks, wooden trains, boxes of lead soldiers, more boxes of puppets in bright costumes and a four-foot high stuffed elephant on wheels that I dragged upstairs to show Granny, who said curtly "it was your mother's." To be dismissive like that was unlike Granny, who loved to talk. I only learned the story of the elephant a half century later from the baby books.

Neither Granny nor Grandpa ever talked much about Mother, which was strange because they were both prodigious story-tellers and I was a good listener. Mother never had anything to say about growing up either, except occasional angry comments to Carol, who relayed them to me. Mother had no story-telling ability at all, unless you count raunchy limericks she learned and soon forgot. As much as I loved *Sucasa*, Mother detested it, and it took me years to discover why. How she could have grown up in that elegant house, with those parents, surrounded by so much family lore and achievement and despised it all was a mystery that took me years to unlock.

Dad, William West Goldsborough, Jr., hated it, too. There are pictures of him at *Sucasa* after their marriage in 1933 and up until 1936, the year I was born, but never after that. What happened? In all the years we visited *Sucasa* from wherever we lived, Dad never came with us. That might be natural enough in most families where mom takes her brood summers to the family homestead while dad stays home and works, but my dad never really worked. He worked at his deals and his schemes and his bets, but it wasn't real work.

He didn't need to work because like everyone else in the family he lived off Oliver money, though would never admit it. Why he never accompanied us to *Sucasa* remained a mystery for years.

§

In this extended clan of Shields, Olivers and Crittendens, Mother stands out. All three of her children understood that from an early age. She was christened Caroline Jackson Crittenden, the same name as Grandpa's mother, the wife of the governor of Missouri, Thomas T. Crittenden. I have a beguiling photo of the two Caroline Jackson Crittendens, both females dressed in white linen, Mother age four, her Grandma age seventy-five, posed together, cheek-to-jowl, Grandma looking peevish, Mother, always uncomfortable with other women, looking devilish, as though she fully understood the life to come. She and my uncle, James Oliver Crittenden, grew up as the only children in *Sucasa*, a house big enough for a dozen children. Granny and Grandpa might have had a dozen children, but they got started late because they had to wait so long. Granny was thirty-eight and Grandpa forty-four when Mother was born, and Jim was born three years later. Baby Jim called his sister "Caca", short for Caroline. Granny, who spoke French, wisely transformed it to Coco, which became her permanent nickname, though never used by her parents.

The baby books shed light on Granny's feelings about Mother's birth. They are hymns to baby Caroline as dotingly loving as if she'd descended from heaven. There'd been an earlier baby girl, also Caroline Jackson Crittenden, who died, and Granny clearly feared she was too old for more child-bearing. Then came this "gift from the angels," as she described the new baby, born June 23, 1910, the exact day of her fourth wedding anniversary. What other sign from heaven did she need that this baby would live and thrive? The delight at the birth spills over from page to page of the baby books until it becomes, knowing Mother as I do, almost, nauseating.

If I go to the *Sucasa* album, I see her playing with her brother in the nursery—she was six when the photos were taken, and Jim was three. They're riding a hobby horse or sprawled on the floor in little cotton nighties playing with blocks and stuffed animals. In the background are children's bookcases with some early Potter books (Beatrix, not Harry) on the shelves, those pretty, smooth-covered miniatures with watercolor reproductions of *Peter Rabbit, Mrs. Tiggy-Winkle, Piggling Bland, Mr. Jeremy Fisher, Mr. Tod* and other anthropomorphized animals I came to know. Mother and Jim spent a great deal of time in the nursery, always tended by a nanny, surrounded by the toys I later found under covers in the ballroom.

I dip into the baby books to give some early flavor. There's a remarkable entry spread across two baby books for June 10, 1914, just before Mother's fourth birthday. Baby Jim Crittenden would have just turned one year that summer, but still Granny dotes on Mother. She kept three baby books on Mother—not sequential but simultaneous—but no baby books on Jim.

I felt ever since my baby rested her little new born head on my breast that she was the most wonderfully sweet and fair and pure baby that ever had been. Everyone has spoken of it from the very first. Her expression is all sweet, angelic purity. Even tramps on the street turn to look after her, and whenever anyone asked her—ever since she was first able to talk—'whom do you love, Caroline,' she would say, 'everyone.' That has been the key note to her whole little life. If she has any pleasure, she instinctively wants to share it with 'everybody.' When she starts to pray it is for each and every one she knows. At Shields, whenever she was going for a drive with her Grandmother Oliver in her carriage (a great treat for she adores horses), she would forthwith invite every Italian laborer working on the place to, 'come and go, too.' I used to be so and feel sure her dear Daddy in his big generous nature was, too.

And then this:

Mr. Hood (Mother's gardener) used to look at her and say— even when she was only a few months old—that she 'seemed to be thinking.' Since she has grown more I have found that little brain of hers entirely too active—for must not the little body develop first— so our every effort has been to hold her back. She never forgets. Her little brain seems indeed filled high with a store of thoughts: And to make them quiet, health-giving thoughts has been a constant effort of ours.

These entries are both revealing and puzzling. Granny's explanation that baby Caroline loved "everyone" is exactly right. As an adult she treated strangers little different from friends and family, in fact generally treated strangers with more warmth and interest than friends and family. I would amend Granny's observation only this way: Mother did not love everyone equally, but was indifferent to them equally. And any love she might have had for horses did not survive early childhood, nor did the praying.

The second part of the entry is puzzling: Since the only way Granny could know Caroline's head was filled with thoughts would be to hear them expressed, what was this almost four-year-old saying that so disquieted Granny? She has just written down that baby Caroline is sweet, fair and pure. Now she says the brain of this angelic creature is filled with thoughts that are neither quiet nor health-giving. Caroline's brain is too active, and she must be "held back." This strange entry may provide a clue, however faint, to Mother's eventual revolt. She was kept out of Miss Dickinson's school in Sewickley until she was seven, something Mother later told Carol she deeply resented. Other girls attended Miss Dickinson's at six, but not Mother. Granny kept her home to work on quiet, health-giving thoughts.

I doubt that religion had anything to do with the extra year of home-schooling or Mother's lack of health-giving thoughts, for Granny was

Mother, Grandpa, Jim and Granny, 1916.

pious but no zealot. The family went to Shields Presbyterian every Sunday, but *Sucasa* was no *Kykuit*, the Rockefeller mansion above the Hudson where John D. Jr. convened the children every morning for bible study and inculcation of the Protestant work ethic. I never heard Grandpa utter a religious thought, and if he liked going to church Sundays it was because it was the social thing to do, he was the church treasurer and it might just be possible to hear a good sermon before Sunday dinner from the Reverend Henry Browne, his best friend. Church in those days is what you did on Sunday mornings, keeping in touch with your neighbors and the village before the age of television and football. One didn't necessarily need a religious disposition to be a church-goer, just the desire to keep a sense of spirituality in a world going increasingly secular and cosmopolitan.

If religion didn't take with Mother it was because she didn't deal in abstractions. Any attempt to talk about "things" with her—including transcendental ones—normally led to the response, "get off it." As a four-year-old, some version of that sentiment was perhaps what led Granny to work harder on "quiet, health-giving thoughts" with baby

Caroline. They would have had their conversations on the sun porch, a pleasant room off Granny's bedroom, which, like the breakfast room below it, faced southeast and was normally bathed in sunlight. It was where they sat mornings to read and write and sew and practice the things little girls learned at the time, all things Mother detested. She never read books, never wrote me a letter in her life and sewed only when she had to, for example, during the war when we lived in Wichita and the nanny Granny sent from Pittsburgh after Billy was born hated flat, dry, boring Kansas and returned home.

There would be no coddling when Mother had children of her own, no sun porches, nannies or baby books. For Mother, unlike Granny, children were a necessary encumbrance of family life, objects meant to be maintained not out of choice or love but inevitability. As a reaction to her parents, who had raised her meticulously, Mother took minimal interest in our educations and manners. Sojourns at *Sucasa* were designed so she could to turn us over to grandparents and servants and not have to think about us until it was time to return to wherever we were living. She regarded marriage as the same sort of necessary encumbrance, one that women endured in those days whether they liked it or not. No woman in her milieu and certainly not in her family had ever remained single.

From the parents of her friends, Carol learned that Mother's disappearances during our *Sucasa* visits each summer were to look up old boyfriends, ones also feeling encumbered by marriage. The moeurs of Sewickley would be transformed in a single generation, from Granny and Grandpa's, which was of the highest respectability, to Mother's, which regarded respectability as stuffy. The explanation for this generational revolution was not just money, for Granny's generation was as wealthy as Mother's. It was *idle* money. Previous generations made the money. Their children lived off it, which left them with too much time on their hands. Then came the Depression, which, as in the case of my father, disinclined people to look for work, especially if they didn't need to.

If inherited money created certain social inclinations, so did it influence characters. Mother, for example, was never guided by any rules I could ever discern. She had broken the rules as a girl, first at *Sucasa*, then at boarding school, then by eloping—twice—and saw no reason not to continue to break them as a married woman. She never bothered to set rules for her children, and Dad was no better. Whatever rules we learned came from the grandparents and from *Sucasa*, and we took them back with us to wherever we lived. As a boy on the beaches around Playa del Rey I noted that Mother actually enjoyed it when I got into a scrape. Carol never got into any scrapes, which was a great disappointment to Mother. By the time Billy came along she'd given up. She wanted miscreant children to validate her own impulses, and we weren't up to the task. She regarded us all as "stuffy," her favorite word, with me the stuffiest of all, and liked nothing so much as to shock us, preferably in front of an audience.

Psychologists talk of reaction formation: Sometimes we see what we hate in our parents and become the opposite—like Jesse James, son of a Baptist minister becoming the worst murderer in Missouri history. But such reaction in my family before Mother was unknown. Granny and her mother, Grandmother Oliver, were by all accounts ladies of similar taste, habit and character who would live together until Granny married at age thirty-four and then in houses separated by only two hundred yards on the same estate until Grandmother Oliver died. From *The Crittenden Memoirs*, it's clear that Grandpa was the same sort of Kansas City gentleman his father had been, a chip off the old block; and Senator John Jordan Crittenden, of Kentucky, who raised Grandpa's father, Thomas, the future governor of Missouri, was no different. Henry Huston Crittenden, Grandpa's brother, who penned the memoirs, shows on page after page the esteem in which the brothers held their family.

But Mother reacted to her family like the body's immune system to an antigen, rejecting almost everything that Shields, Olivers and Crittendens represented—family, work, home, culture. The one thing she did not reject was money. As a boy, I sensed the gulf separating Mother from her parents because that same gulf had opened between us. Rebel, yes, generational change is part of the natural course of things, but why do it so crudely, so selfishly, in ways, as we shall see, so clearly intended to hurt and destroy. That's not rebellion, it is revenge.

In political science a century ago there was something called Namier's law, an idea holding that European nations were destined to be enemies of their neighbors and friends of their neighbors' neighbors: Spain was France's enemy and Germany's friend; France was Germany's enemy and Poland's friend; Germany was France's enemy and Italy's friend, and so on. Alliances required leapfrogging.

Could it be the same in families—leapfrogging parents to embrace grandparents? Perhaps it applies to place as well and explains why the things that attracted me to *Sucasa*—beauty, tradition, order, permanence—were the same ones that drove Mother away.

We don't know why some children take after their parents and others react to them. It's not virtue versus vice, for children can reject a parent's virtue as easily as they embrace its vice. If some reaction is natural, why is it sometimes strong to the point of rupture, and without apparent reason? Why do some children resent their parents for the very fact of being their parents, while their siblings hold them in loving affection?

The parent favored A, creating resentment in B, says the psychologist. Cain killed Abel because the Lord preferred Abel—at least that's what Cain thought.

But what if the parent didn't favor A, but actually favored B or maybe neither? The Lord didn't really prefer Abel, just liked Abel's mutton better than Cain's broccoli. No big deal. Lots of people don't like broccoli. Cain took it wrong.

Three things enter the mix, say behaviorists: genes, environment and the X factor, the child's own uniqueness, the greatest variable.

In Mother's case, the X factor simply overwhelmed everything else.

SUMMER'S START

A short description of the crossing of the country by train, arrival at Sucasa, and the possibility that a former railroad to Mexico becomes an airline.

Union Station, Los Angeles, 1940.
Courtesy of Security Pacific Collection / Los Angeles Public Library.

When we moved to California after the war, our migrations to *Sucasa* were thanks mainly to the Super Chief, greatest of trains. Few people flew in those days and certainly not cross-country with three children. We'd drive from the beach downtown to Union Station, Carol would look around to see if any movie stars were entraining with us and Mother would charge me with watching Billy, almost five-years old in 1947 the year we took our first Super Chief. Dad dropped us off, but didn't come inside, leaving the porters to trundle the baggage into the station. I didn't know it at the time, but Dad looked forward to his summers of freedom.

I liked going downtown, which even for a kid of ten was easy enough in those days. The Pacific Electric buses rolled along the coast from Redondo to Hermosa to Manhattan, swinging by Playa del Rey after El Segundo before heading inland toward Culver City and Los Angeles. For a dime I could ride to Culver City for the movies and hang out outside the MGM or Hal Roach Studios. For a quarter I could ride downtown to Grauman's Chinese Theater or Clifton's Cafeteria, with the waterfall inside; or with one transfer go to the Farmers' Market on Fairfax or Gilmore Field, across the street, where the Hollywood Stars played baseball. Wrigley Field, where the Angels played, was downtown on Avalon Boulevard, named after the village on Catalina Island where Mother had taken us on the ferry and I'd seen the Chicago Cubs train. We'd only been in California two years but I knew we'd stumbled onto something special.

I loved what we had, but hated being so far from *Sucasa*. Maybe I was only ten, but I already could appreciate life's refinements, some-thing bohemian Playa del Rey definitely lacked. Mother would pack us up—two small suitcases for three kids and two large suitcases for her—and we'd be off. The train pulled out at four o'clock, and I'd have forty hours to romp. With its red and yellow locomotive looking like some fierce Aztec bird, the Super Chief chugged through Pasadena and Cucamonga before setting fast course for the Mojave Desert. Next stops: Flagstaff and Albuquerque.

There's never been a train like the Super Chief. A real train ride, like a real ocean cruise, needs time and space. The Europeans, I discovered later, have great trains but you're not on them long enough to get the feel of a cruise, when the object is the getting there as well as to get there. And unlike America, Europe has civilization everywhere so you never have the feeling of being alone, deep at sea or in space. A real

The Sante Fe Super Chief being serviced at the depot, Albuquerque, New Mexico, 1943. Photo by Jack Delano. Library of Congress, Prints and Photographs Division, FSA-OWI collection, LC-USW361-679.

train ride needs a continent to cross, flora and fauna to be studied under your mobile microscope and enough time cut off from the real world and your real life to dig down deep into things.

As a kid cooped up with travelers who tended to congregate in only three cars—diner, observation and lounge—I had certain rights. Because most families were heading west in those days, there were few kids on the train. Sometimes Carol, Billy and I were the only ones on the Super Chief, and I was the only real kid because Carol was a teen-ager and Billy still a baby. As the boy on the Super Chief I became a center of attention, like a dog at a cocktail party. Men would pull me over to show me a card trick or try to explain the Continental Divide, porters would poke me and old ladies buy me cokes in the lounge car just to sit with them. We always had a drawing room with four beds, the one overhead which was mine. I'd climb up at bedtime, tie the heavy curtains together for privacy and lie awake in the dark as we clickety-clacked across country. It had the feeling of a space ship, quiet and dark, and I stayed awake as long as I could.

But we hit Albuquerque at six in the morning, so I had to be ready.

I didn't tell anyone I was getting off the first time, just decided to slip out before the others were awake. The porter, whose name was Leon, told me the station was full of Indians, and I couldn't miss that. Granny had a collection of arrowheads from the Iroquois tribes around Sewickley, and if I could arrive with something from Albuquerque Indians she'd be impressed. I set my mental alarm clock, and as the train slowed down in the quiet of the desert morning I popped awake. Skinny and lithe, I slipped on my clothes, dropped down, grabbed my sneakers and moved out of the darkened room, quiet as an Indian. Mother had the curtains drawn on her lower berth, Carol was deep in some teenage dream, Billy lifeless and I was out the door with a small click. The porter, Leon, the first black man I'd ever met which is why I remember his name, was chatting in the vestibule with passengers. The train stopped, I hung back until everyone was off and jumped down.

"Where do you think you're going?" he demanded.

The porters were impressive in starched white jackets and stiff railroad caps. Each man, up and down the train, stood guard by the squatty yellow metal stool he'd placed on the platform for passengers.

"The station," I said, "to see the Indians."

With a dozen arches along the front and a high tower in the middle, Albuquerque station was as beautiful, no question, as Union Station in Los Angeles, though a lot smaller. It was a ways away, across several lines of track, and the thought occurred that a westbound train might arrive to cut off my line of retreat, but I had to take the chance.

"You get back on that train. Where's your mama? She know you're out here?"

"She's asleep."

I was dashing before he could stop me. They'd never leave without me. Besides, I'd listen for the conductor's whistle. There was always a whistle.

I made it back, but just barely. I'd gone out to the street scouting for the Indians, who were disappointing, didn't hear the whistle and was dashing back across the tracks as Leon and the conductor stood arguing about something and glaring. Everyone in the compartment was still asleep as I slipped back into my berth, excited by my adventure.

§

By breakfast—Mother made us wait until the second sitting at 8:30— I was starving. She always dressed up in a suit and high heels on these trips, even for breakfast, and would change later for dinner, depending on whom she met. Carol, Billy and I were already at the table, Billy fiddling with the stainless steel sugar bowl while Carol read the menu to him. I tried to count the telephone poles as we zipped by, but lost track. A sign said someplace called Lamy was coming up, but I knew the Super Chief didn't stop again until Colorado, or maybe it was Kansas.

Heads lifted up as Mother made her entrance. She'd been a beautiful young woman, and still was attractive, especially to men. The pictures of her taken around *Sucasa* when she was growing up are of fashion-magazine quality. One series, taken when she was thirteen but dressed and made up to look older, did appear in a magazine. In those pictures she poses in various sunny rooms around *Sucasa* wearing different dresses, shawls, shoes, hats, her brown hair tied in ribbons and eyes always cast down in the maidenly manner. The thing that strikes me about the pictures today is their softness. Young women today, even the most elegant ones, are hard-bodied and streamlined, athletic. They exercise, tone-up, build muscles. Mother, who never exercised as a girl, had a softness, even pudginess to her, and when she finally dieted and Dexedrined after she married Burnie Adams, she got flabby because there weren't enough muscles down there underneath.

"Mother," whispered Carol, "look over there."

"Where?"

"Straight ahead of you, on the other side, three tables down."

"Who is it?"

"Peggy Ann Garner."

"It is, isn't it? Much better complexion than yours."

"Mother!"

"She's about your age, isn't she?"

"Mother, she's fifteen, maybe even sixteen."

"Is that her mother with her?"

"I think so. She's supposed to be mean."

"Very stylish, though. Look at her shoes. . . real alligator."

"She was so good in *A Tree Grows in Brooklyn*."

I didn't know what they were talking about until I heard that. "I didn't like that movie," I said.

"You're too young to understand it," said Carol.

I was about to respond when I looked up and caught sight of uniforms approaching. It was Leon and the conductor. No question where they were heading, their eyes were fixed straight on me as we zoomed across New Mexico.

Silently, they stopped, swaying slightly as they hovered over the table. The conductor glanced down at his clipboard while Leon stood back a step or two, looking outside, looking uncomfortable. The conductor wore a baggy blue jacket not half as impressive as Leon's snazzy white one though I liked his conductor's hat, which looked military. He was small and wiry, normally the meanest sort. Standing over Mother, he looked at me slantwise.

"Mrs. Goldsborough?"

Mother looked up and batted her brown eyes. I scrunched down some in my chair.

He pointed at me with his clipboard. "Is this your son?"

Decades later, having known hundreds of parents and hundreds of children and having had two children of my own not to mention various nieces, nephews, cousins and the rest, I know that the question— "is this your son"—foretells by its tone how the parent will respond. If it is indeed your son, you normally answer, "yes, sir." But the inflexion of the inquiry determines whether your response will be enthusiastic or more like one elicited under torture. By his tone, the conductor showed he'd not stopped by to wish us good morning or announce I'd won the Super Chief lottery.

Mother as teen model. Sucasa breakfast room, 1924.

Mother's eyes narrowed on me, and she licked her lips to make the lipstick shine. She cleared her throat before looking up again.

"Yes," she said. "This is Jimmy."

"Madam, do you know that Jimmy left the train at Albuquerque, alone, without parental supervision, went into the station and almost missed the train. Do you know that we had to hold the train for Jimmy?"

I didn't like the emphasis on my name, but elected to stay silent.

Mother stared at me expressionless as she considered the information. "That's impossible," she said. "He was in the room, asleep with me."

The conductor's nose was too big for his face making his glasses ride high so he had to bend his head at a sharp angle to look down, like a predatory bird.

"I don't think so," he said, slowly, with inflection. He was bending over me, and I could smell his rank breath. I hoped Mother smelled it, too, because she had a thing about bad breath. "I think Jimmy snuck out. What about that, Jimmy?"

Snuck. I hated the word. Snuck meant guilt. I hadn't snuck out, I'd slipped out, quietly, like an Indian.

Mother stared straight at me, her mouth puckering. "Jimmy, is that true?"

Billy almost five, stared up at me like I was Captain Midnight. Across the table, Carol was looking down the aisle, no doubt wondering whether this scene would queer any hope of meeting Peggy Ann Garner. I fiddled with the menu. Silence engulfed the dining car, just a few hushed whispers up and down the aisle. I wondered if Peggy Ann, out of vision behind me, was watching. For the first time in my life, I was center stage, and I rather liked it.

I nodded—a short, quick nod indicating acknowledgment, not guilt.

The conductor began his soliloquy:

"Madam, it is forbidden for children to leave the train unaccompanied by adults. Imagine that the porter had not seen him go." He turned around. "Isn't that right, Leon? Imagine that the train had left without him." He was soaring now, aware that he, not me, held center stage. "Imagine that Jimmy had disappeared in the station in Albuquerque.

Indian country! Imagine all the things that could happen if we did not have a rule that says children are forbidden to leave the train unaccompanied by adults."

Mother stared at me silently, clueless, as usual, what to say or do. The thought of me disappearing in "Indian country" clearly did not exercise her. I saw her weighing its pros and cons. Sometimes her lack of quick thinking hurt us but just as often it helped. In this case, silence presented a chance to get out of this without any deals. The conductor seemed puzzled by her failure to act the aggrieved parent.

He waited, Mother waited, I waited, Peggy Ann waited. Everybody waited.

The conductor blinked first, and I realized he didn't have any bullets in his gun. "Well," he muttered, "I'm sure you'll see this doesn't happen again. I would hate to have to report you."

"Of course, Conductor," said Mother. "Thank you very much."

"Idiot," she hissed when he was gone. "In front of all these people! That was embarrassing."

Since Mother broke all the rules herself, she certainly wasn't going to worry about me breaking a few. Whenever she tried to act the disciplinarian it turned out badly because by the time she'd thought up a punishment she'd usually forgotten the crime. The one bad thing about the Albuquerque incident was that it had embarrassed her. Embarrassing Mother, which wasn't easy, always led to retribution.

That's the way it was on those trips. We'd gone back to *Sucasa* for the summer as long as I could remember, taking the Super Chief three times, the summers of '47, '48 and '49, and I made it back to the train every time. Before that, when we lived in New York, Connecticut and Wichita, we'd taken shorter train trips to *Sucasa*, ones I don't much remember. Mother said if I ever missed the train, she wasn't coming back for me, even in Indian country, and I believed her. But I had to investigate the stations. Eventually I'd been in every station where the Super Chief stopped, collecting city pennants along the way, including ones with strange names like La Junta and Trinidad.

I knew I was a lucky kid. I not only spent summers in the greatest house ever built, but got to spend eighty hours going and coming on the greatest train. My best friends at El Segundo Elementary—Bobby Beathard, Eugene Wray and Patrick Murphy—had never ridden the

Super Chief. Nor had they taken a plane, as I'd done once, flying from Wichita to Los Angeles. They were mostly typical kids, either native Californians or from families that came west after the war and had no eastern homestead to return to. We were different that way, splitting our lives between the beaches of Playa del Rey and the woods of Sewickley; between the proletarian chaos of postwar Southern California and the regal order of Sewickley's Presbyterian establishment.

The contrast enlarged our horizons. Did it make us a touch schizophrenic as well? I can speak only for myself.

We arrived at Chicago's Union Station after breakfast and had an hour to get over to the Pennsylvania Railroad for the eight-hour trip to Pittsburgh. Stewart, the chauffeur; or Douglas, who would replace him (those were their family names, though I didn't know it at the time), would meet us at Pittsburgh's Union Station in the black Buick sedan with the roll-up glass between front and back, suitcases would be loaded up and we'd be off down Ohio River Boulevard.

Between 1940, when I was three, and 2008, I cannot count the times I made that thirteen-mile drive along the river from Pittsburgh to Shields and the exhilaration I felt each time—even when I knew, as at the end, there would be no one waiting. I knew every inch of the boulevard, every sound and sight along it, from the dark and grim Western Pennsylvania penitentiary to the hum of cobblestones on the turnabout off the Neville Island bridge, named after General John Neville as Granny told me so many times, whose descendants married the Shields, who married the Olivers, and so on. General Neville served with Braddock and Washington on their march to drive the French from Fort Duquesne and later was commandant of Fort Pitt. As Washington's regional tax collector, he played a key role in the ignominious Whiskey Rebellion.

Up the hill after the Neville Island bridge, dropping down to Haysville, then more cobblestones up the ramp to Beaver Road for the short trip through Osborne and Sewickley, past the Edgeworth Club and Edgeworth school, where I started the eighth grade after Mother's divorce, past the stone wall and winding driveway leading to the Ethelbert Nevin house, past the curved, yellow-brick wall around the old horse trough as we entered Shields. Then came the sweep past the stone pillars and former gas lamps (by then electric), up the hill to the gravel driveway leading to *Sucasa*, the great house with its tall chimneys reaching for the sky. There under the front portico, never failing,

Caroline Jackson Crittenden as a young woman, 1930.

Granny stood waving her handkerchief as the car approached, Grandpa discretely in the background. We'd arrive by eight on those warm summer evenings, I'd spot the fireflies, which didn't exist in Southern California, and begin planning my first day.

§

The first morning was the only time we all met for breakfast. Grandpa liked to preside over the first breakfast, hear from us all, what we wanted, what we expected, what was new. Mother hated it, and we knew we'd never see her at breakfast again, but the first day was ritual. Edith, the downstairs maid, would have the breakfast room set for 8:30; Bobby and Dicky, canaries in separate brass cages, would greet us; the *Post-Gazette*, an Oliver newspaper in the days it was known simply as the *Gazette*, sat on the brass table rack waiting for Grandpa; and six places were set, with mine always facing outward, toward the tennis court, the rose garden and the sweep of trees and grass leading across the estate, up the hills to the farm and the deep woods beyond.

For me, *Sucasa* was a house of exceptional warmth. I'm not sure why that was so, for the furnishings were not of the sort we would describe as warm today, that is, soft, comfy furniture in over-stuffed rooms with lots of bright colors. *Sucasa's* furnishings were antique, ancient even—Persian carpets, Venetian tapestries, dark silk drapes and valances, portraits of ancestors and Tuscan villas, early American furniture in which you mostly sat straight, colors tending to browns and faded scarlets. But the rooms were big and light, the ceilings high and windows tall in bright white frames, letting sunlight inside in summer and reflecting light off the snow in winter. Each of the house's thirty-five-odd rooms was a separate, individual place, a space lit up not only from outside light but by the character of the people who belonged there. Even the broad hallways had their character, with mahogany tables loaded with embroidered runners and exotic bric-a-brac, plus strange objects like the Chinese gong that Grandpa sounded each night to announce dinner. And below all the rooms was the vast basement ballroom.

With windows on three sides looking out on trees and lawns, the breakfast room, facing east like the sun porch above it, was the sunniest of all, and the chirping of Bobby and Dicky added to its warmth. The breakfast room—we also took lunches there except on Sundays when we adjourned to the adjoining dining room—was made for pleasant and lingering family meals, though that's not always what took place.

If ever there were parents and children who had less to say to each other than Mother and me, it was Mother and Granny. This was a mystery that took me years to unlock, and I cannot say I was particularly aware of it at age ten other than that while Granny's conversation with me was always interesting, with Mother it consisted mostly of awkward silences as though both were afraid that too much talking would lead into forbidden territory.

Grandpa, for his part, was a normally sunny man willing to let whatever bygones there were be bygones. He would talk about his great uncle, Senator Crittenden, who'd tried to head off the Civil War; or about the senator's sons who fought as generals on opposite sides in the war; or about his father, Governor Crittenden, and his hunt for Jesse James; or about Mexico. How Grandpa loved to talk about Mexico, where he'd served with his father, the consul general. Granny would tell Bible stories or ones about the Leets and Shields who'd acquired the lands, fought the Indians and built the homesteads; or about the Olivers who owned railroads, iron mines, steel mills and newspapers. I never knew either grandparent to run out of a story to tell. There was no television in those days, just a Philco floor radio in Grandpa's den and books in the tall shelves in the drawing room. Story-telling was still a primary form of entertainment.

They were listening to us chatter about the Super Chief while we waited for Mother to make her appearance and breakfast to begin. Grandpa had his tie and jacket on—I never saw him dressed otherwise—but was not going to Pittsburgh that day. He was half-listening, half-reading the *Post-Gazette*, which was propped on the brass rack whose flat back consisted of a rooster standing on an arrow-shaped weather vane marked NEWS. Very clever, I thought.

Hearing Mother in the hallway, Granny hit the foot buzzer for Edith.

Edith, whose last name I never knew, was a long-faced woman of indeterminate age whom Granny had found somewhere "upstate," who lived on the third floor and had been the downstairs maid at *Sucasa* forever. Like Grandpa, Edith never altered her mode of dress: She wore a shiny black uniform fronted with a lacy white apron and kept her black-gray hair in a permanent chignon under a hair net. As devoid of color as was Edith, Mother was a summery palette that morning, dressed for going places. She eyed me fishily as she came in. Edith took our orders, mostly for eggs, for *Sucasa* had a large chicken coop.

Grandpa looked up over his reading glasses when Edith was gone.

"Caroline, your children look like they could all put on some weight. What's wrong, California still on rationing?"

"I'm trying to lose weight, Daddy."

"We'll fatten you all up this summer, right Jimmy? I bet you don't weigh a hundred pounds. You come up with me after breakfast and I'll weigh you. We'll weigh you again before you leave, and I'll give you a quarter for every pound you gain."

Grandpa turned eighty-one that year, the first summer I really got to know him thanks to some long walks. He'd been athletic as a young man and still was spry. Granny had pictures of him in her bedroom as a young horseman, jumping over fences and playing polo. They still kept horses up at the farm, but Grandpa hadn't ridden much since a polo accident in Mexico City. He'd met Granny in Mexico while serving as vice counsel with his father, who was appointed counsel general by President Cleveland after stepping down as governor of Missouri.

Granny had nothing athletic about her. She was a small, bosomy lady clad in chiffony dresses down to her ankles who walked on the outsides of her white shoes. Grandpa loved exercise as much as Granny hated it, and though both took walks, Grandpa's were much longer, down to the Ohio or up to the farm or to Little Sewickley Creek. Even on long walks, Grandpa was always dressed in jacket, vest and tie and never without a cane, of which he kept a large collection, along with umbrellas, in a porcelain stand by the front door. On her walks, Granny was content to tour the immediate grounds, staying on the brick paths or strolling through the rose garden and greenhouse. The Oliver house was gone by the late Forties, so she couldn't visit her mother anymore, but she still led Carol and me on occasional walks to the Shields house, beyond where the Oliver house had stood, to visit ancient Aunt Mina, short for Wilhemina.

"What's Red up to these days?" Grandpa asked Mother.

"Red" was my father, William West Goldsborough Jr., the "Red" coming from his flaming James Cagney hair and I guess a little from his Welsh personality, of which I inherited none. My brother Billy, also red-headed, was William West Goldsborough III, but my given names and brown hair came from the Olivers. In any case, though I didn't know all the details at age ten, something between Dad and Grandpa, like between Mother and Granny, hadn't clicked, and Dad didn't come to *Sucasa* anymore.

"He's fine," said Mother, evasively. "Looking after his affairs."

Something in what she said caused Granny to look up at Grandpa, who was staring at Mother over his glasses.

"Affairs?" he said.

"He wants to start an airline to Mexico."

Breakfast room, 1915.

Grandpa took off his reading glasses. "An airline to Mexico. . .? with what. . .? your trust funds?"

"Will," said Granny. "Remember how we met."

We fell silent as Edith brought the orange juice, freshly squeezed, with lots of pulp and not cold. Frozen food had not yet reached Western Pennsylvania.

"How did you meet?" I asked.

"We met in Mexico City," said Granny. "Your grandfather was serving there and my father, your great-grandfather Oliver, took me on a trip from Pittsburgh to Mexico City where he wanted to build a railroad."

"*Wanted*?" said Grandpa. "We did build it. "The Kansas City, Mexico and Orient Railway. . . chartered April 30, 1900. . . bankrupt in 1914. . . cash short. . . you can remind Red of that. Where's he getting the money?"

"I don't know," said Mother. "He has partners."

"The man needs a real job."

"Not Red," said Mother, finishing her juice. "He's too busy for that."

That struck me as funny, but nobody laughed.

"What happened to the railroad?" I asked.

Grandpa stared outside toward the tennis court, a faraway look in his eyes. "You know," he said, "they're going ahead with it. The Mexicans are finishing it, and good for them. Some day it will reach the Pacific, over I don't know how many bridges and through how many tunnels, across mountains, gorges, rivers. It will be the most spectacular railway in the world. We'd have cut four hundred miles off shipments between Kansas City and the Orient. It was before the Panama Canal, you know. We started it, others finished it. . . history of human progress. . .

His voice trailed off as Edith arrived with coffee and a large bowl of fruit salad—apples, melon, cherries, apricots and berries mixed together—all from the estate. She poured coffee for Mother and Grandpa and set the silver coffee urn by Grandpa.

"Now," said Mother, when Edith was gone again, "I want to talk about the summer. . . starting with you, Jimmy." She had that look in her eye again. "I was on the phone this morning. You're going to summer camp."

My mouth dropped in disbelief. The retribution.

"I'm not," I said.

"You are," she said.

The grandparents looked back and forth with silent interest.

"I'm not," I repeated. "I've never had to go to camp before."

"You're ten, almost eleven."

"What about Carol?"

"Girls don't go to camp," said Carol, unhelpfully. "Boys do."

"What about Billy?"

"At five. . . ?"

"I won't go. It's not fair. . ."

Grandpa, a former boy in this house full of women, was my only hope. "Grandpa, don't let them send me to camp."

Grave of Lieutenant J.J. Crittenden, 20th Infantry at Little Big Horn. Original photo taken 1877, one year after the June 25, 1876 battle. From a postcard by Herbert A. Coffeen, Pub., Sheridan, Wyoming; original photo by Stanley J. Morrow.

My plea echoed around the silent room. Bobby and Dicky eyed us suspiciously, not used to this much excitement at breakfast. Was there a chance?

"Why send him to camp?" asked Grandpa. "Let him run. Where will he ever have anything like this again?"

"No," said Mother, "it's settled. Do you know what he did on the train? He got off at Albuquerque and disappeared. They had to hold the train."

"They did not and you know it!" I said. "They said they did, but they didn't."

"In the middle of Indian country," said Mother.

"Indian country. . . !" sputtered Grandpa. "Now hold on. The Indian wars are over. Maybe Cousin John died with Custer, but Albuquerque is no more Indian country today than Sewickley."

"We had a cousin at Little Big Horn. . . ?"

I'd spotted an opening. I'd done a fifth grade book report on Custer's Last Stand.

"Senator Crittenden's son, John Jordan, Jr. You don't know that? Caroline, why don't you keep your children informed about family? Jimmy, we'll walk down to the river after breakfast and I'll tell you some things."

"I'm glad that's settled," said Mother, who'd already forgotten how we got onto Indians. "Now Carol, you. . . what are your plans?"

"I'm meeting Jenny at the Edgeworth Club for lunch," she said. "All the girls are coming."

"Billy," said Mother, "you'll spend the day with Granny."

"And you, Caroline?" said Granny.

Edith brought out toast on silver trays covered with starched linen napkins and china plates bearing hard butter balls, which she had rolled into perfect little orbs in the pantry using fluted wooden paddles. She poured more coffee for Mother and Grandpa and soon returned with plates of scrambled eggs and bacon, though Grandpa always took his eggs soft-boiled in a cup, and Granny didn't eat eggs at all, sticking to the toast. Jars of apricot, raspberry and strawberry preserves, all put up from fruits from the estate, were placed on the table.

"I have calls to make for a week," she said.

"Caroline," said Granny, who'd been mostly silent until then, "don't forget your family. Everyone wants to see you—the Shields, Todd and John Oliver, Uncle Dave, the Robinsons, Cousin Virginia doesn't have long left."

"Oh, Mother, I didn't come back here to see a lot of cousins. I'm having lunch with Rosie Richardson. I'll let you know."

"They're all invited for Sunday dinner," said Granny. "Make sure you plan for that. It's your family."

"Fine," said Mother, "I'll see them at Sunday dinner."

"They're coming to see you and your children," Granny persisted. "They want to keep in touch. They want to hear about California."

Mother was about to respond, but Grandpa laughed. "They'll be dying to hear about Red's plans for a Mexican airline. What's he call it? It have a name yet. . . ?"

"Ramsa," said Mother.

"Where's it fly?"

"Los Angeles, Mexico City and the Yucatan."

"Sounds like the Kansas City, Mexico and Orient Railway. That lasted fourteen years. How long you think Red's venture will last?"

"I couldn't say," said Mother.

"Maybe you can drum up some investors for him at Sunday dinner," said Grandpa with a chuckle. "What about that, Amelia? Maybe Uncle Dave will sell some of his G.E. Or the Reas, about time they sold some steel, don't you think? Airlines, now that's the thing of the future. Come to think of it Caroline, I thought you told me Red was through with airplanes. He sold his Beech stock after the war, didn't he?"

"He thinks commercial airlines are here to stay. And there's nothing in Mexico."

"Man always was full of ideas. Too bad he can't make any money. Should have stayed with his seat on the stock exchange."

"His chicken business did all right," I said.

"What. . . ?"

"Frozen chickens from Mexico."

"What. . . ?"

"It's the latest thing in California, he says," said Mother. "They freeze them in Mexico, fly them up in frozen containers and sell them frozen. You keep them frozen until you use them."

"Where do you keep them frozen, Caroline?" asked Granny.

"You rent frozen food lockers," I said. "He's got a bunch. I've seen them."

Grandpa was staring back and forth from me to Mother, fixing finally on Mother. "He's not serious," he said.

"He has partners."

"It works," I said. "You can freeze everything—chickens, fish, vegetables, fruits like strawberries and oranges. You can drink orange juice the year round."

Grandpa fell quiet a while, occupying himself with his soft-boiled eggs and toast and catching a bit of runny yolk in the chin folds running down from his mouth. Granny motioned to him, and he dabbed it off with a napkin and swallowed some coffee. He was ruminating.

"Amelia, when's the last time we were in California?"

They locked eyes as Granny thought about that one. "On the way to the Orient, Will. . . 1932. . . We stayed a few days in San Francisco."

"How would you like to go back?" he said, after a moment. "They say Los Angeles is a lot like Mexico City."

FLYING TO THE YUCATAN

An example of the many postwar opportunities in California for a smart businessman with Eastern connections.

Venice canals and oil wells, 1929. Playa del Rey hill in the distance. Photo by Adelbert Bartlett. Courtesy Santa Monica Public Library, Image Archives / Carolyn Bartlett Farnham Collection.

Red Goldsborough sat on Bunny Warren's front patio, watching the waves break beyond the broad stretch of white sand in front of him. Free for the first time since he'd arrived in California, he was spending a lot of time at Bunny's in Manhattan Beach. Smart, self-confident and easy-going, Bunny was a relief for him. They'd met a few months before at Pancho's, a Mexican restaurant with a good piano bar up on Highland Street where he went from time to time. He'd greeted Joaquin Acosta, the piano-playing son of Catalina Acosta, our Playa del Rey piano teacher, and suddenly this attractive redhead was on the barstool next to him. "Love that red hair," he said with a friendly smile, she'd laughed, and that's how it started. She was divorced, had a son away in the Navy, made a good living as an escrow officer and owned her own house on the beach.

He'd been for a 7 a.m. swim, showered and was taking breakfast on the patio overlooking strand, beach and ocean, feeling as good as he ever remembered. A few other brave hearts were in the water, which wouldn't hit seventy until noon, but cold water never bothered him. Most of the early birds up and about were content to stroll the strand for exercise, heading at a brisk pace toward the Manhattan Beach pier for coffee, doughnut and newspaper. The pier, a half-mile north of Bunny's, was already busy, and the smell of fish alive in the early morning air. It had the makings of a splendid day, sans the usual morning fog—or marine layer, as they liked to call it. He watched a fishing boat push off and saw a group at pier's end with lines already in the water. That's how they'd spend their day, staring at lines dangling in the water and drinking beer. He understood the beer, not the fishing.

Bunny was gone when he'd got back to the house, leaving him bacon, scrambled eggs and an English muffin in a still warm oven. "See you Friday," said a note on the table, "I'll make the reservations today. Love, B." The reservations were at the Solana Beach Motel for opening day of Del Mar track season.

Single again, he was looking forward to the summer. It wasn't that Dad didn't love his family in his own indifferent way, but, like Mother, he loved the idea of family more than its actual existence, which tended to interfere with his private life. Mother's insistence on returning to *Sucasa* each summer gave him freedom, and he knew how to use it. It was her decision; she knew he'd never go back, never set foot in *Sucasa* again. They'd both known that since before the war. Meeting Bunny at

Pancho's had simply been a stroke of luck. He'd hit the Trifecta with her and had every reason to believe his luck would carry over to Del Mar.

Most husbands and fathers—we'd heard Mother remind him often enough—went to work each morning, as Dad had done in New York and Wichita, but things changed when we came west. Dad's view was that California was an embarrassment of riches, a place with so much postwar opportunity that a smart guy didn't have to go to work each morning. A smart guy came up with the ideas for others who went to work each morning. California wasn't like New York, where you had to show up every day just to keep up with the crowd. California was virgin territory, ripe postwar pickings for guys with ideas. You decided which deals had the payoffs, make the right plays and waited to cash in. Dad's only problem was that he lacked the capital to make all the plays he wanted. Oliver income paid the bills and took him to the track, but provided no capital. It was one of the things he had against Grandpa.

Dressed in his usual summer slacks and Hawaiian shirt, he climbed into the green Buick convertible we'd bought in Rye the summer of '41, the last models produced before Detroit converted for war. Decrepit by '47, it suited Dad, who loved convertibles. He'd driven it from New York to Wichita in the spring of '42 and on to Los Angeles in December of '44 and would drive it until salt air corrosion turned it into white dust. Top down, he gunned up the coast toward Playa del Rey, a fifteen-minute drive through Manhattan Beach and El Segundo. On Main Street, El Segundo, he passed our schools, high school on the right where Carol went, grammar on the left, which was mine.

We were lucky kids, Dad told us. California schools were first rate, especially El Segundo, a town owned by Standard Oil. The name El Segundo derived from the presence of Standard's second refinery, built in 1917 to accommodate the oil strikes from Long Beach to Venice. Standard poured money into its schools so the children of its workers would grow up smart and loyal, the same thing Andrew Carnegie did for Pittsburgh, Dad said. However good Pittsburgh's public schools were thanks to Carnegie, Dad himself had gone to the private Shadyside Academy and then to Exeter. That was before the Depression changed things for the Goldsboroughs.

He pulled up steep Vista del Mar in Playa del Rey and stopped in front of our brown-shingle house on Montreal Street. Mother had found the house while we were staying in a motel on Wilshire for Christmas of '44 after arriving from Wichita. It was four bedrooms with a large enclosed patio overlooking the ocean. Two-and-a-half years later we still paid the same hundred-dollar-a-month rent we'd paid at the start. I knew about the rent because Carol and I carried the checks to Captain Stone's house on our walks up Vista del Mar Lane for piano lessons with Mrs. Acosta.

Queenie, the half-chow, half-mutt Mother bought because dogs went with children, ambled out of the iceplant to greet him as he parked the car. Dad wasn't Queenie's favorite family member, but they got along well enough. Inside, he pulled some Milk Bones out for her breakfast, grabbed the newspaper he'd picked up from the lawn and headed for the patio. He swung open the fence shutters and dropped down into his favorite redwood chair. From there he could see the full sweep of Santa Monica Bay—Catalina to Point Dume, beyond Malibu. For his morning swims, he could be at the beach with a five-minute trot down the hill, not quite as convenient as Bunny's, but good enough. It refreshed him and helped work the booze out of his system. He glanced at the stock pages, but his attention went back to the ocean. It was already a sweet day. They were all sweet in California.

Back in the car, Queenie was in before he could shut the door, lonesome, looking for company. What the hell. He'd put the top up when he got to E. F. Hutton's, and she could sleep all morning. That's all she did anyway. They crossed the stone bridge over Ballona Creek and zipped along the coast road, dog on the cracked rear seat, paws on the faded canvas top, red fur ruffling as she howled madly into the ocean breezes. He passed the churning oil wells to the east, iron mantises, mixing oil smells with the salt air, not unpleasant, unique to Venice. With its canals, arched bridges and gondolas, Venice was to be a replica of the real thing. Then they'd struck oil, turning the canals into grease. You still saw an occasional gondola stuck in the muck.

Weekday mornings started with the same open-air drive along the coast to the Hutton office on Wilshire in Santa Monica. It was the life Dad loved. No trains, no subways, no crowds, no snow, no mush, no rush. He'd watch the ticker tape for an hour or so, occasionally make a trade, then cross the street to the Black Bull for a lunch of roast beef sandwich and one highball. I'd gone with him enough times. At ten, I already knew how to sit on a barstool, despite dangling legs. On this particular morning he had to decide between going to the track or to

Santa Monica Bay, 1935.
Courtesy Santa Monica Public Library Image Archives.

the bank after lunch. He'd told Tom Morris and Jim Collins, his Ramsa partners, that he'd meet them at the bank but was really thinking of Hollywood Park, where the season was closing and he liked the race card.

He would never leave California. Coming west from Wichita instead of heading back to New York had been a risk, but it had worked out. He loved the casual life. Wichita was a prison to be endured during the war—making Beech planes was better than fighting Japs—but it was bleak, dry and boring. Five minutes in any direction got you outside the walls, but there was no place to go—no relief, no escape, just more bleakness for hundreds of miles. Thank God for bootleggers. The war over, he couldn't stay in Wichita, couldn't go back to Pittsburgh, wouldn't go to *Sucasa*, didn't miss New York and so packed up and brought us where none of us had been before.

Opportunity in California was everywhere, but beyond that was the exhilaration of life itself. Living on the ocean changed the way you looked at things. The sameness of Wichita—farms, fields and flatness in all directions—made you feel insignificant, another ant in the colony. The ocean was a changing, pulsating organism reminding you that you were alive. Serene and blue in August or chopping with rough white horses in January, it could calm you or bring the blood up. *Saturday Evening Post* ads showed couples diving through California waves, not trudging through Kansas corn fields. There was nothing about California he didn't like. People had been streaming into Los Angeles since the war ended, with no sign of stopping. Soldiers and sailors liked what they saw as they shipped out and came back to stay. With money and people rushing in, there were big fish to be caught, especially for a smart Eastern operator.

He parked under some palms on a side street off Wilshire, muscled the rusted top up and rolled the windows half way so Queenie couldn't get out. Inside the brokerage, he nodded to a few pals and took a seat in one of the red leather arm chairs. He glanced at the ticker to check the markets and unfolded the racing sheet from the morning paper. He felt good about the day, though he liked his chances better at the track than in the markets. He caught the eye of Joe Messick, one of the brokers, sitting at his desk by the window. Joe was an admirer, impressed that Red Goldsborough owned a seat on the New York Stock Exchange but was smart enough to lease it out and come west. Joe, with his bad eyes, had spent the war pushing papers in New York and hated it. He was an Angeleno who'd come back as soon as he could, though working Wall Street hours in California meant rising with the roosters—if there were any roosters in L.A.

The markets were dead so he kept his eyes on the racing form and figured he'd better decide. He'd told Tom Morris he'd call at eleven and it was already 10:45. He weighed the pros and cons of going to the bank, jotting them down in his neat, thin ink script on the pad he kept for calculations.

> Pro: Ramsa was their new company and he should be with his partners when they got the loan.
>
> Pro: His New York Stock Exchange membership was part of the collateral.
>
> Con: They already had his signature, and Tom could handle the rest.
>
> Con: He had the third, fourth and fifth races at Hollywood Park down cold and could make a few hundred simoleons on those races alone.

The choice came down to a meaningless gesture versus a few hundred dollars. He had to drop Queenie off anyway. It was no choice at all, and he phoned Tom to tell him he'd meet him at home for drinks that evening to go over their plans.

§

Relaxed in linen slacks and a long-sleeved lime silk shirt, Tom Morris was at his Steinway as he walked in. Morris lived off Sunset in West Hollywood in one of those flowing, ranchero houses built in the twenties when Hollywood was still getting its legs. He'd bought it from a scriptwriter during the Depression for $10,000, and it was now worth three times that and rising each day, an easy, if boring, way to make money. The front yard was mostly cactus and other ornery-looking succulents through which a path wound to a gate in bougainvillea-covered walls and into an inner patio leading to the portico of the house. The screen door slammed behind him, and he moved into the cool inner sanctum of the hall, eyeing the walnut staircase and banisters and pausing to listen to Morris' playing, something slow and sad.

"Listen to this," he called. . . "just came to me." He was humming along. It was all chords, mournful and low.

"Sounds familiar."

He played on a bit, red lips puckering, mustache twitching. Then he stopped abruptly. "Shit. It is familiar. It's Chopin's *E-Minor Prelude*. I didn't know I knew Chopin's *E-Minor Prelude*. I don't know it and can't play in E minor"

"Geniuses think alike."

"I've always had an ear."

Morris left Chopin and headed to the bar. He was a short, dapper man who walked quickly and always wore a smile. He'd become Dad's best friend, maybe his only friend, in California, though the two men had nothing observable in common, other than being about the same size. He had a law practice dealing mostly with the Hollywood crowd, though it bored him, and was extremely sociable, far more than Dad. "What're you drinking?" he called.

"G and T. How'd it go today?"

"How'd you do?"

"Nosed at the wire from a big day. Won two C's. Going to Del Mar for the opening next week."

"Don't forget you're a working man again."

"The track is work."

Morris laughed as he poured the drink, and they settled onto a leather couch facing doors opening onto a rear patio canopied by a large rubber tree stretching toward the property wall. Thanks to heavy walls, low ceilings and a minimum of windows, the Morris house, like most ranchero houses, stayed remarkably cool on hot July evenings. The descendents of the *Californios* knew how to construct, knew how to build houses with thick walls and leafy trees and small windows that kept the heat outside. It could be a problem in winter, but not in West Hollywood, the sub-tropics.

Always the good host, Tom had set out almonds and olives on the oak coffee table. He raised his glass. "We're in business, Red. Here's to the three of us. Here's to Ramsa."

They heard the screen door slam and looked up to see burly Jim Collins. "Save that toast."

"Save it hell," said Morris. "We'll make another."

"Missed you today, Red."

"Red was hitting the ponies. Two C's worth. I figure he owes us a La Cienega steak dinner. Mix your own, big Jim, and pull up a chair. We've got fifty grand and some serious planning to do."

Collins mixed a vodka tonic, picked a coaster off the pile and headed for the easy chair facing the couch. He bent to scoop some almonds while the smaller men watched him maneuver his large frame into the chair. With broad shoulders, wavy blond hair and easy smile, Collins looked like he belonged in pictures, though a growing paunch and too-florid complexion suggested his movie career might not last much longer. He'd been a test pilot with Beech in Wichita and helped sell Dad on coming west after the war. They'd hooked up with Morris, Jim's pal since USC days, and made some money on frozen food lockers. Now they were ready for something bigger.

"Two C's?" Sounds like you're treating us to that steak dinner."

"Still mooching, eh? Just like Wichita."

"Now, boys," said Morris, "Rule is we go Dutch or not at all."

"Hell," said Red, "dinner's a business expense."

"We've got fifty grand, a name, one pilot, no crews, no mechanics and no planes," said Morris, laughing. "What kind of business is that?"

"I told you, I've got two DC-3s in Ontario," said Collins. They've got Burma Road miles, but look sound. If they test OK we can get them for $10,000 each, financed."

"I told you. . . we need four planes," said Red. "How do you operate a scheduled airline between two countries, three cities and 2,500 miles with two planes? One's in for repairs and we're down to a single plane. That's not an airline, it's a charter."

Collins lit a Chesterfield, inhaling deeply and picking a morsel of tobacco off his lip. He was dressed in his usual wrinkled beige cotton suit with the knot of his tie halfway down his shirt. This was not his first vodka of the day.

I'm not arguing," he said, "but you've got to do better than a couple of C's at the track if we're going to have four planes. Four planes means eight pilots, at least, plus navigators, attendants, ground crews, the rest. . . ."

"In three cities," said Morris.

"And two languages," said Collins.

"Red's right," said Morris. "We need four planes. Can you get more DC-3s?"

"Not around here," said Collins. "And not for that price."

"They don't have to be DC-3s," said Red. "We could have two big planes and two small ones. Maybe Walter and Olive would sell us a couple of Twin Beeches."

"Nine passengers?" said Collins.

"To start, why not? Everyone going to Mexico City won't go on to Merida."

"You call Walter," said Collins, "we never got along."

"I'll call Olive," said Red. "She likes me. She'll do it."

"Why do women like you?" said Collins. "You're short and ugly."

"You ever done it with a redhead?"

Collins laughed. "I'll dye my hair."

"Girls can tell."

They laughed, and Morris rose to refill drinks. Overhead, the ceiling fan turned slowly enough to count the blades, creating a waft more sensed than felt. Though Dad would never move from the beach, he loved Tom's house. Like its owner, it was solid and friendly, and Dad already had met a few Hollywood stars like John Carradine and Bill Boyd at Tom's parties.

He was known as a smooth, shrewd and reasonable lawyer, and most of his business came from sorting out contract disputes between actors, agents and studios. Sometimes he'd have them over to mix with his own friends. His bar was well-stocked and if you wanted to sing he could play almost anything as long as you sang in F-sharp or something close. He was a sociable man who'd never married because he preferred the company of men, though that's not to suggest he didn't have girlfriends. He and Dad had hit it off right away. Morris liked offbeat people, and there was something in Dad's Wall Street swagger that appealed to him. Dad had ideas, and Morris, whose law practice sometimes bored him, was always looking for ideas.

Finishing their drinks, they bundled into Morris' Cadillac convertible for the short drive to Lawry's La Cienega and a working dinner.

$

Southeastern Mexico, from Tabasco to Belize but especially Yucatán and Quintana Roo, was screaming to be opened up for growing American tourism in 1947, but the Mexicans had scarcely touched the peninsula since the days of the Mayans. Development was going to take American capital and know-how. The Ramsa partners had already flown in and out of Mérida and Campeche checking on connections and explored to the east where the Gulf of Mexico turns into the Caribbean Sea and jungles are replaced by white sand beaches stretching on for miles. There was an undeveloped spit of land off a fishing village called Cancún that looked like Miami must have looked in 1913 when Carl Fisher put up money for a bridge to an empty spit of land across Biscayne Bay and named it Miami Beach.

Put a bridge and few hotels at Cancún and run some tourist packages from Los Angeles and you'd have a unique product: luxury plus history; Miami plus Mayans. Who could resist such a place? If they could open

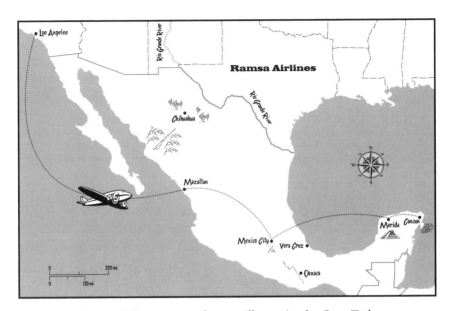

Ramsa Airlines proposed route. Illustration by Gene Toth.

up the peninsula by air from Los Angeles, think what they could do from Florida and Texas, hundreds of miles closer. Havana and Miami, controlled by the mobs, needed competition, and Las Vegas, except for a gangster-run hotel called the Flamingo, hardly existed. With its mixture of climate and archeology, Yucatán was the place. Sun, surf and sex followed by an outing to the pyramids. The brochures wrote themselves. Ramsa couldn't miss.

They finished their steaks and sat back, content. They'd divided up responsibilities: Collins would drive to Ontario to check on the DC-3s; Red would call Olive Beech in Wichita and get on the trail of surplus Twin Beeches. Morris would contact L.A. airport, still a tiny operation at Mines Field on Sepulveda looking for clients and ready to rent space to anything with wings. They now had a legal airline partnership called Ramsa, a name purchased for $1,000 from a bankrupt Mexico City airline flying Piper Cubs to Acapulco and Vera Cruz. They had $50,000 in the bank and were about to buy two planes. They were airline men, and it was time to get operational.

"Something's nagging at me," said Morris over coffee.

The waitress dropped off the bill, and Red picked it up.

"Forget it, Red," said Collins. "You could lose it back tomorrow."

"I'm doing numbers tomorrow." He laid down a hundred dollar bill.

"Hey," said Morris. "Dutch."

"Expense account dinner."

"You and your numbers," said Collins.

"That's what's nagging me" said Morris. He and Collins were smoking and finishing their coffee.

"What's nagging you?" asked Collins.

"The numbers. We buy the DC-3s and we're down to $30,000, with payments to make. Say it costs us another ten grand to get two Beeches."

"Maybe Olive will lease them."

"Maybe," said Morris. "Still, it's more incumbrance. And we still have to hire staff, rent space in three places, buy equipment and pay our own expenses. Probably we have to advertise. And there will be *mordidas* to pay in Mexico. And you know what? We have no income. We can easily go through thirty grand before we have a single paying customer."

"I'll work out a budget," said Red.

Collins looked at Morris. "What are you saying?"

"I'm saying we're underfunded."

"That's all the bank would give us," said Collins.

"Until we start earning money," said Morris.

"Which is when we don't need it anymore," said Red.

"Banks are perverse," said Collins. "Bankers are perverts."

"The rich are perverts," said Morris.

They laughed and fell silent and watched the waitress, young and cute in a flouncy, mid-thigh skirt and obviously looking to be discovered, wend her way back from the cashier with change. She also watched them. Lawry's was popular with the Hollywood crowd, and one day some guy—and it could be any of these three—would be her break. She had to be careful; she met a lot of phonies. She also had to be alert. The little one with the mustache looked like an agent. The big blond could be an actor, and the redhead paid the bill.

Dad at Sucasa (far right) with (left to right) Millie Oliver, cousin Amelia Neville Johnson, Jim Crittenden, Mother with baby Carol and unidentified friend with one sock only. Sucasa, summer 1934.

"Damn good steaks," said Collins, wanting to wrap his arm around her bare thighs. She had a fresh, freckled face and thick, sandy hair down halfway down her neck.

"I'll tell the chef." She placed the change down on a plate.

"That's yours, honey," said Red, pushing the plate toward her.

"What's your name?" asked Collins.

"Iris," she said.

"From?"

"Iowa."

"Iris from Iowa," said Collins. "That's cries for a lyric."

"You guys in pictures?"

Morris laughed. "Afraid not, honey. Just business."

"Now why'd you have to go and say that?" said Collins. "You want us to be in pictures, we're in pictures."

She smiled. Blue eyes, corn-fed complexion, she'd have to watch her weight later, but for now everything was in full bloom. "Thanks for the tip. Very generous."

"Remember us when your famous, honey," said Collins.

"And I will be."

She left for another table. "Quit drooling," said Morris. "You are married men."

"Let me drool," said Collins.

"Speaking of married men," said Red, watching Iris. "I had a call from Coco."

"Give her my love," said Collins. "And how are things in Sewickley?"

"Will Crittenden is curious about Ramsa."

They stared at him. Collins, who'd never met Grandpa, felt he'd known him all his life. In the five years he'd known Dad, three in Wichita and two in Los Angeles, he'd heard the name enough to regard him as an intimate. He knew that Will Crittenden had met his wife in Mexico City and taken over the family steel fortune when the Oliver men died. He knew that, unlike most others, Crittenden had come out of the Depression whole. He knew that the war, thanks to his positions in steel and heavy industry, had made him a wealthy man.

Morris knew less about Crittenden. He'd heard his name and knew Dad wasn't on good terms with his father-in-law, but didn't know the whole story. Tom Morris was not a speculative man. He was an operator who knew the law and did not look to motives as much as actions. He knew that Mother had trust funds that were set up so Dad couldn't touch them, or at least not touch the principal. He knew that Dad's resentment came from the fact that while Grandpa had full control over his wife's trusts, he had denied to Dad such control over Mother's trusts.

Collins broke the silence. "I believe you said Will Crittenden is interested in Ramsa? May I ask how Will Crittenden knows anything about Ramsa?"

"Coco said she mentioned it."

"And?"

"He wants to come out here."

"When?"

"End of summer."

"He wants to invest?"

"He's never given me a red cent. He never will."

"Hold on," said Morris. "Maybe you don't get along with your father-in-law, but why be negative? Give the guy a chance. What exactly did Coco say?"

"That Ramsa came up, and he's is curious. That's all she said. He met his wife in Mexico City fifty years ago. Her father was on a trip to discuss a railroad deal with the Mexicans. It didn't work out."

"Maybe he's nostalgic and wants to recoup," said Morris. "The railroad didn't work so do it with airlines. Get well on the next race, so to speak. Maybe he figures Mexico owes him something. This could be sweet."

Red shook his head. "I came out here to get away from all that. Crittenden wants me in a house in Westchester County, riding the 6:30 to Grand Central with a lot of other schmucks. The man inherited a fortune and did nothing but sit on it. He thinks everyone should be like him, catching a train to a desk. If everyone in Pittsburgh had been like him there'd be no steel industry. No oil industry. Those guys knew about risks. Crittenden will come out here to listen. He won't give us a nickel."

§

Queenie joined him on the patio after breakfast the next morning. It was another clear day, and he swung open the shutters and sank into his favorite redwood chair with the newspaper. He'd skipped his morning swim for he had business to do. It was only ten o'clock and heading for a scorcher downtown, but there were always nice breezes at the beach. He imagined life in the Wall Street brokerages—one o'clock and the poor slobs sweltering at their desks, gasping for a waft of air from the fans. . . or worse, working the floor of the exchange, sweat running down into eyes and armpits. His eyes feasted on the scene in front of him—blue ocean, great arc of beaches sweeping around Santa Monica Bay past Malibu to Point Mugu. Down the hill, he saw people riding the waves by the Westport Beach Club, our club, where he, always an unclubby man, never set foot.

He was startled the first time he'd seen that view because the mountains went dead west past Malibu and then abruptly ended. . . like dropping off the ends of the earth. Reality was that the land bent northward after Point Mugu as the coastline climbed toward Santa Barbara and

Point Conception. Or was it *Concepción*? He was learning some Spanish. Who or what was conceived at Point Conception? Point Conception was also the Hollister Ranch, but surely the Point preceded the ranch. He should have gone up with Coco and the kids to visit the Hollisters last year, but that was more of her Sewickley crowd. One of the Sewickley Olivers, Coco's cousin Becky, married a Hollister, uniting Pittsburgh steel with California's largest ranch. The rich got richer. He wondered if Hollister had control of his wife's trusts.

He glanced at the newspaper headlines. July, '47, Europe was nasty, and nobody ruled out war. Truman was pledging money, but only Western Europe was interested. One by one, Eastern European nations were being locked behind an "iron curtain," as Churchill called it. He wondered if it would be harder to find surplus planes. He checked his watch: It was just after noon in Wichita, too early to call Olive, who'd still be in the cafeteria. He wanted to get her just after lunch, when she'd be well fed on Salisbury steak or meatloaf—was there a difference?—and alone with the ledgers. He knew her schedule because for nearly three years he'd occupied the office next to her, and she was military in her punctuality. He watched Queenie jump up, paws on the window ledge, black ears back, eyes squinty, ocean breezes ruffling her red fur. Even dogs preferred California. He stroked her back. He wasn't a dog lover, but Queenie was all right.

Olive Beech had helped keep him out of the war. He'd been thirty-two at Pearl Harbor with two children and Coco pregnant with Billy. There were no marriage deferments. As a broker, he'd been dealing for some time with Olive on the phone, recommending Beech stock to his clients and taking a fair position himself—thanks to Millie Oliver's munificence. When Olive offered him a job—she ran the company while Walter built the planes—he jumped at it. Beech was adapting its civilian aircraft for both the Navy and Army Air Force.

Walter and Olive Beech were not especially sociable sorts but were decent and progressive Midwesterners, and when he left Beech at the end of '44 they shook his hand and told him to stay in touch, which, thirty months later, he was about to do. He'd been little more than a bookkeeper, but the Beeches knew he'd helped them when their stock was low and, postwar, it had become a high-flyer. If he had to do it over he wouldn't have sold his Beech, at least not all of it. It figured that the end of the war would depress the aircraft industry, only it hadn't. He'd been wrong about that. The civilian industry took over from the military, and Beech had doubled since he sold.

He never cried over cashing out too soon. The mistake was to cash out too late, something he rarely did. He was a trader, moving in and out of positions, making money on shifting valuations based on changing fundamentals or good buzz. He could never be a Will Crittenden. The fun was not just the money, it was the excitement, the action, same reason a horse race beats the lottery. Winning with action showed that you were smarter than the others, not just luckier. Beech stock had helped finance the move to California, the frozen food lockers and now Ramsa. He had no regrets about selling Beech. There were better ways to make money than sitting on stocks or clipping coupons.

He laid down the newspaper and checked his watch again: Twenty after. . . just a few more minutes. Olive was a fast eater.

A SECOND ENCOUNTER

*Amelia's outing with a strange young man, an
unexpected opportunity, plus a necessary account
of the settling of the Sewickley Valley.*

*Major Daniel Leet, circa 1810.
From cabinet card by Rothwell, Washington, Pennsylvania.*

The summer of '47 was a new experience for me at *Sucasa*, and not because Mother tried to send me to camp. That summer I was ten—double digits—and my grandparents took a new kind of interest in me. It's not that they'd ignored me in previous years, but it was just the usual interest grandparents have for children, not the interest they have for people.

I'd always been left free to romp the estate, hang out with the hands and generally just be asked to show up for dinner and maybe lunch. But that summer, the grandparents began to seek me out. Carol and I had long crawled into Granny's four-poster mornings for stories, but the summer of '47, when Carol was thirteen, she stopped coming. It would be just Granny and me for stories, and I began to hear new ones. Until then, she'd told mostly adventure stories, mainly from the Bible and American history. The Bible stories were the Old Testament standards most of us hear at one time or another—Joseph, Jacob, Jonah, Noah, the usual suspects, so to speak. The New Testament stories always came with a moral, for Granny liked morals. Some of her frontier stories were variations on Cooper's *Leatherstocking Tales*—though I didn't know that at the time—which were kept in wall bookcases in the drawing room. But they weren't all from Cooper, for she knew plenty of local Indian lore and told stories to go with the arrowhead collection she kept on a shelf in her room.

The summer of '47 was when she first asked if I wanted to hear stories about growing up down the path in the Oliver house, which was torn down in '44, and about her sisters and brother and how she met and married Grandpa. Surely she'd told Mother these stories as a girl, but Mother either forgot them or wasn't listening for I never heard a word about any of it from her. Granny wanted me to know more about the family, she said. Looking back, I suspect both grandparents had concluded that neither Mother nor Dad were instructing their children in family matters or how to grow up right, so it would have to be done at *Sucasa* or not at all. I can't argue with that.

That summer Grandpa gave up going to Pittsburgh each day. He still went downtown to his office in the Henry W. Oliver Building on Smithfield Street once or twice a week, and sometimes I'd ride along when Stewart drove him to Sewickley Station or to meet the 5:30 commuter back from Pittsburgh—trains having ceased using the Shields Station during the war—but mostly Grandpa hung around *Sucasa*

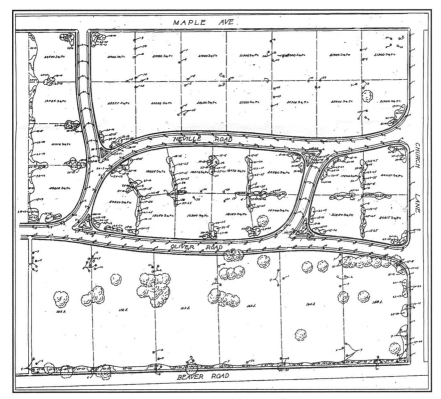

Olmsted plan for Shield's township, 1905.
Courtesy Sewickley Valley Historical Society.

taking care of the estate. With time on his hands, he began to invite me on walks with him.

He was a big walker and had mapped out three favorites, ones he'd taken alone since Uncle Jim had grown up. The best one, and the longest, was down the hill to Church Lane and on to the Ohio River, but he also liked to cross Woodland Road and climb up to the farm. If he wasn't up to the high farm hills that day or it had rained and the cow pies made the trek too treacherous, we'd go down Woodland to Little Sewickley Creek and come back by the lily pond. Little Sewickley Creek (Big Sewickley Creek was about a mile farther down Beaver Road) cut along the bottom of the estate on the east side on its way to the river.

I loved the lily pond. I knew none of its story at the time—how James Oliver had hired the Olmsted Brothers of Massachusetts, sons of Frederick Law Olmsted, the architect of New York's Central Park, to create

Picnic party at the "Lily Pond", 1921.

a kind of mini-Central Park for his family. The lily pond was a broad, landscaped area stretching along Little Sewickley Creek on the lower part of the estate. A winding dirt path with sharp U-turns got you to the bottom, and the first and only time I decided to leave the path and cut straight down the hill in short pants I got the worst case of poison ivy I've ever had, so bad I was bathed in calamine lotion for a week and barely left my room. No corticosteroids in those days. Why didn't someone tell me, I pleaded? The truth is, the last boy they'd had around the place was Uncle Jim, and they'd forgotten how boys were.

At the bottom of the path was a steel-trestled footbridge across the creek, and on the far side the lily pond—actually two large ponds full of fish, lily pads, reeds, croaking frogs and flitting water bugs, everything surrounded by grass and sleeping mistily in summer hazes under a canopy of high trees. Between the ponds stood an octagonal gazebo, its barky arches looking out on slopes stretching down to the ponds. Topped with a pagoda roof, the gazebo had a large pine table and chairs where picnickers could retreat in case of rain.

Attracted by the ponds, I sometimes went down there alone, which Granny didn't like. She told me how her brother Leet had gotten stomach cramps during a swim up Big Sewickley Creek and nearly drowned. Like so many children in those days, I grew up believing the myth of

Jim and Mother with nanny on path to lily pond, 1916.

"stomach cramps"—be sure to wait an hour after eating—that endures thanks to mothers and grandmothers. The truth is that Granny was plain afraid of water and would have preferred that her father never heard of the Olmsteds, just as she disapproved of the pool built for Leet in the Oliver house annex. I doubt she ever swam in her life, though Grandpa had been a big swimmer.

The lily pond wasn't much used in my time—the grass not mowed, wild crocuses invading here and there, the gazebo a bit creaky and even the creek bridge showing holes in it—but it was easy to imagine what a splendid place it had been. Besides the picnics, they'd held family reunions there and garden parties and birthday parties for Mother and Jim with lots of Oliver cousins. Each time we went down there, Grandpa would remind himself to tell the hands to spruce up the place. With three grandchildren in summer residence, maybe it could be brought back to life.

By the end of the summer of '47, I knew more about my grandparents than I knew about my parents. To find out what happened to my parents I first had to know what happened to my grandparents. Had I gone to camp that summer, I would have missed a great deal of the story, for the bus picked me up the first day of camp at eight a.m. But Mother's attempt to deprive me of freedom at *Sucasa* came to nothing. When I missed the bus on the second day, the camp director called Sewickley 12, *Sucasa*'s phone number. Since Mother wasn't up yet, they got Grandpa, who said he'd send them a check. Instead of learning about camp, I spent that summer learning about Leets, Shields, Olivers and Crittendens.

§

Amelia Neville Oliver, my grandmother, eldest daughter of James and Amelia (Millie) Shields Oliver, was twenty-five years old in 1897, still a spinster, and showing every sign of remaining one. Of quiet and artistic personality, she didn't particularly mind. Of course, she wanted children—what else did women do in those days?—but she had little brother Leet to care for, thirteen years younger and like her own child. Leet was named after Major Daniel Leet, the patriarch who'd surveyed and acquired much of the land in Sewickley Valley in the 1790s and whose daughter Eliza married David Shields, Amelia's great-great grandfather. To everyone's surprise, baby Leet, Millie Oliver's last child, came along in 1885, when Millie was 38, the same age Amelia would be when Mother was born twenty-five years later. After three daughters, the Olivers were overjoyed to have a son who, in his time, would take over their business affairs. There was a shortage of sons among the Oliver brothers, and women didn't enter business in those days.

The James Olivers lived on Ridge Avenue, which is on Pittsburgh's North Side today but was still part of the town called Allegheny in 1897, across the Allegheny River from Pittsburgh. With the vast Shields property ready and waiting downriver thanks to Major Daniel Leet's purchases, it didn't take long for James and Millie to build a country home just down the path from the 1854 Shields "homestead," where Millie had grown up. Finished in 1883, the Oliver house, three stories

James Oliver, 1878. From cabinet card by Sarony, New York, New York.

of white brick and shingle, stood for sixty-one years, or until soon after Millie Shields Oliver died in 1943, aged ninety-six.

Arriving from Wichita the summer of '44, it was a shock to find nothing but mounds of grass where the Oliver house had stood. Until then, nothing on the estate had ever changed for me, but it was clear enough why the house was torn down: When James Oliver built his house in 1883, gas lamps still were used in place of electric lights, water closets in place of modern plumbing and wood fireplaces in place of central heating. Grandmother Oliver's thick drapes were not for aesthetics but to help control the temperature. To modernize the house would have cost more than a new one. And who was to live there?

James Oliver was one of four brothers, all pioneers in Pittsburgh industry. The brothers and two sisters were the children of Henry

Oliver, a saddler from Dungannon who immigrated to Pittsburgh in 1842. Henry was not "black Irish," the impoverished Catholics driven out of Ireland by English feudalism and the potato famine of the late 1840s, but a prosperous Protestant businessman of County Tyrone who immigrated because he was an unhappy Whig in a constituency gone Tory. A friend back from the States told him that Pittsburgh, gateway to the American West, was the place for a smart Irishman, so Oliver packed up wife, children and two domestics, boarded a ship at Liverpool and set out for New York and Philadelphia, whence on to Pittsburgh by the Pennsylvania Canal. Pittsburgh was where the Ohio River started, and in that pre-railroad era the Ohio was the only access to the Mississippi and Missouri Rivers, which was as far west as you wanted to go. By the end of 1842 Henry Oliver had opened a grocery at the corner of Third and Smithfield.

Over the next generation, iron, railroads, war and steel—in that order—made Pittsburgh into the great city it became. The discovery of iron deposits came first, and the arrival of the Pennsylvania and Baltimore and Ohio Railroads in the 1850s meant Pittsburgh could ship its iron and coal to places the rivers didn't go. During the Civil War Pittsburgh became the "arsenal of the Union" and, the war over, a band of Scotch-Irish immigrants led by Andrew Carnegie transformed it into America's "steel city." Carnegie's coup was to invest in the new Bessemer steel process during the depression of 1873. While other businesses pulled back, Carnegie expanded, and when the economy picked up again he was ready to become the world's largest steel producer. Cleverly, he named his huge Monongahela River works after J. Edgar Thomson, president of the Pennsylvania Railroad, which had an insatiable demand for steel rails.

Carnegie wasn't alone. Two other sons of Scotch-Irish immigrants, Thomas Mellon and Henry Oliver, Jr., also played a role in the rise of Pittsburgh into America's steel capital. Thomas Mellon and his sons, Andrew and Richard, became the city's bankers, providing funds needed for the demands of Pittsburgh's new industrialist class. Henry Jr., the sharpest of the Oliver brothers, was the first to see that the new "soft" iron ores discovered in Minnesota's Mesabi field would work in Carnegie's Bessemer process. Carnegie was unmoved when Oliver got control of the Mesabi and wrote to friend: "Oliver's ore bargain is just like him—nothing in it. If there is any department of business which offers no inducement, it is ore. It has never been profitable."

Henry Oliver, Jr., 1878. From cabinet card by W. Kurtz, New York, New York.

Even the great Carnegie could be wrong. With the help of Mellon loans and John D. Rockefeller's Great Lakes barges, the Olivers brought their Mesabi ore to Pittsburgh, and soon Carnegie's Thomson works was dependent on it. By 1892, Carnegie recognized his error and ordered Henry Frick, the "coke king" who had become Carnegie Steel's chairman, to buy half the Oliver Iron Mining Company. A few years later, Carnegie and the Olivers sold their remaining steel and iron interests to J.P. Morgan, who formed the United States Steel Company. Carnegie sold his company for $492 million in U.S. Steel bonds and preferred and common stock, the largest price ever paid until then. The Oliver Coal Mining Company was sold to Morgan for a mere $182 million.

With his steel fortune, Carnegie turned to philanthropy. "The man who dies rich, dies disgraced," he proclaimed from his castle in Scotland. Having but one child, Carnegie could afford to be charitable. The six Oliver siblings—four brothers and two sisters—with many more children than Carnegie and less than half the wealth, had more practical concerns: David, had sixteen children; Margaret ten; Mary Frances, nine; George, seven; Henry Jr., one; and James four, including Amelia, my grandmother, who in the summer of 1897 had just returned from art school in New York to the family's home on Ridge Avenue.

Two of the mansions along Ridge Avenue belonged to the brothers, Henry Oliver Jr. and James Oliver. James' house, where Granny was born in 1872 (and Mother in 1910), was down the street from Henry's house, which was on the hill side of Ridge, just two blocks from the home of Benjamin J. Jones, of Jones and Laughlin Steel. William Kendall Thaw, who made his fortune in freight transport, lived nearby. Thaw had ten children by two wives, including Harry Kendall Thaw, a handsome young man one year Amelia's senior.

Granny loved to talk about our Scotch-Irish heritage. There was a tinge of prejudice in it for she always mentioned that the Olivers, like the Mellons, were from County Tyrone, and therefore Protestants, not Catholics, and imbued with the Protestant "work ethic." It was what had led them pick up stakes in Ireland (whither they had been sent from Scotland by English kings to dilute the Catholic presence) and come to America, where the possibilities for success, defined as making money, were greater. Making money, she always said, was not inconsistent with a good Christian life as long as you lived modestly and gave something back.

The Ridge Avenue families had more in common than just heritage and steel. Many of them played the great Scotch-Irish game of golf, most of them tended toward the Presbyterian faith—a gentler derivative of Calvinism—and were members of Third Presbyterian, on Sixth Avenue, just across the Seventh Street bridge from Allegheny City in Pittsburgh. In other words, they worked, played and worshiped together. James Oliver was an usher at Third Presbyterian, his wife Millie sometimes played the organ there and daughter Amelia had known young Harry Thaw at Third Presbyterian Sunday School since they were children.

§

One Sunday in June of 1897, as Granny told her story, she was home from art school in New York, and Millie informed her she had invited young Harry Thaw to lunch with them in Shields. Harry was an eligible young bachelor from a respectable and successful family, and both

James B. Oliver and Amelia N. S. Oliver house on Beaver Road in Edgeworth with pool annex in background, 1930.

James and Millie were fond of him, despite his eccentricities. The merging of the Oliver and Thaw fortunes was an idea that had entered the minds of both James Oliver and William Thaw, if for no other reason than the Olivers had produced mostly daughters and the Thaws mostly sons.

Personally, Granny said, she had nothing in common with Harry Thaw, but in those days, families, status and propinquity were sufficient for marriage. Love was a welcome addition to the equation, not a necessary one. Granny described herself as pious and artistic, shy in the extreme and most comfortable in the company of her own family. For his part, Harry, robust and boisterous, had been expelled from Harvard for unspecified transgressions and subsequently tried various jobs in his father's businesses. He was successful in none, but the senior Thaw hoped marriage would help him to find his focus.

William Thaw wanted Harry to marry her, Granny said, though he would have preferred he marry her cousin Edith, the only child of Henry Oliver Jr., the wealthiest of the Olivers. Edith, however, had just married Henry Robinson Rea, a young man whose prominent Pittsburgh family had pioneered the tin-plate rolling machinery industry and had grown as fabulously wealthy as the rest of their industrious Scotch-Irish brethren.

Inviting Harry that Sunday had been her father's idea, Granny said, and her mother saw no reason to oppose him. Millie had some sympathy for Harry despite his reputation. It was well known along Ridge Avenue that William Thaw could be overbearing with his children. Millie knew how fortunate she was to have a spouse with as much equanimity as her James. All the Oliver brothers were like that, but James was surely the champion.

As for Harry, Millie thought it possible that his uninhibited personality, whatever its causes, might be just what Amelia needed. She loved her eldest daughter deeply, but sometimes felt she needed to be pushed. She saw Amelia's art classes as nothing more than a pleasant diversion. Millie penned a whimsical note to William Thaw indicating that her failure to invite the parents to accompany their son with them to Sunday dinner in Shields was not meant as a slight, but as an opportunity. William responded in the same vein, saying that he understood perfectly.

The Olivers and Harry Thaw boarded the train at Allegheny Station after church that summer Sunday of 1897, and following a forty-minute trip down the Ohio detrained at Shields. The party was met at the station, where leafy Church Lane meets the banks of the Ohio, by Samuel Tucker, employed by James Oliver as groundskeeper and coachman, and transported to the summer house. Both James and Henry Jr. had summer homes in the Sewickley Valley, though James had the additional advantage of having married Millie Shields, whose family, thanks to Daniel Leet and David Shields, was the valley's largest property owner.

Five hours later, following a dinner that Granny remembered precisely—lamb, mint sauce, creamed potatoes, string beans and honeydew melon—and walks by everyone around the estate, they returned to Shields Station to catch the 7:30 train back to Allegheny. It had been a lovely day and it would remain light in the Sewickley Valley (though not in Pittsburgh) until after nine o'clock. One hour later, mother and daughter sat sipping tea in the drawing room at 701 Ridge Avenue to discuss the day's events.

"He is a strange man, Mother," said the daughter. "I do not wish to see Harry Thaw again."

Millie, a practical, down-to-earth Shields with little of the Oliver romanticism, considered Amelia's words. "I saw nothing strange about

*Edith Anne Oliver, almost 8, and and Leet Oliver, age 3, August 1888.
From cabinet card by Scott, New Brunswick, New Jersey.*

him today," she said. "He is spontaneous and entertaining, not a bad combination. Your father rather likes him."

I've seen enough pictures of Granny as a young woman to know she was not unattractive. Though petite, she had a nice figure and her face was pretty. She did have, as did so many children in the days when orthodontics was as unknown as anesthetics, rather buck teeth, a condition that kept her from smiling as much as she might have liked, though that, too, as can be seen in photographs, has its charm. More than either of her sisters, Fanny and Edith, though not more than brother Leet, Amelia represented a blending of the fine bone structure of the Shields and the robustness of the Olivers.

"It's just a feeling, especially when we were walking," she told her mother. "We walked to the end of the path and then along the grass toward the old schoolhouse." In telling the story, Granny would pause to remark that they had walked precisely where *Sucasa* would be built eighteen years later.

"It was such a fine day," she said. "The squirrels were scampering and birds chirping. I saw a goldfinch and a red crossbill. Have you ever seen a crossbill in Shields, Mother?"

"I'm sure I wouldn't know," said Millie. Granny's love of bird-watching was one quality she did not inherit from her mother.

"The way he looks at me—not in the eyes directly, but... you know..."

Millie said nothing.

"And some of the things he said, were... well, I can't describe them any other way but as strange."

Amelia sat back in the velvet chair and looked at the portrait of her father hanging above the mantelpiece. Focusing on him, as calm and gentle a man as she could imagine, might help her understand precisely what it was about Harry she disliked... more than merely disliked, in fact. He actually scared her.

"He expressed some feelings toward his father I thought should not have been expressed. To have such feelings is bad enough, but to express them, even indirectly, to someone outside the family is unimaginable."

Millie Oliver considered asking her daughter what young Harry had said, but thought better of it. Instead, she said: "Are you quite sure you understood him?"

"Quite sure, Mother. And it made me uncomfortable. And his looks made me shudder. I hope you won't invite him again."

"As I said, Amelia, your father quite likes him."

"Oh, Mother. . . ."

They fell silent a moment, Millie grasping her daughter's thought.

"Of course I didn't mean to suggest your father would ever go against your wishes. But are you quite sure you're giving Harry the benefit of the doubt? He seems to think quite a lot of you."

Amelia Neville Oliver (Mrs. William J. Crittenden), 1892.
From cabinet card by Roseti, New York, New York.

"I don't think so. I don't think so at all. He did ask, though, if he could call on me when I'm back in New York. He plans to spend more time there in the fall."

"What did you tell him?"

"I told him Miss Summers did not allow gentlemen visitors. . . which is not true, but seemed to satisfy him."

Millie Oliver finished her tea. The lamps had been lit since they arrived home, though these were already the long days of summer. As bright and sunny as it had been in Shields, as the train passed Neville Island and approached Pittsburgh, they could see the sooty darkness that constantly enveloped the steel city.

The mention of New York reminded Millie of something she wanted to say.

"You know, my dear, you may not be going back to Miss Summers directly. Your father hasn't told you, but I know he intends to. He is planning another trip to Mexico thanks to his correspondence with young Mr. Crittenden. He intends to ask you to accompany him."

Three years earlier, on an excursion to Mexico City, the family had been entertained by Consul General Thomas T. Crittenden, the former governor of Missouri. Amelia had met young Will Crittenden, who assisted his father as vice counsel. They had strolled together through the lush consulate gardens off Paseo de la Reforma, the broad new avenue built by the executed "Emperor" Maximilien to resemble Paris' Champs Elysees. As she took leave of him, the young man asked if he might be allowed to write her, and she responded that she would be honored.

For three years they corresponded, somewhat irregularly for Will Crittenden was a busy man in a lively environment. When his father, with the election of the Republican McKinley, returned to Kansas City, Will stayed on in Mexico to start his own insurance business. In the time they had corresponded, Amelia often wondered about her feelings for Will Crittenden. She was flattered that such an attractive and popular gentleman would be interested enough to begin a correspondence— the first time she corresponded with any man outside her family. For a while, she'd found herself dreaming both of him and of Mexico. With time, however, and few prospects of ever seeing him again, she persuaded herself it was an infatuation based on a short acquaintance in an exotic place. How could they ever meet again? And without meeting again, how could their relationship grow?

Granny came back to this story many times over the years, and their correspondence added more details. The letters bore witness to the couple's growing attachment, but also displayed vast differences between them. Will was pious in his way, which was in his favor, but also a romantic son of Missouri who had fallen in love with Mexico and made his home there. Amelia was a Yankee with deep roots and family responsibilities in Pittsburgh. Their destiny seemed to be to remain distant correspondents until Will's heart was captured by another—most likely someone with more glamour and certainly more propinquity than Amelia Neville Oliver of Shields, Pennsylvania.

Now, unexpectedly, at the end of a very unsuccessful day in the company of Harry Thaw, opportunity was presenting itself: of course Amelia would accompany her father on his return to Mexico to discuss these new business opportunities.

Her return that summer to Mexico City was a pivotal point in her life and therefore all our lives. Following her second meeting with Will Crittenden, their letters took on a more personal tone. Even as their feelings grew, however, Amelia kept her distance. In their correspondence, I found no hint of personal commitment until near the end. As the eldest daughter, Amelia's responsibilities were first to her family, something Will understood. Tradition smiles on first-born sons, but first-born daughters carry a burden, especially when their mothers have children late in life. Born into a prosperous family, Amelia never became the quasi-domestic that was the fate of first-born girls in less-favored families, but more was expected of her than of her sisters. Frances, called Fanny, four years Amelia's junior, had always been helpful, but was fragile of health. In 1897, Edith Ann, sixteen, already was an exotic creature, but still every bit a child.

Her brother, Leet, the dauphin, who turned twelve that summer, was the joy of her life, the young Apollo, "all harmony of instrument and verse... all light of art or nature." How she loved him and feared for him, for so much depended on him. When he went on camping excursions up Big Sewickley Creek, where the masters taught boys to swim and boat, she was sick until he was safely back under her wing. She was alarmed when the annex was built at their Shields home so he could have his own swimming pool. She doted on him. When she prayed, as she did nightly, she asked God that if something had to happen to their family, let it happen to her. She could be spared. Leet could not.

$

There was something louche in how the Shields obtained their Sewickley lands, no doubt about it. That's not something Granny ever told me or something Millie ever told her. I doubt either knew the truth or would have believed it had they been told.

Like so many who had served in the Continental Army during the Revolution, Major Daniel Leet came out of the war in bad financial shape. Men like Leet, who had been with Washington at Valley Forge, had gone for months, even years, without being paid in real currency. As the war dragged on and the Continental Congress ran out of gold and sterling, the army was paid in something called continental script, which depreciated over time. By war's end so much script had been issued that it was worthless and the men refused to accept it.

The Pennsylvanians had a brilliant idea. The state wanted people to move westward, over the Appalachians to the new frontier along the Ohio River. Pennsylvania was land rich and cash poor so why not pay the soldiers in land? There was a problem, however: The lands in question belonged to the tribes of the Iroquois nation. The tribes had fought alongside the defeated British and were not in the best position to negotiate, but when they met the Pennsylvanians at Fort Stanwix, New York, in 1784, they were well-informed enough to demand gold, not script, for their land. Pennsylvania scraped together $5,000 in gold certificates and for that price obtained, in the Treaty of Fort Stanwix, 750,000 acres of land in the form of a triangle with its apex at Pittsburgh and two sides running up the Ohio and Allegheny Rivers to a point equidistant from Butler, fifty miles to the northwest. The purchased lands were then offered to the former soldiers of the Continental Army.

With their script, veterans bought something called "depreciation certificates." The number of certificates a soldier could buy depended on three things: how long he had served, when he had served (because depreciation was more rapid toward the end of the war) and his rank. In addition, certificates were negotiable, meaning that veterans could use any gold or sterling of their own to buy certificates offered for sale by other veterans.

For about six hundred dollars, Major Daniel Leet, who had been sent by Pennsylvania to officially survey the Sewickley Valley after the war, acquired his first piece of land along the Ohio, a lot of 212 acres in what is today called Leetsdale, in 1791. Leet was from Philadelphia and during the Revolution had become friends with a Philadelphia silversmith named Thomas Shields. When Shields' son, David, married Leet's daughter, Eliza, Leet offered his Sewickley Valley lands to the children as a wedding present. By that time, he had augmented his purchases with six more lots along the Ohio, each one containing between two hundred and 250 acres. Seven lots, comprising some 1,500 acres in all, were passed to the newlyweds, David and Eliza Shields.

To my knowledge, no one, either inside or outside the family, ever raised any question about that sequence of events, which show Major

David Shields, circa 1810.
From cabinet card by Rothwell, Washington, Pennsylvania.

Daniel Leet to be exceedingly generous (in addition to exceedingly valiant, for he subsequently led war parties against those Ohio Valley Indians who rejected the Treaty of Fort Stanwix). Leet spent his hard-earned gold to buy a rich swath of land along the Ohio and immediately turned it over to his daughter and son-in-law while he himself languished in modest circumstances in a cabin in what is now Washington County, Pennsylvania, but was then part of Virginia.

As I would discover in the archives of the Sewickley Valley Historical Society, the truth suggests more guile than generosity in Leet's actions. Pennsylvania law prohibited surveyors from acquiring the lands they officially surveyed—a reasonable restriction. The truth is that Major Daniel Leet's putative largesse was really a means of providing cover for lands surreptitiously obtained. As their official surveyor, Leet had no right to any of those 1,500 acres along the Ohio's the east bank, lying roughly between today's Ambridge and Sewickley. To conceal the subterfuge, he signed the lands over to daughter Eliza and son-in-law David Shields.

Leet remained in his cabin until near the end of this life, only moving in with David and Eliza in their house, *Newington,* in the township now called Shields, midway between Sewickley and Leetsdale, in 1827. In time, David and Eliza divided up the land bonanza among their own children, eventually populating the Sewickley Valley over nearly two centuries with many more Leet and Shields progeny than the magnanimous major ever could have possibly imagined.

Passing the Flame

*Correspondence between Shields and Mexico
City sheds light on a marriage's long delay.*

*Grandpa's den at Sucasa, 1915. Governor
Crittenden's portrait hangs over the mantel,
and portrait of James Oliver on the far wall.*

By avoiding camp that summer I not only learned about the family, but was free to explore *Sucasa* as never before. The ballroom yielded the greatest treasures, but there wasn't a room or closet that didn't get my attention. Granny's sun porch, directly over the breakfast room, was full of exotic glass objects on an array of small tables, from finely blown deer and giraffes on spindly legs no thicker than toothpicks to heavy paper weights with exotic scenes sculpted inside. From the sun porch, I could creep up the back stairs to the third-floor maids and storage rooms, where, standing on a chair, I could see through the dormers to the Dashields locks, named after David Shields, on the far bank of the Ohio. I respected the maids' rooms on my wanders, though I might sneak a peek inside if Edith or Mabel or Rose, not expecting visitors, had left her door open.

On the first floor, Grandpa's den by the front door was good for snooping, its walk-in closet filled with a musty, leathery, tobacco smell from shoes, raincoats, cigars, golf clubs, tennis racquets, a croquet set and other interesting things accumulated over the course of a man's life. In Playa del Rey, there were no closets like that. Another "room" I liked was the walk-in steel wall safe, located in the butler's pantry between the kitchen and main hallway and opened only on special days, like Sundays and holidays, when company was invited. Grandpa opened it using a secret combination, one he didn't reveal to anyone, not even me. Filled with shelves of gleaming glass dinnerware in gold filigree and eighteenth century Thomas Shields silver, the safe was a magnet for me. I would stand inside, carefully keeping one foot outside, as Grandpa brought out the treasures.

§

The rediscovery of letters and baby books from the ballroom fifty years later in the attic of Mother's third and last Playa del Rey house was a stroke of luck. Carol and I had been finishing up her move to the nursing home in Palm Desert, the movers had come and gone and I was making a final walk through the sad and empty house now up for sale when I spied a trap door in the ceiling of the upstairs laundry room. Standing on the washing machine, I pushed the door open and, on tip-toes, stared into a dim and dusty crawl space. Two heavy cardboard boxes, the kind movers use, were just within reach. Pulling on one, a shower of dried mouse turds rained down on me. The boxes had been stowed up there since Mother bought the house after Burnie Adams died in 1968.

Quilt given by Mrs. Henry Clay to Mrs. J. J. Crittenden in 1842 when J. J. Crittenden replaced Clay in the U. S. Senate.

How could these boxes have come so close to being abandoned? One contained a five-piece silver tea set, the date 1785 clearly engraved on it, and a letter from Granny stating that this was

> *The silver service of Major Isaac Craig and Amelia Neville, his wife (1785), given by Amelia Neville Craig's father, General John Neville.*

The set bore the marks of Philadelphia silversmith Thomas Shields— the same silver Grandpa used to haul from the safe at *Sucasa*. Alongside, wrapped in a yellowing plastic bag, was the quilt from Granny's four-poster. Rich in colors, with some thirty tableaux sewn into its squares, it was the gift of Mrs. Henry Clay's quilting circle to Mrs. John Jordan

Crittenden when Crittenden replaced Clay as senator from Kentucky in 1842. It hangs today in the Kentucky State Museum in Frankfort.

The second box contained the baby books and letters, which I recognized from my childhood explorations in *Sucasa*'s ballroom. The baby books, three of them, cloth-covered and fragile, were marked, *Our Baby Book*, *Babylogue* and *Baby's Biography*, copyrights 1891, and two in 1907. They contained page upon page of entries in Granny's meticulous handwriting, praising heaven for delivering her such a beautiful baby. The letters represented the long correspondence between Granny and Grandpa, between Shields and Mexico City. Here was the epistolary thread that held their twelve-year-long courtship together, the key to so many family mysteries.

Should I read them? Granny had kept them for a reason. They were meant to be read by someone, so why not me? I knew of them, she had often spoken of them, so it was no violation. It was surely no accident I found them before they were lost forever. How, I wanted to know, could a relationship have been sustained so long by letters alone? Between Amelia's second trip to Mexico and their marriage in 1906, they did not see each other for nine years. When they married, they had seen each other only twice in twelve years. Mexico City, a place I have lived, has many diversions, and I doubt my grandfather was the man to deprive himself. Yet for a decade he wooed my provincial grandmother a world away in Shields, never flagging; and she was content to wait just as long. Why did they wait? How could she be sure he would propose? How could love survive so long on the strength of letters alone?

Amelia's interest in their correspondence was understandable. Shy, insecure, beset by domestic duties, surrounded by demanding family, restricted by the conventions of Western Pennsylvania Presbyterian society, she could escape and romanticize by means of these exchanges with this gentleman in his exotic habitat. What struck me most was that the relationship had endured without any formal commitment. Either party, but especially Amelia, had every right to expect that the next letter would be a "Dear John" or "Dear Mary." But that letter never came. Amelia, surrounded by cousins in provincial Shields, surely had fewer prospects than Will; but Will, however more exciting his life must have been, was as assiduous in the correspondence as she.

In modern times, such an ages-long, long-distance dalliance by post could not exist. The couple would phone daily, rendezvous in Florida or the Caribbean and all questions would be answered. The issues of Amelia's duty to her family and Will's duty to his business would be resolved by jet planes. He could be in Pittsburgh in hours, leaving his business for days rather than weeks. Moreover, and most lamentably, because the Internet has replaced letters, there would be no record of this tender but agonizing romance, one sustained over a decade by correspondence alone. There would be no way to communicate the story a century later to descendants—like me—who might be interested. Letters can be preserved and remembered. Who keeps e-mails?

But why seek to interpret the letters? They speak for themselves, shedding more light on their story than I could possibly do. Both grandparents were prodigious storytellers, so it should be no surprise that their letters were both instructive and entertaining, touching on many themes I would hear later lying in Granny's bed or on walks with Grandpa. I begin with excerpts from a letter written by Granny in that fine, forward-slanting ink script I came to know so well. For if Mother never wrote letters, Granny was a great letter-writer. Why would a letter-writing mother have a daughter who never wrote? Another mystery. This letter is dated June 6, 1903, and deals with an issue surfacing throughout their long correspondence: physical separation. It has been six years since they last saw each other and they write in that familiarly formal— or is it formally familiar?—tone of the era. Will has been thrown from his horse during a polo match and narrowly escaped permanent injury, a story I would hear many times from his own lips. He has just left the hospital to return to his home in Lomas de Chapultepec.

The address on this letter, like all of them from Amelia, is: Mr. William J. Crittenden, Apartado 2027, Mexico, D. F.

My Dearest Will,

You poor dear! How I long to be at your side and offer you comfort. I cannot imagine anything more exciting than a polo match, and it is a wonder there are not more injuries. A concussion and paralysis, however brief, are terrifying things, and the thought that your spine hit the horse's knee makes me think how fortunate we are you did not fall under the animal's hooves. I shudder at the thought! You must tell me how long you will be convalescing and if there is anything we can send to speed your recovery. . . Will, your letter brought me to tears, and they were not just over your terrible injuries. How I would love to fly to your side in Mexico—enchanting Mexico!—but it simply cannot be. Daddy depends on me so much these days. Fanny is with us in Shields for the summer with her baby—Amelia Neville, named for me—I am so proud! And Edith is just back from Europe. She has met an Italian marchese, and it sounds terribly serious. In addition to this, Daddy is slowing down and needs more attention. Leet has been accepted at Yale, and I am acting as his tutor this summer. How I would love to have you here to meet everyone. But I know you cannot leave your affairs. It is our destiny to dream. . .

The intervals between postmarks averaged about a month, longer early in the correspondence and then somewhat less. That would be sufficient time for the post offices of two countries to do their jobs, for the recipient to read and absorb the contents, compose an answer and turn it over again to the post offices again. Will's response is dated July 4, 1903:

Dear Amelia,

Thank your for your latest. It cheered me greatly. I am writing you today, July 4, Independence Day, after returning from a reception at the embassy. It seems like only yesterday that the Governor and I arrived here fresh from Kansas City determined to launch a new era in relations between our two nations, and it already has been a decade. I can't say we accomplished much, but I put the blame squarely on the Mexicans. Diaz is little less than a dictator, and I fear that things will not improve between our two nations until he is gone. . . I hobbled around the familiar paths, aided by friends, thinking of the time you and I walked together in these same gardens. Sometimes I feel we are like people marooned on different islands with no boats at hand. We are in neighboring countries, not even separated by water, and it proves impossible to see each other. I understand the reasons you must remain with your family, and forgive me if I seemed selfish in my last. But the body heals and the spirit with it. Whatever the doctors say, I intend to resume riding. Of course, I will come to you when I can. I will come and sweep you off your feet and we will fly back to the Mexico we both love. Tell your father I am extremely frustrated with the obstacles the Mexicans keep throwing in our paths concerning the railway. I have dealt with them now for nearly ten years, officially and privately, and I can tell you that on this matter I have found them at their most difficult. . .

Grandpa at Sucasa, 1915.

It's clear from this letter that Will has become an agent of sorts for the Kansas City, Mexico and Orient Railway (KCMOR), just as it was he who had originally acquainted James Oliver in the project. By 1903, they've been at work on the line for six years, and, as the letters make clear, have encountered severe obstacles. They've issued stock and received a small subsidy from the Diaz government, apparently intrigued with the idea of opening up Topolobampo Bay for U.S. shipping to the Orient. The railway would cut four hundred miles off the transit of Midwestern livestock and grains then shipping through California to the Orient. One of Will's letters throws some light on the matter. In a letter dated November 18, 1903, I find this paragraph:

> ... the notion that Kansas wheat and Texas herds could by-pass the Rocky Mountains and Western deserts by going through Mexico made sense to me from the moment I first heard it from Arthur Stillwell; as did the idea of providing competition to the Gould lines and bringing down his exorbitant Midwest shipping rates. The provincial Mexicans are just as enthusiastic, but there are problems in the capital. As I have emphasized in my correspondence with Mr.

Oliver, our plans are appreciated more in Chihuahua and Sinaloa than in the capital. Diaz offers no more help. He has centralized all decision-making around him, and that, ultimately, will be the end of him. It is what makes Mexico so inefficient. . .

It's clear from this that Will Crittenden was corresponding with James Oliver as well as Amelia during the period. The mention of Arthur Stillwell is intriguing. This nineteenth century adventurer had taken over a Mexican railroad project abandoned by Albert Kinsey Owen. Imitating his more famous brother, Robert Dale Owen, founder of the socialist colonies in New Harmony, Ind., and Economy, (now Ambridge) Pennsylvania, Albert Owen had founded his own socialist colony in Topolobampo with some six hundred colonists come down from the States. To serve the colony, he was granted a concession by Mexico to build a railroad along the desolate Northwest coast. When both colony and railroad failed, Stillwell took control of the railroad charter and turned to Will Crittenden—and his connection to Pittsburgh steelmen through the Olivers—to reach potential U.S. investors for a railroad reaching across the Sierra Madres.

Amelia, too, was interested in the railway project—perhaps because through it she had renewed her relations with Will. Will's letters also show he has involved his own father in Kansas City, where, as former governor of Missouri he might help speed along the project at that end. The trouble, however, was not at that end. As history would prove, Will was right about the government of Porfirio Diaz, soon to be brought down by the Mexican Revolution, putting an end for half a century to the railroad project. As Grandpa said, the history of human progress is that great projects are left by one generation to be completed by another.

Conceived a century earlier, the railway would be completed in 1961, when the Mexicans themselves—just as other passenger railroads in North America were shutting down—laid the final track to the most spectacular railroad in the Western Hemisphere and perhaps the world. I have ridden on the *Chihuahua al Pacifico* Railway, *El Chepe*, as it is known, a four hundred-mile journey from Los Mochis (Topolobampo) to Chihuahua, a line with too many bridges and tunnels to count, one that rises over a mile into the sky as it crosses the Western Sierra Madres and literally takes your breath away. I have sat in its air-conditioned cars as we disappeared into mile-long tunnels

and crossed over thousand-foot gorges and told the Mexican travelers
around me that part of the story they didn't know—how the railroad's
origins went back more than a hundred years, back to men like Owen,
Stillwell, Crittenden and Oliver, men who had the dream but ran out
of money and into the Mexican Revolution.

Amelia writes on October 10, 1904:

Dearest Will,

  *How I wish you could have been here. I am sure there has never
been another wedding like it, at least not in Shields. My dear
sister Edith, that radiant child, was magnificent, and the train of
her dress must have reached ten feet. The bridegroom, Alfredo, il
marchese, was as regal as the King of Italy himself. Our little church
(Alfredo, grâce a Dieu, is not Catholic) was more splendid than it
has ever been, thanks entirely to Mother. The carriages paraded up
and down Church Lane, discharging their cargoes of Italians and
Americans in formal attire, many of the Italians in uniform, which
seemed out of place in peaceful little Shields. The Olivers were out en
masse, including Aunt Edith, still in mourning from Uncle Henry's
untimely death. Daddy is still greatly affected by the loss of his older
brother, such a pillar of the family. It has put added burdens on the
entire family, but especially him. . . The weather held out for the
wedding. . . October thunderstorms are not unknown in Western
Pennsylvania. I've not yet seen the photographs but am sure they
will be magnificent. The trees along Church Lane were dressed in
their finest colors. Daddy, who is not well, had tears in his eyes as
he walked beside dear Edith, which I saw clearly for he kept his
gaze on me the entire length of the aisle. His tears made me cry as
well. Leet, back from Yale, caught everyone's eyes, including those
of the Italian girls, who are so beautiful I almost wondered if there
would be another wedding before we were done. . . Afterward, the
carriages took us to the reception at the Allegheny Country Club,
and we danced away the night. Oh, Will, I danced many times, and
spoke French to those in the Italian party not fluent in English, but
I was thinking of you constantly. My dancing partners could not
know it but each one became you! Well after midnight, I collapsed
in bed and shed more tears, mostly tears of joy. Edith, my baby,
married now and leaving for her new life in Rome! She is so happy.
If ever an Oliver was born to marry a marchese and live in Rome,*

it is Edith. Fanny would have been completely unsuited, and, as for me, dearest Will, I cannot imagine being so far from you. Shields is already too far. And now Leet has gone back to school. Alas, summer is over and we are settling in for winter. . .

I try to imagine Will Crittenden in his sunny garden in Lomas pondering this missive about Edith's wedding to Alfredo, Marchese Dusmet de Smours, whom Edith had met on a visit to Geneva. Does Will see himself as Alfredo standing at the altar of Shields Presbyterian while Amelia comes down the aisle on James' arm? Or does he shudder at the prospect of leaving the Mexico he dearly loves for a place so new and strange to him? At this point, he has never set foot in Shields or Sewickley and knows about them only from what Amelia has told him. Surely he would have noticed that no sooner was Edith's wedding over than the couple left for Rome. The wedding takes place where the bride chooses, but the place of residence is where the groom chooses. Perhaps Will faltered, as I did, at the phrase "mostly tears of joy." The word "mostly" surely was not used inadvertently, for Granny was always very precise. The word emphasizes the underlying tone, which is melancholic. Amelia is joyful at her sister's triumph and at the dashing figure cut by young Leet with the *ragazze*, but is herself forlorn in the arms of the Italian officers and comes home to throw herself on her bed to weep "mostly" of joy. She finds her solace not in rounds on the dance floor, but in letters to Mexico.

It is now 1905, eleven years since Will and Amelia first met in Mexico City. Nothing really has changed except Will has turned thirty-nine and Amelia thirty-three. He has lived for eleven years at the center of American society in the Mexican capital and is still unattached and uncommitted. He is a dashing and clubby man in a worldly city, but has maintained this private relationship with shy Amelia for all these years without really committing himself. The Olivers might have thought this odd, perhaps even caddish in days when relationships were defined by behavior rather than behavior by relationships, but Will was deeply serious about Amelia. Still, he has not proposed, and they are not engaged.

He is the one more at fault for the ambiguousness, but my view is that he was not taking liberties so much as digging in his heels about leaving Mexico. It had been his home and place of business for a dozen years. He would not leave, and as long as Amelia could not leave Shields, their mutual affection could be expressed only through correspondence, which, fortunately, was sufficient to sustain it. Perhaps because Will had lived in Mexico so long, he felt, in the Mexican style, that things would await *mañana*. Amelia would still be there.

He could have been wrong about that. Amelia might have met a Ridge Street or Shields neighbor more acceptable than Harry Thaw. Granny once spoke of a morning in 1905: The Olivers were in their Shields home, where they lived almost exclusively because of the effects of Pittsburgh's foul air on James' health, and she had just come down for breakfast. Her father was already at the table, which overlooked the broad lawns sweeping down toward Beaver Road, lawns that in ten years would be shared by *Sucasa*. James Oliver had given up smoking the Cuban cigars he dearly loved—more obtainable since the Spanish-American War made Cuba a U.S. colony—but years of smoking and Pittsburgh living had affected his breathing, which came in short, quick breaths into lungs with only a fraction of their former power.

He greeted her and, wordlessly, passed her the *Pittsburgh Gazette*, owned by his brother George. Allowing her time to cast her eyes over the front page photos and story, he asked: "How could I have been so wrong about that young man?"

The photos were of Harry Thaw and showgirl Evelyn Nesbit, whom one story unkindly identified as the former mistress of architect Stanford White and actor John Barrymore. The couple had been married the previous day in Pittsburgh's Third Presbyterian, where Amelia and Harry had met as children and where Millie sometimes played the organ, though not for Harry and Evelyn.

Amelia gazed the longest time at the photo of Evelyn—in marvelous white décolletage—and read the newspaper description of her by Irwin S. Cobb as "the most exquisitely beautiful human being I ever looked upon." She did not respond to her father. There had been no mention of Harry Thaw in the family since that unfortunate luncheon nearly a decade earlier, though all knew he had turned into an irresponsible rake. As she read, she recalled that Harry's father, William, their recently deceased Pittsburgh friend, had left Harry twelve million dollars in his will with the stipulation the money be held in trust "until such time as he shall prove himself responsible."

Perhaps now Harry would never get it. On the other hand, perhaps marrying, even to a showgirl, made him responsible. It would be for the Thaw trustees to determine.

There is a possibility, it must be said for I heard it often enough from my father, that Will Crittenden married Amelia Oliver for her money. One could seek to explain their long epistolary courtship as Will's attempt to string shy Amelia along while seeking a more exotic partner among the many wealthy American families that passed through the Mexican capital. But I came to know my grandfather far better than my father knew him and I cannot imagine Will Crittenden being so caddish. It was simply not in his nature. I prefer to think of it as a ten-year commitment that endured precisely because it was so strong and which was consummated as soon as circumstances permitted. Why else, once the obstacles removed, did they marry so quickly? We know, too, that marriage was more significant a century ago than it is today. Engagements went on for years awaiting the right circumstances. Divorces did not happen. Couples and families took great care because the commitment, once made, was irrevocable.

Their correspondence was by no means limited to *les affaires du coeur,* but shows that both correspondents also had *les coeurs aux affaires.* There are very few subjects of general interest they did not touch on over the passing years, including business, railroads, literature, politics, culture and religion. That both families were Presbyterian, and that both Will and Amelia were church-goers gave them a strong point in common—though I must add that Grandpa's religion was more of the sociable kind, more an aesthetic than a spiritual thing.

On one subject, however, they had some mild disagreement, and there are hints of future problems in letters written during that summer of 1905. Will had this to say:

> . . . *You mention the Republican tradition of the Olivers, that the city of Pittsburgh has never voted for a Democrat in its history, and state that your community's faith in the Grand Old Party is being tested by President Roosevelt. As you know, I come from a long line of Democrats (though Senator John Jordan Crittenden was technically a Whig, a political animal now extinct), and it pleases me to have a man in the White House willing to take on the trusts. A "trust-buster" I believe they call him. We should be happy to have in this President someone we both can like—you because he comes from your party and I because he governs like someone from mine.*

Granny on wedding day, June 23, 1906.

The comment shows the good humor with which Grandpa tackled most issues, and I can see the twinkle in his eye as he penned that paragraph. Granny, who normally lacked Grandpa's sense of fun, in this case was not to be outdone:

> ... As I have mentioned before, dear, I keep all your letters in the safest place imaginable, the secret drawer of my secrétaire. However, faced with your subversive sentiments on the subject of the gentleman in the White House, I now wonder if that drawer is secret enough or if I shall have to burn the letter. Perhaps you can offer me advice on this matter.

The bantering tone ended in a letter dated November 30, 1905.

Dearest Will,

Terrible news! Daddy died last night. I am devastated. . . We all were with him when he went, Mama, Fanny, Edith, Leet, Uncle Dave, Uncle George. Though we'd seen it coming, the shock is every bit as great. Uncle Henry gone last year and now Daddy, both barely into their sixties—O pray that two is all the Lord calls. He will be buried Friday at the Allegheny Cemetery, where Mother today ordered the stone. Grandpa Henry and Grandma Margaret Oliver already are buried there. . . Now the burden of the family business falls entirely on Leet, only in his second year at Yale! Leet loves science so, but I fear it is not to be. Uncle George already has taken him aside and Leet understands what he must do. The poor dear boy, but families take precedence over the individual, do they not, Will? It is very difficult for me to imagine life without Daddy, the kindest, most loving of men. Mother is holding up, but I know how she feels inside. She just won't show it. The Shields are stoics in this sort of thing, definitely more than the Olivers. In that, I am more an Oliver. . .

Will's short response to Amelia is dated January 19, 1906. He apologizes for the delay and states that he was traveling and did not receive her forwarded letter until he had arrived in Chihuahua. He hopes she has received his telegram and that of his parents and reiterates his deepest sympathy and condolences. He states that he is still in Chihuahua and will reply in more detail when he returns to his home in the capital.

But why could he not reply in more detail from Chihuahua? The mails run from there, too. But Will Crittenden was facing his moment of truth. He had long felt that it was James Oliver, not Millie, who kept Amelia in Sewickley. He had no hard facts for that, only his interpretations of her letters: "Daddy is slowing down," "Daddy needs my attention," "Daddy depends on me." Having met James Oliver twice on his visits to Mexico and having corresponded with him as well as his daughter, Will understood Amelia's attachment to her father, by any standard an exceptional man. Hadn't Amelia stated that she was "more an Oliver?"

Will barely remembered Millie Oliver, a small, straight-forward woman who came to the consulate with her family on their first visit and was escorted around the grounds by the governor. It was not Millie who kept Amelia, the last Oliver daughter to marry, at home. It was James. It was not a willful act to deprive his eldest daughter of her right to marry, but Amelia's sense that he needed her and depended on her, though he would never have admitted it, even to himself. It was not just duty that kept Amelia at home—families take precedence over the individual, she said—but a sense of tenderness between father and daughter that did not exist between mother and daughter, a sense seen in Amelia's use of the familiar "Daddy" compared with the more formal "Mother."

I suspect that Will's delay in writing following James Oliver's death was not a result of being in Chihuahua but of not knowing what to say. If he is right that James' existence was the primary obstacle to marrying Amelia and bringing her to Mexico, he has just seen that obstacle removed. Should he now propose? Is that what he has waited for all these years? And could he propose so soon after the event or would a proposal now appear opportunistic? Will's conundrum does not answer the question raised by my father—whether he married for money or love—but for me that question is answered by the letters. Will loved Amelia, had been waiting for her and now the wait could end.

Or could it? Even if Will was right that Amelia now was free to leave Shields—what if they had waited too long; what if the time for marriage had passed them by and James' death meant Amelia, the eldest, unmarried daughter, must now remain as a companion for her grieving mother? They had not seen each other in nine years! Will's delay in answering Amelia is best explained by his need to sort these issues out. When he is done, he proceeds as he must, writing on February 6, 1906:

My Darling Amelia,

More than two months have passed since your father's untimely death and my thoughts have been with you constantly. James Oliver was an excellent and exceptional man. I know how you must grieve. People like us, whose fathers have lighted our way, are among the most fortunate. I am blessed that the governor, several years older than your own father, has been given a long life, but the grief I will feel when he is gone, like the grief you now feel, will be proportionate to my love for him. Dearest, I feel our time has come. We have waited so long, separated by great distance but bound by mutual affection. There have been times for me over the years, as there must have been for you, when I wondered if our moment would come, or if we were condemned, by the nature of things, to live our lives apart, perhaps even with others. But through our correspondence we have remained close—indeed grown closer. Separate duties and long separation could not break the bonds. What I wish to know now, dearest, is if you will have me; if you will allow me to come to you and your family, to make you my bride and return with me to my home in Mexico. . .

It's all there, isn't it? He's laid his cards on the table in the most honorable of ways—grieving for her father, offering to come to her side, asking for her hand and stating—as a condition, for it surely is one—that they return to Mexico. Will Crittenden has his business and his independence in Mexico and is not one to become an employee in Oliver enterprises. In that, perhaps there was something of Harry Thaw in him. Independent people do not join family firms. Grandpa spoke to me often of his life in Mexico, and it was always clear he intended to remain there. Amelia never asked him to settle in Shields. How could she? He had no more ties to Shields than she had to Kansas City. He would have been as much an outsider in her town as she would be in his. Mexico City was the perfect compromise, the perfect setting, for the newlyweds.

Amelia wrote on March 3, 1906:

Dearest Will,

You cannot imagine my joy upon reading your last. Daddy would be so happy! He so respected and admired both you and your father and always hoped we would marry some day. I love you with all my heart and confess that I have done so since the first day we walked in the gardens of the Consulate. . . That we have waited so long has allowed the roots of our love to grow deeply into the soil so that once intertwined they will be inseparable. Mother is thrilled. Tell me when you can come, and we will begin arrangements. The sooner you arrive the more happiness you will bring to us all. . .

Joining and Parting

*Two versions of a story agree that a most happy
event is followed immediately by a tragic one with
unanticipated consequences.*

Shields Station, circa 1890.

In her four-poster stories, Granny told me of her father's death and how she and Grandpa were married soon afterward. When I told Grandpa what she'd said, he listened carefully as we walked and then fell silent. It was August, the weather had been hot and humid bringing out crickets and fireflies at night, and we were picking our way through cow pies to the woods above the pasture on the way to the farm. The cows munched and eyed us warily, swishing at flies. Despite their warm and fuzzy image, cows are especially unsociable beasts. When we approached they simply turned their heads away with a bored shake and a moo, too lazy even to move their oafish bodies. We stopped a moment at the crest while Grandpa cleaned his rimless glasses and caught his breath, before heading into the woods along the path leading to the farmhouse and stables.

"There are some things you should know," he said, and for the rest of the walk and others to follow told me the story as he remembered it, his version differing from Granny's not so much in substance as in impression and detail. It was the first time I was given a glimpse into the selectivity of memory and the relativity both of truth and experience. What I set down here is necessarily an amalgam of what both grandparents told me, against the background of what I would come to learn on my own.

On June 2, 1906, Will Crittenden boarded the morning express from Mexico City's central station bound for Monterrey, connecting to Nuevo Laredo and Laredo, the start of the four-day journey taking him to Pittsburgh. He might have detoured through Missouri—able to ride his own KCMOR line from Chihuahua to Kansas City—but he'd already informed his parents of his plans and would see them soon enough at the wedding. It's easy to imagine his nervousness: forty years a bachelor and about to marry a woman he has met twice in his life in a place he has never been, surrounded by people he mostly doesn't know. He was comforted to know that his family would be there, father, mother and both brothers. He was also comforted in knowing he and his bride would be leaving soon after the wedding to return to Mexico City. Amelia had agreed immediately. Will's business affairs were in the hands of his Mexican staff, which was about to be tested by its leader's first extended absence.

He had four train changes to make, at Monterrey, Laredo, Dallas and Chicago, but had a compartment booked through to Chicago and

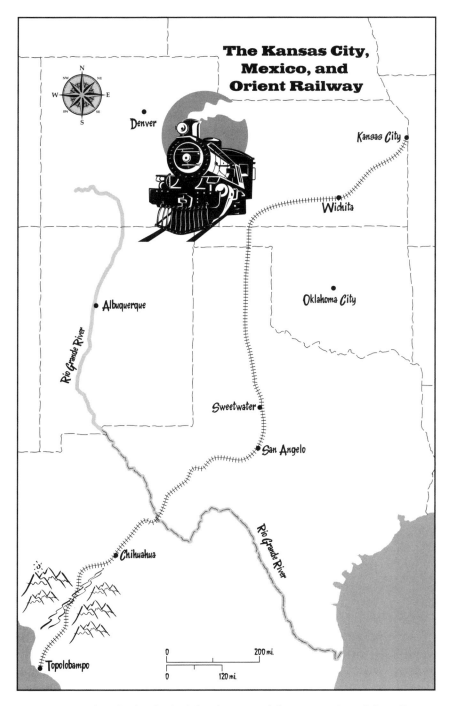

KCMOR Railroad. The final Chihuahua-Topolobampo section of the railway ran into the Mexican Revolution and was not begun. Illustration by Gene Toth.

always had enjoyed first-class train travel. He had Mark Twain's *Following the Equator* with him, perfect company for the journey, plus a supply of maps, cigars, pens and stationery. Having taken these trains before, he knew he had generally good food to look forward to. He contented himself by thinking that in three weeks he would be back on the train with his new wife heading in the opposite direction. A calm and practical man, Crittenden nevertheless was a little giddy with the thought he soon would be married. The longer you wait, friends had told him, the harder it is to adjust. One gets used to living alone. He'd packed a bottle of Kentucky bourbon with him to help make the adjustment.

The maps were a diversion, letting him trace the route the KCMOR was to follow over the Sierra Madres from Chihuahua to Topolobampo. He had no idea what state Oliver affairs were in following the deaths of two of the brothers, Henry and James, but assumed the family's interest in the railroad would continue. He had brought James into the project and had every intention of keeping the family involved. While in Pittsburgh, he planned to meet with Leet, home from Yale, and with his two surviving uncles, David and George.

KCMOR track already had been laid in Texas from San Angelo to Del Rio, connecting to Wichita in the north and Chihuahua in the south. West of Chihuahua, however, where they faced the Sierra Madres and two hundred miles of daunting mountains, rivers and gorges, no track had gone down. They were cash short, but the idea was sound: Midwesterners wanted to get their products to the Orient, and the routes to California were too slow and expensive. Work had resumed on a canal across Panama, this time headed by Americans, not French. A completed canal would be a boon for the Midwest, but was still a dream. Railroads were reality. The Olivers were the perfect partner for the enterprise, active in the steel industry but railroad men in their own right, having started both the Pittsburgh and Lake Erie, and Pittsburgh and Northern Railroads.

It was to be no ordinary wedding. Will had known Amelia for a decade, but it had been like knowing a character in a book, depending mostly on one's imagination. Their long correspondence had drawn them closer, but it remained an epistolary affair, not one of intimacy. And if their correspondence revealed affinities, so did it reveal differences. Politics, for one. The Crittendens were solid Democrats, and the Olivers—in fact, most of Pittsburgh and Sewickley from what Amelia had written—were Republicans. In one letter to Amelia, Will explained how the last-ditch effort of his great uncle, Kentucky Senator John Jordan Crittenden, to avert the Civil War—known as the Crittenden Compromise—was rejected by President Lincoln because Lincoln, a Republican, remembered Crittenden's support for Democrat Stephen Douglas in the famous Illinois Senate race of 1858. Douglas won that election, though Lincoln won the popular vote. The nation was still in the days of indirect Senate elections, as it remains today for presidents, with equally lamentable consequences.

"Hands off!" Lincoln wrote Crittenden on July 7, 1858, in a blunt invitation to stay out of the Illinois contest. The senator's response of July 29 informed the future president that his support for Douglas "did not include a single particle of personal unkindness or opposition to you," which indicated Crittenden well understood that this bumptious Illinois lawyer had a political future ahead of him.

The Crittendens' Democratic Party roots ran deep. Thomas Crittenden, Will's father, had been elected to Congress and then governor of Missouri as a Democrat. Later he was appointed counsel general to Mexico by President Cleveland, a Democrat. Both the Kentucky and Missouri Crittendens had opposed the Civil War and fought with the Union, but they were Whigs and Democrats, not Lincoln Republicans.

Will was a Southerner riding into a Yankee stronghold. True, Missouri and Kentucky were not the Deep South, and Pittsburgh, gateway to the West, was not Yankee New England, but the differences between their families and between their states were substantial. The Crittendens had been political and military animals throughout their history, while the Olivers were men of business and industry.

Will's story of Senator Crittenden's two sons in the Civil War had astonished the Olivers since none of that clan had borne arms. Senator Crittenden's sons, Thomas Leonidas and George Bibb, served as generals on opposing sides, the only such case in the war. They met in the same Kentucky battle, Mill Spring and Logan's Crossroads, January 19, 1862, when the Tennessee secessionists tried to invade Union Kentucky. In *The Crittenden Memoirs*, compiled by Henry Huston Crittenden, Grandpa's older brother, there is a moving account of how Senator Crittenden, "receiving the communication that the two armies were assembling for battle and that a beloved son was a participant on either side, as a member of Congress, secured a special permit and under a flag of truce visited them both on the eve of battle."

How that story excited my imagination. I imagined Billy and me opposing each other on the ramparts of some great battle. Could a brother kill a brother? From Granny, I knew about Cain and Abel, a story that seemed to me more fable than truth. But Grandpa had personally known the two Crittenden generals, his cousins, sons of his great uncle, the senator.

I had an image of General George B., sword flashing as he led the rebel advance, coming upon General Tom L., defending the Union lines.

"Stand aside," demands General George B.

"In a pig's eye," replies General Tom L.

Could they kill each other? Could I kill my brother? It was a quandary I resolved by establishing that generals don't actually fight, but sit on steeds high in the hills observing the battles below. Anyway, I knew that both brothers survived the war. General Tom L. even survived his own son, Lieutenant John Jordan Crittenden, his father's namesake, killed with Custer at Little Big Horn.

Another of Grandpa's stories stirred my youthful interest just as powerfully. It concerned the death, in Havana, of his uncle, Colonel William Logan Crittenden, older brother of his father, the governor. Uncle Bill, as Grandpa called him, had signed on to an expedition against Cuba in 1850 led by Narciso Lopez, a Venezuelan adventurer whose stated goal was to liberate Cuba from Spanish rule. Lopez had strong support in the American South, which saw him as a tool for their annexationist plans to bring Cuba into the Union as a slave state. The Cuban sugar economy was built on slave labor, and as the U.S. domestic quarrel over slavery heated up, it was the South's goal to assure that every free state brought into the Union was matched by a slave state.

The Lopez-Crittenden expedition was an eerie precursor of the Bay of Pigs invasion more than a century later. As at the Bay of Pigs, the invaders assured their U.S. supporters the Cubans would rally to them and victory would be swift. As at the Bay of Pigs, they received little Cuban support and were swiftly captured. Lopez was garroted at Havana's Fort La Punta, opposite Morro Castle, before 10,000 people, September 1, 1851.

Colonel Crittenden, educated at West Point and a veteran of the Mexican war, was accorded a soldier's death. He and his men were shot, in groups of five, by a Spanish firing squad, August 16, 1851. Grandpa

LINCOLN AND J. J. CRITTENDEN

SENATOR CRITTENDEN deemed it his duty to side with Stephen A. Douglas in his contest for U. S. Senator against Mr. Lincoln as the following correspondence will show:

(A. Lincoln to J. J. Crittenden)*

Springfield, Illinois, July 7th, 1858.

To THE HONORABLE JOHN J. CRITTENDEN.

DEAR SIR.—I beg you will pardon me for the liberty I take in addressing you upon so limited an acquaintance, and that acquaintance so long past. I am prompted to do so by a story being whispered about here that you are anxious for the re-election of Mr. Douglas to the United States Senate, and also of Harris, of our district, to the House of Representatives, and that you are pledged to write letters to that effect to your friends here in Illinois, if requested. I do not believe the story, but still it gives me some uneasiness. If such was your inclination, I do not believe you would so express yourself. It is not in character with you as I have always estimated you.

You have no warmer friends than here in Illinois, and I assure you nine-tenths—I believe ninety-nine-hundredths of them—would be mortified exceedingly by anything of the sort from you. When I tell you this, make such allowance as you think just for my position, which I doubt not, you understand. Nor am I fishing for a letter on the other side. Even if such could be had, my judgment is that you would better be HANDS OFF!

Please drop me a line; and if your purposes are as I hope they are not, please let me know. The confirmation would pain me much, but I should continue your friend and admirer.

Your obedient servant,

A. LINCOLN.

P.S.—I purposely fold this sheet within itself instead of an envelope.

* Biography of J. J. Crittenden by his daughter, Mrs. Coleman.

Text of Abraham Lincoln's letter to John J. Crittenden. Reproduced from The Crittenden Memoirs, *1939, by Henry Huston Crittenden.*

would read from the letter the colonel wrote to his uncle, John Jordan Crittenden, then serving as attorney general in the Fillmore cabinet. It is brief and to the point:

> *Dear Uncle:*
>
> *In a few minutes some fifty of us will be shot. We came here with Lopez. You will do me the justice to believe that my motives were good. I was deceived by Lopez. He as well as the public press assured me that the island was in a state of prosperous revolution. I am commanded to finish writing at once. I will die like a man.*
>
> *W. L. Crittenden*

The differences between the Olivers and Crittendens were real ones—political, geographical, professional, economic—and such differences normally weren't bridged in those days. But if real differences existed, similarities of view and character helped draw Will and Amelia together. Amelia's letters stress how family always comes first, followed by church and community. Starting meagerly with Henry Oliver's grocery store, the Olivers had built an industrial empire that could be sustained only if each family member worked at it. Will understood that to mean Amelia could not leave her family until Leet was ready to take over from his father.

On religion, they were mostly alike, neither giving much thought to minor differences among the Protestant sects. In a letter written to his father from Mexico, Will asked something he'd never asked him before: Had sectarian differences made any difference in his marriage? The governor replied thus, a passage found in *The Crittenden Memoirs*. One sees where Grandpa got his sense of humor:

> *Your mother is a member of the Christian church, a firm believer in its tenets and doctrines. I have always been an old school Presbyterian of the bluest faith, whose beliefs are as firmly fixed as the color of the Ethiopian or the spots of the leopard. Still we always thought it far more important to ourselves and our children to attend to our duties as man and wife than to idly discuss the differences between the two systems of theology, believing there was good enough doctrine in each to save us if we were otherwise worthy of salvation.*

§

The train pulled into Pittsburgh's Union Station shortly after break-fast June 6, 1906, and Will headed with his suitcase into the station to await his trunk. A man in livery approached and asked if he had the pleasure of addressing Mr. Crittenden from Mexico City. Assured that he had that pleasure, he introduced himself as John Henderson, the Olivers' coachman, who was to take him to Ridge Avenue. A few min-utes later they were in the carriage and heading over the Allegheny River under the sweeping steel cables of the Seventh Street Bridge. Will noted motor cars here and there, something still non-existent in Mexico City, but most of the traffic, including trolleys, was horse-drawn. He noted that the sky was unusually dark, though it had been a bright spring day as he'd taken breakfast in the dining car coming up the Ohio.

In twenty minutes, the Oliver carriage carried him from Union Sta-tion into a driveway leading off Ridge Avenue toward an elegant white-stone house. As they approached, he saw Amelia, tending a garden, turn to face them. Though it had been eight months since James Oliver's death, she was dressed entirely in black.

They clasped hands and stood for a moment, wordless. How strange it must have been! How many other couples have had a courtship quite like theirs, conducted entirely by mail? One imagines arranged mar-riages between strangers—some poor princess sent against her wishes to marry a foreign prince for *raisons d'état*—but this was no arranged marriage. This was a voluntary union of two lovers who over the course of a long courtship had spent perhaps one hour alone. On the basis of that hour and countless letters they had decided to spend the rest of their lives together. As they clasped hands, both were aware it was the first time they had touched.

Amelia had Will's baggage sent upstairs and, saying little, led him inside and along a hallway into the drawing room, where Millie, book in hand, sat waiting. The high-ceilinged room was somber—valences and curtains pulled back to let in what little light there was from the dark skies outside. At one end of the room stood a grand piano, and the opposite wall was adorned with bookcases. Millie Oliver, sitting stiffly on a settee, was also dressed in black, strange, Will thought, with the wedding so close. He took her thin hand, and she motioned him to sit in the chair facing her. She was erect, subdued and appeared frailer than he remembered.

"Mr. Crittenden," she began, "may I offer you some tea?"

He thanked her, but declined.

"Fanny," said Mrs. Oliver quickly, "my second daughter, has died, and we are in mourning again. The wedding, however, will go on a scheduled."

He looked with astonishment from one woman to the other and quickly offered his condolences.

Amelia's younger sister had died giving birth to her second child four days earlier and had been buried the previous day. Fanny's three-year old daughter, Amelia Neville, Amelia's niece and namesake, had left that morning with her grieving father, whose business affairs were in Washington. A year after losing her uncle Henry and eight months after losing her father, Amelia had lost her sister. Will's eyes went to the full-length portrait of James Oliver over the mantle. Dressed in a dark cutaway frock and white waistcoat, posing under a copse of trees, Oliver stared directly at the portraitist, gaze clear and self-assured. With a thick mustache and body tending toward corpulent, he looked every bit the steel tycoon. Will Crittenden had spent more time with James Oliver than with the daughter he was about to marry. The deaths, coming so close together, clearly had taken their toll on the family.

An awkward silence engulfed the room. As he waited for the ladies to speak, Will heard a door shut, and a young man soon appeared, approaching them across the drawing room with a loping stride. This was Leet Oliver, the dauphin. Will was relieved finally to see a smiling face in Pittsburgh. Leet, he noticed, was not dressed in black.

How many times did I hear the story of their first meeting, and how Leet, twenty years old and back from Yale for the summer, had tried to be subdued in the circumstances but could not hide his natural ebullience. At that age, one bounces back, and Leet had the comfort of youth, his mother and two other sisters to ease the blow of Fanny's loss.

David Leet Oliver was what the French call *espiègle*, a word derived from Germany's legend of *Till Eulenspiegel*, a particularly clever and lively young man with a touch of the devil in him and a shadow over his fate. He was the only one of the Oliver family to attend college and had just finished his second year at Yale, where he achieved honors of every kind—academically, in sports and as a member of the best clubs. He was dressed in tan knickers and a sweater and looked like he was heading for an athletic event of some kind, which, in fact, he was, a

Shields Presbyterian Church and Shields Mausoleum, 1907.
Courtesy of Sewickley Valley Historical Society.

golf game. His mother and sister might have disagreed with his planned activities coming so soon after a death in the family, but would never have interfered.

Will felt instant liking for his brother-in-law to be—a beautiful boy, athletic, exuberant, with blond hair tumbling across his forehead. The dark room, shrouded in mourning, brightened instantly. The women emerged from their shells as the men shook hands. Leet turned their minds from funerals to weddings, reminding them with his presence why their guest was there. He laughed, looked you in the eye, and Will saw he had the gift of frank curiosity—unusual at a time when social convention among new acquaintances required reticence and discretion. Such curiosity could be patronizing in some, but not in Leet Oliver. He was genuinely interested in all things. When family responsibilities called on him to shift his academic interests at Yale, he had broadened them to include both science and business, rather than substitute the one, his love, for the other, his duty.

The next ten days were a whirlwind. The Olivers moved back to Shields, while Will remained on Ridge Avenue, where his own family would be staying. He was on the train each day to Shields, met by the coachman until he informed him one day that he preferred to walk. Summers at *Sucasa* I came to know every foot of ground along that stretch between Shields station and the estate. Grandpa described the first time he made that walk, a fine day in June of 1906:

Detraining, he stood alone as the train pulled out, enjoying the rush of the Ohio over the shoals where the Dashields dam and locks would be built thirty years later. Then he started up leafy Church Lane, still dirt in those days, past the house of Rebecca and Hannah Shields, old-maid daughters of Eliza and David. He passed the church parsonage, the manse as the Presbyterians called it, which in my day was the residence of the Reverend and Mrs. Henry Browne. Beyond the parsonage came the Shields mausoleum and church, and he stood a moment to admire the architecture and imagine his coming wedding day. Shields Presbyterian, finished in 1864, was built by Eliza because she disapproved of the organ in Sewickley Presbyterian. Shields Presbyterian received its first organ only after her death, thanks to Millie Oliver, her granddaughter, and over only pro-forma objections from Rebecca and Hannah, who did not share their mother's Calvinistic interpretation of Presbyterianism. Not only did Shields get its own organ, but Eliza, in her mausoleum residence next door, could occasionally hear her own granddaughter playing it.

On two occasions, Will had detrained at Sewickley, one stop before Shields, and was met by Leet in his new car for a drive up Blackburn Road to the Allegheny Country Club, finished four years earlier. Leet was a top player on Yale's golf team, and if Will was less experienced at golf than at polo, he nevertheless had entertained U.S. champion Willie Anderson at Mexico City's *de los Pinos* course and played the game. Though he was twice Leet's age and no longer had the spontaneity of youth, Will, to Amelia's great joy, struck up an immediate friendship with her brother.

Leet took him on rounds to meet an endless supply of Shields and Olivers, including the redoubtable Captain Dave Shields, his uncle, who'd fought at Gettysburg and knew the story of the Crittenden generals and of Colonel Crittenden, shot by the Spaniards in Havana. Although Leet planned on moving into his father's Pittsburgh offices after Yale, he had no intention of staying glued to a desk, and the knowledge of having a sister and brother-in-law in Mexico City appealed to him. Will lost no time bringing up the KCMOR project, and Leet was keen to learn more. He quizzed Will on other opportunities in Mexico, perhaps opening vacation resorts so Americans could take advantage of the growing rail network between the two countries.

Pennsylvania Rail Road Station at Sewickley, Pennsylvania, circa 1910.
Photo courtesy of the Sewickley Valley Historical Society.

Will found Leet standing by his car the first time he detrained at Sewickley, and they clamored back in for the drive to the Heights. The sporty red car was wide open in front and to the sides, like a buggy, and Leet handed him a set of goggles. His father, he explained, had bought the car, a 1905 Model F Cadillac, shortly before his death, and only Leet and the coachman had driven it. When he was away at school, it sat in the carriage house, as the women refused to ride in it.

They headed up Broad Street, wide avenue shaded under a canopy of elms and sycamores stretching from the Ohio River to Sewickley village. It was a clear and warm June morning, all the more remarkable because there had been no sign either of sky or warmth on the train from dark Pittsburgh. Leet honked the air horn as they crossed Beaver Road and turned onto Blackburn to begin the slow climb up to the Heights.

"All this," he said, sweeping his arm as they chugged up the hill, "belongs to Uncle Henry, the brains of the family, or more specifically, now belongs to Aunt Edith, his widow. Unfortunately, Oliver men seem to die young." He rapped on the steering wheel. "Knock on wood."

The car proceeded smoothly, if slowly and loudly, up the hill, about as fast as a horse at gallop. The road at bottom was asphalt, but turned to gravel and dirt as they climbed. On both sides, deep woods encroached, the road's two lanes cutting along a narrow ridge through tangles of trees above and below. They were deep in the woods now, road and car the only sign of man's presence. Around a bend, they saw a one-horse carriage plodding down the hill, and Leet hailed the coachman.

"Coming back, if we don't get stuck behind something like that, I'll show you how fast this thing can go. I've had it up to thirty-five coming down. You need goggles at those speeds because the wind waters your eyes. They'll have to put some kind of wind shield on motor cars if they make them go any faster." He laughed. "Great car, but you should see the one my roommate has at Yale. New Model N Ford his father bought when he made Phi Beta Kappa. Ford will make a fortune on that car. Costs five hundred dollars. Goes forty miles an hour. Coming down this hill, I could get it well over forty except for the turns. This Caddy cost twice that. Ford has a technique for making cars he says will keep driving the price down. . . says one day every family will own a motor car."

It was Will's first extended motor car ride. "You have a wonderful family," Leet told him as they reached the crest and clattered onto the road soon known as Country Club Lane. The Crittendens had established themselves on Ridge Avenue for the wedding and been twice down river to Shields to meet the Olivers. "Three boys and no girls. Practically the opposite of my family—three girls and one boy."

"I had a little sister," said Will. "Caroline. . . Carrie. She died of diphtheria."

"I know how it feels," Leet said after a moment. "Fanny's loss will hurt for a long time. . . she was a dear girl."

§

The wedding was held at Shields Church June 23, 1906, with Millie Oliver at the organ to play Wagner's *Wedding March*, which Eliza, in her mausoleum residence next door and anyone else on Church Lane would have heard, for the doors to the church remained open on a sunny day starting the new summer. Two years after Edith's wedding to Alfredo, the fleet of carriages for this Oliver marriage was supplemented by a handful of motor cars, all of which, the ceremony over, began the steep climb up Chestnut and Blackburn Roads to the Allegheny Country Club. The third and last of James Oliver's three daughters was now married.

An orchestra was brought down from Pittsburgh, and the celebrating went on into the night. Crittenden brothers danced with Oliver and Shields daughters; Leet Oliver danced with his mother, sisters and a great many cousins. George Tener Oliver, one of the two remaining Oliver brothers—who would be U.S. senator from Pennsylvania in three years time (and remembered for legislation putting the "h" back in Pittsburg)—spent much of the evening in discussion with Governor Crittenden. According to Grandpa, Uncle George wanted to know the precise details of Jesse James murder, which, as *The Crittenden Memoirs* record, cost the governor his job. Captain Dave Shields, who'd fought at Gettysburg and lost a brother at Chancellorsville, cornered Grandpa by the buffet to talk about the Civil War until Granny rescued him.

Three days later, after many long walks around the Oliver estate, traversing the very site—and they could have had no inkling—where *Sucasa* would stand in ten years, Will and Amelia descended for breakfast on the morning of their departure. Leet had left the previous day for New Haven, and the newlyweds would entrain from Pittsburgh the following day for Mexico. On the breakfast table, folded at the place where James Oliver had habitually sat but which had been Will's place since the wedding, was the *Pittsburgh Gazette*. Taking his juice, he noticed the banner headline. Reading it over quickly, he passed it to his wife.

"I believe you knew this gentleman."

She read and gasped. Harry Thaw, her onetime friend, had shot and killed a man.

"Good Lord," she said, reading aloud: "'He ruined my wife and then deserted the girl,' Thaw told the police. 'I can prove it.'"

The dead man was the famed architect Stanford White, whom the newspaper unkindly identified as one of Mrs. Thaw's former lovers.

She set the paper aside and stared at her husband. "He walked up at Madison Square Garden Theater and just shot him. I know that theater. Horrid, Will, horrid! That man was in this house. . . at this table. Mother invited him for lunch. I never could stand him. . . even as a little boy. But this. . . I never would have imagined this. . ."

The partings were poignant. Millie Oliver had lost a husband and daughter, a second daughter was on her way back to Rome, her only son had returned to Yale and her eldest daughter was leaving for

Mexico, which was hardly closer than Rome in those days. A house not long before vibrant with life would soon be as quiet as the Shields mausoleum. Two days earlier, gathering in the drawing room for Leet's departure, Will had seen the tears his wife shed bidding her brother good-bye, the parting eased somewhat by Leet's assurances he would soon visit them in Mexico City.

Now it was their turn. More tears as Amelia exchanged good-byes with her mother. In his short stay in Shields, Will had come to recognize Millie Shields Oliver as a stoic and resourceful woman, noticing she took departures rather more easily than Amelia. There remained an ample supply of Shields and Olivers in the neighborhood to keep his mother-in-law company.

They spent the night at Ridge Avenue and were driven the following day to Union Station for a ten o'clock departure for Chicago, the carriage bearing three more trunks than when Will arrived. The rest of Amelia's things were shipped by Railway Express. He'd booked drawing rooms through to Mexico City, and this trip, rather than the few days in Shields, would be their real honeymoon. He'd enjoyed himself in Pennsylvania, but was ready to leave. It was more than three weeks since his departure and in that time he'd had no news of his affairs. That was not bad news, for he was to be disturbed only on urgent matters. Still, it would be good to return to work again.

The train to Chicago was the first calm they'd known since his arrival. Alone, they discovered they were easy together. Both were avid readers, and they could sit side by side, tomes in hand, perfectly comfortable without exchanging a word. Years later, they still had that same easy companionship. We would repair to Grandpa's den after dinner and sit by the floor Philco listening to *Amos and Andy* and *The Shadow* while he smoked his cigar and read the *Sun-Telegraph*. Granny and I played cards, *Fish*, *Old Maid* or double solitaire. Saturdays after lunch they listened to the Metropolitan Opera, never exchanging a word.

They changed trains in Chicago, and were pulling into Oklahoma City by breakfast. Will noticed that the more distance between them and Shields, the more his wife opened up. This was a woman, he realized, deeply in love with her family but who needed distance to find herself. He was not much different himself. He would have done anything for his mother, father and brothers and never was happier than when surrounded by them. But a certain reticence and even stiffness came over him in family that he didn't feel on his own. They were alike in that way.

The train arrived in Dallas late the second afternoon. They forwarded their luggage and boarded a cross-town carriage for the Laredo station. Arriving, rather than sit in the muggy heat of the station, they asked the conductor if they might board early, as the train did not leave for another hour. The train stood in the shade, and they could open the window onto the platform for circulation.

A porter showed them to their drawing room, elegantly appointed in turn-of-the-century style, and they slumped down on the cushioned banquette, exhausted but happy. Soon they would be home in Mexico. Mexico! Together in Mexico after so much waiting. The few times I heard Granny pronounce the word, a sad look came into her eyes and she faltered. It was Grandpa who couldn't stop talking of Mexico. How close they had been! How different things might have been!

How gloriously happy they must have been sitting quietly on that train, waiting, daydreaming, anticipating, glancing out the window while awaiting the exhilarating cry of the conductor: "All Aboard!"

They would never hear that cry. The conductor was at their door, rapping and announcing a telegram for Mrs. Crittenden.

Will passed it to his wife, who took it insouciantly, expecting more belated congratulations. So many cousins! She opened the familiar yellow Western Union envelope. It was from Millie.

Reading slowly, she shuddered and gasped, dropping the telegram to the floor. She swooned and collapsed as Will, stunned, reached for her. Steadying her, he picked up the telegram and read.

"Leet killed New Haven motor accident STOP Uncle George leaving to bring him back STOP Funeral Monday STOP Return immediately STOP"

"Good Lord!" he cried.

Amelia was sobbing and shaking so hard he feared she might go into convulsions. He held her and rang for the porter, who quickly returned with water and smelling salts. He helped her with both, and the shaking subsided, though her body continued to jerk spasmodically. She had not spoken a word since opening the telegram.

Amelia was inconsolable, her mind already locked in a shroud of grief it would never fully dispel. Will must have been close to shock

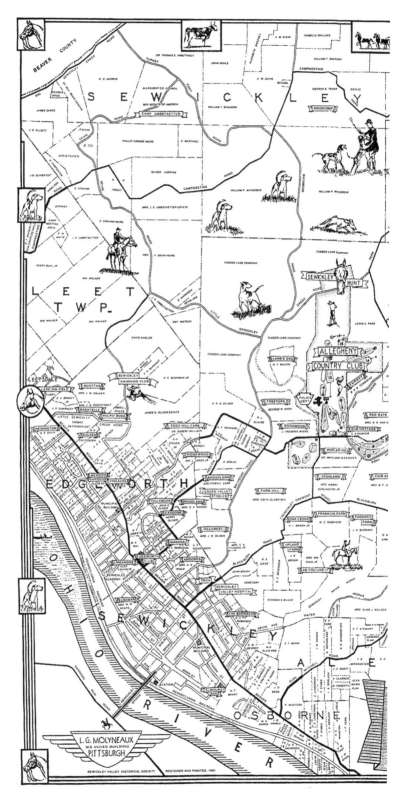

Molyneaux map of Sewickley Valley, 1935.

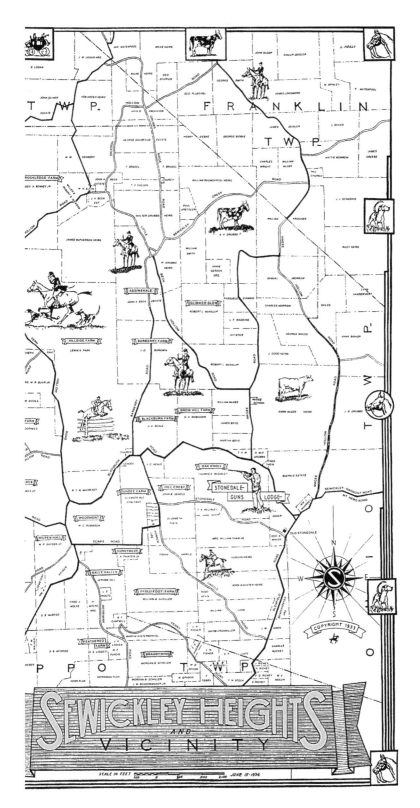

Courtesy Sewickley Valley Historical Society.

himself, grieving not just for his wife's lost brother but unable to escape the thought that everything had changed in a trice. They had boarded the train only moments before rich with joyful anticipation that finally—finally!—they were off for the life in Mexico that had eluded them so long.

Sitting there those endless moments, did he consider sending her back alone? How long does it take a lifelong bachelor to understand he no longer is one person, but two? It was three weeks since he'd left Mexico, and to return to Shields meant days, even weeks, of delay before his return. But if that thought passed through his mind, it surely was quickly and angrily rejected. If the telegram had announced that Will's brother—Henry or Tom Jr.—had died, would she not have accompanied him to Kansas City? But even as the thought crossed his mind—or perhaps because of it—he knew this was more than just returning for the funeral. Would she even return with him now? Could he expect her to?

Leet dead! The beautiful golden boy on the threshold of life, carrying the hopes of his family, snuffed out in a motor accident. Coming back from golf that day, Will had seen Leet's reckless side, the car careening down from the Heights with the gaping hillside below them. His friend's car, he'd said, a reward for making Phi Beta Kappa, went even faster. Forty miles an hour he'd said, almost the speed of a train with nothing to protect you, nothing to hold on to. . . sitting up there on the seat like you were driving a stage coach, but going twice as fast. Was it his Phi Beta Kappa friend's car that Leet died in? Did his friend die as well?

Will was now the only man in Amelia's immediate family. Of James Oliver's robust family of a year ago, the patriarch was dead, the only son and one daughter had died within the month and two other daughters had decamped for Rome and Mexico City. So much had depended on Leet. With Amelia still clinging to him, he rang for the porter and ordered their trunks removed. They would put up in Dallas for the night. He felt a cold dread come over him as he considered their future. What terrible, terrible luck. Selfish thoughts crowded through his mind, and he struggled to shut them out. It was too soon to think it through, but he sensed that everything was different.

Money and History

An unfortunate Sunday dinner, the house of the dead, a new golf ball, and the baby books, plus a short account of how the great families of Pittsburgh came to their wealth and what they did with it.

Granny's bedroom with Henry Clay quilt, 1915.

My grandparents' storytelling gift was inherited from their parents. It's not surprising that so many people in those days were story-tellers, for storytelling was a main form of entertainment. At *Sucasa*, the bookshelves were crammed with the works of the great storytell-ers—Hawthorne, Cooper, Twain, Dickens, Scott, Austen—and as the new century came along, so did radio. Reading and listening, far more than movies or television, involve the imagination, which is the secret of storytelling. Summer mornings at *Sucasa*, I'd slip out of my room and tiptoe down the wide hallway, past the slatted white outer door to Grandpa's bedroom, past the sweeping stairway and the steady tick-tock of the grandfather clock from the landing, to Granny's door at the end of the hall.

I'd rap softly, she'd whisper come in and I'd find her propped up on her pillows, always with a book, long gray hair falling down across her shoulders. The first time I saw her that way was a shock for she never wore her hair down during the day. She'd mark her place while I circled the bed and slipped in the far side. From her I learned the pleasures of reading in bed in the mornings. "The happiest part of a man's life is what he passes lying awake in bed in the morning," said Dr. Johnson, and Granny would surely amend that to include women. An ancient Shields bed warmer with its long wooden handle and copper pan leaned against the fireplace. Sometimes we heard the muffled sounds of Grandpa fusting about, but his rooms were separated from Granny's by a short hallway and two closed doors. I'd lie on my back, hands cupped under my head on the pillow. Granny would sometimes ask what I wanted to hear, but mostly just start right in.

Of all the family stories I heard, none were about Mother. It seemed strange to me, for once Granny started there was no end to her family lore. The nurturing of children is such an integral part of family exis-tence that parents generally die to talk about offspring, imposing sto-ries on anyone who will listen. And children want to hear about their parents, both to satisfy curious minds and for more practical reasons, sensing that knowledge of how their parents acted when they were our age could prove useful.

Between the baby books and Mother's adulthood something went seriously wrong. As a boy, I understood how distant they were and assumed it was how they'd always been. The baby books, however, remove any possibility of that—the love between baby Caroline and her parents is too well documented. But something clearly changed along the way. In a good many summers at *Sucasa* and a few autumns and winters as well, I cannot recall Mother ever doing anything with her parents, any sign of affection between them or even any notable conversation. No, that is not quite right. I remember one conversation—or one "event," more precisely—though I wish I didn't. I must say a word about that before returning to the baby books.

§

Sunday dinners were always a production at *Sucasa*. There would be guests, a chicken or duck slaughtered or maybe a roast, and a morning ride for me with Stewart, the chauffeur, to Sewickley Ice to pick up ice for making ice cream, which we did in the "ice room" off the hallway inside the back door leading to the kitchen. In my time, *Sucasa* had a large built-in refrigerator in the storage pantry (to be distinguished from the butler's pantry), but the "ice room" is where Sewickley Ice used to make its deliveries and where Sunday ice cream was always made. For me, refrigerators for years were "ice boxes" because that's what parents and grandparents called them.

Ice carefully stowed in the car, Stewart and I would swing back through Shields to pick up Simpson, a tall, mustached Englishman, and his wife Amanda, who'd worked as butler and maid for Millie Oliver and were brought in on Sundays and special occasions to help out at *Sucasa*. Errands done, Stewart would circle the roundabout to pick up Granny and Grandpa for the drive down the hill to Shields Presbyterian. I attended church with them, which was a compromise, for while I hated Sunday school in the nearby "white chapel," I enjoyed the church organ and singing and didn't mind the Reverend Browne's sermons, some based on stories I already knew, thanks to Granny.

Our errands finished this particular Sunday, Stewart pulled the Buick up to the porch promptly at 10:45. Grandpa checked his watch, replacing it in his vest pocket, gold fob glittering. He donned his hat, picked a cane from the porcelain stand by the door, Granny emerged from the powder room—long, satiny ladies' room in faded rose colors off the front hall just down from Grandpa's den—and we were off for church. Carol was away somewhere, Billy too young and as for Mother, I didn't even ask. I cannot remember Mother ever going to church with us in Shields. Since the church was just down the hill, a distance Grandpa and I walked many times on our way to the river, I sometimes wondered why we didn't walk, but Granny didn't like walking as much as Grandpa did. She was also, I discovered on walks with her, very slow.

Shields Presbyterian is an imposing gray-stone structure once covered entirely with ivy. Set back slightly from Church Lane, the first thing you notice about it are three slim, lancet-arch windows, looking from a distance like three hooded monks. It was built thanks to Eliza Shields, dedicated in 1869 and one of its many stained glass windows bears the inscription: "In memory of Daniel Leet, a soldier of the Revolution and his wife, Wilhemine"—modest enough testimony to her mother and father, pioneers of Western Pennsylvania. Like in all Presbyterian churches, Shields has a pulpit, not an altar, which is what Granny and Grandpa liked about it. Most impressive were the organ pipes, reaching for the heavens in their many widths and lengths like the stalks in the Oliver corn fields just down Church Lane, across from the white chapel.

At age ten, I knew none of the history of the Shields organ: how Eliza Shields, more Calvinist than Presbyterian, believed music was profane and would not allow an organ in her church, and how Millie Oliver, her granddaughter, prevailed to have one installed after her death. But I loved the music, which filled every church crevice and shook the windows up to the rafters. I stood side-by-side, though not very tall, with my grandfather and the other good Presbyterians as we lifted our voices to be heard above the pounding of the pipes. On those Sundays when the music or Reverend Browne's homily was off, which wasn't often, I meditated on the lunch to follow.

I liked Reverend Browne in part for his accent—he was an Irishman from Londonderry—and in part because he liked preaching from the gospels rather than the Old Testament, which always seemed to me more fable than truth. Maybe it's because he was Irish that he identified more with helping the poor than with fire and brimstone. "How terrible for you who are rich now," he would say, quoting Jesus to the well-heeled as they silently squirmed, "you have had your easy life. How terrible for you who are full now; you will go hungry."

This Sunday I would go hungry myself a while. As we filed out—our pew was in the front and we were last to leave—Reverend Browne, taking leave of the parishioners on the front steps, produced an iron key from under his cassock, which he always wore for services, handed it to Grandpa, who passed it to Granny, who gave it to me. With a tug on my sleeve, leaving Grandpa and Reverend Browne talking, Granny pulled me down the steps. We started across the grass toward the stone structure next door, situated between the church and the parsonage.

Shields Presbyterian Church, 2006.

This building, built in gray granite rather than the brick of the church but with the same high gables, had caught my attention on walks to the river. It was, said Grandpa, "where the Shields are buried." It would be many years before I learned how unique the Shields mausoleum was; learned that churchyards normally do not have massive family mausoleums standing next door.

Wearing her funny white shoes with stubby heels, Granny started off around the house of the dead, as she called it, with me in tow, her ankles bending outward into the soft grass so I thought she might topple. We made two tours of the place, Granny chattering constantly. It was a two-story building with one round, opaque window on each side she called *oeil de bouef* and an arched stone entrance with thick, inset wooden doors like those leading into a castle. I was curious. After our second tour, she took my arm, and we climbed the steps to the front door.

"Unlock it," she commanded.

The iron key turned with some difficulty, but eventually the bolt slid and I pushed on the door, heavy and creaky.

Inside was dark and stuffy, the only light coming from the opaque windows and door, which I made sure remained open. On three sides of the tomb I saw large metal drawers, which Granny said once contained caskets removed at some point and placed underground. The stone floor was covered with brass plaques with names and dates of my departed ancestors. Each plaque represented a Shields or someone who had married one. The room was not only dark, but dank, with a smell I didn't think came just from being locked up.

Granny stayed silent, letting me absorb the full feeling of this creepy place. I was interested but also repulsed, my young imagination conjuring up all the things we associate with tombs. Death is a strange thing for a ten-year-old. It exists as a real phenomenon, but not a personal one. At ten, existence is permanent. The thought that I would one day be Granny's age seemed impossible to me, let alone dead. At ten, stories of death are the stuff of fairy tales and wars in far-away places, not real life.

"The granite of this house represents the granite of our family," Granny said, motionless, her long white dress brushing the dusty floor. Her words echoed around the walls. "Don't ever forget that. Your Mother must never forget that, and neither must you nor your family to come. The Shields built this house to endure just as our family is meant to endure."

Poor Granny. As if Mother ever gave a thought to where she would be buried or to being buried at all when she ran off with the cowboy or eloped with my father or disappeared with her Sewickley ex-boyfriends. Entirely of this life, Mother did not have a transcendental bone in her body. Unlike Granny, who left a detailed plan, Mother would leave no burial instructions in her will. She left no instructions for death because she didn't care about it. She would go out dancing. No fear. I give her credit for that.

Granny was not done. "Not all the Leets and Shields are buried in here," she said.

And so I heard the story of her uncle, "young Tom Shields," as he is called. It was years before I understood that she wasn't talking about young Tom Shields at all. She was talking about Mother.

The Shields were what we call today land-poor—all land and no cash. They were farmers, raising their crops in the fertile valley of the region once called Sewickley Bottom because of the two broad creeks rushing from the heights into rich lowlands along the Ohio. At the center of the farmlands was *Newington*, the house where Major Daniel Leet came to

Shields Mausoleum, 2006.

die on land surreptitiously conveyed to Eliza, his daughter, and son-in-law, David Shields. The main Shields income in those pre-railroad days came from provisioning wagon trains heading downriver into Ohio and beyond.

Young Tom Shields was Major Daniel Leet's great grandson. His offense, for which he and his descendents were forever banished from the mausoleum, was to sell land—specifically a narrow five-mile strip running along the east bank of the Ohio between what is today Ambridge and Edgeworth—to the railroads for a right-of-way. This represented a triple offense: The railroads would destroy the rural nature of the valley, damage the Shields' business of provisioning wagon trains, and, most egregiously, require the excavation of the family graveyard along the riverbank where the railroads were to lay their track.

Major Daniel Leet himself was buried on that riverbank, as were Eliza and David Shields, founders of Leetsdale and Shields. Young Tom Shields' own father, Thomas Leet Shields, eldest son of David and Eliza, was also buried there. The whole clan was in permanent residence on the strip of land overlooking the Ohio River and the woods near where George Washington powwowed with the tribes whose help he sought in evicting the French from Fort Duquesne—soon to be Fort Pitt—and the entire Ohio Valley.

Who can blame young Tom Shields today? The offense for which he was banished from the mausoleum could not long have been avoided. The railroads running westward could not be stopped, and soon his own niece, Millie Shields, would marry into the Oliver clan, which owned two railroads and was starting more, including one in Mexico. Tom's offense reflected a conflict that spread across the nation after the Civil War as people pushed westward into new territories and as new states were brought into the Union. It was the conflict between urban and rural America, between Jeffersonians and Hamiltonians, between stagecoaches and railroads, carriages and horseless carriages, farmers and ranchers.

At first the railroads laid but a single track on Tom's land along the riverbank, but a decade later there were four lines and soon four more across the river. The Shields had been futilely trying to preserve rural Sewickley Valley at a time Pittsburgh was filling up with immigrant workers and new industry. Young Tom Shields would have none of it. He knew farming alone could not sustain the valley.

Unable to keep their valley rural, the Shields, thanks mainly to Young Tom, switched tactics, though not in time to earn his entrance into the mausoleum. If they couldn't keep it rural, they would keep it suburban. The industrialists needed a place to live and breathe, didn't they, to escape the soot and grime of the steel mills? The family would develop the valley residentially: They would sell their lands, not for industry but for homes, large homes—mansions and estates. They would fight to control local government, zoning and land use. Maybe they couldn't stop the railroads—why would they even try now that marriage had brought railroads into the family? But transportation was one thing, industry quite another. The question was—how could they assure their pastoral way of life forever, so that future generations, future town councils, future zoning and planning didn't undo all they had done, turning their pristine valley into an adjunct to Pittsburgh's mills and foundries, changing everything green into black? There was so much land. How could they ensure industry was barred forever?

The question soon answered itself:

Nine-hole golf courses like the Allegheny Country Club in Allegheny and the newer Edgeworth Club on Beaver Road in Sewickley (where

Sucasa *dining room, 1915.*

James Oliver was president), had served well enough when golf balls were made of gut and it took a mighty blast with a brassie or baffy to advance a ball one hundred yards. But balls with rubber centers had just been developed, and golf courses needed more space. Pittsburgh's titans of industry wanted a full, Scottish-style, eighteen-hole course, large enough so a good whack at one of the new balls didn't send it through somebody's window. There was plenty of room in the hills above Sewickley, called Sewickley Heights, for an eighteen-hole course. The problem was that getting up to the Heights in a horse-drawn carriage was a feat.

The year 1902, when motor cars first went into production, was the same year the United States Golf Association, under heavy lobbying from the rich and famous, finally approved the new balls. That same year, the eighteen-hole Allegheny Country Club in Sewickley Heights, easily reachable by motor car, opened for business. The list of companies that switched golf memberships from the nine-hole Edgeworth Club to the new eighteen-hole Allegheny Country Club was a who's who of Pittsburgh iron and steel industry: La Belle Steel, Crucible Steel, Carnegie Steel, Clairton Steel, Oliver and Snyder Steel, Oliver Iron and Steel, Schoen Steel, Pittsburgh Forge, Republic Iron Works, Western Bridge

Works. Representatives of nearly every industry in Pittsburgh—oil, banking, utilities, transport, plate glass, ship works, aluminum—were right behind them. They would build their mansions, raise their children and play their golf in the luscious lands around Sewickley, where the air was pure, the water sweet and the rolling hills made for golf.

Industry in Sewickley Valley—never!

§

I've eaten in the world's best restaurants but have never had better meals than Sundays at *Sucasa*. It was as though an entire restaurant was created to serve one meal for family and friends. Everything for those meals was special, from the bite-sized sandwiches sans crust served as hors d'oeuvres in the drawing room, to the home-made vanilla ice cream with chocolate sauce and galettes for dessert. I've had things at that table I've never seen again, or at least never eaten—like beaten biscuits, deep-fried eggplant squares, shaved meatballs in cream sauce, and strange desserts that, while appreciating their exoticism, I never really liked—like prune whip, tapioca, rice pudding, baked apples and angel hair. Give me homemade ice cream and chocolate sauce every time. The vegetables, dairy products and poultry came from the farm, and there was not a way that Viola, the Italian cook from Ambridge, didn't know how to prepare them. Nobody knew a thing about cholesterol, good or bad, and maybe not knowing helped, for some of the cousins, in addition to Granny and Grandpa, were very old.

Except for the visit to the mausoleum, everything had gone as usual that Sunday: Stewart and I picked up ice in Sewickley and Amanda and Simpson in Shields. We'd returned from church. The guests, including the Reverend and Mrs. Browne, had arrived. Mother, over-dressed and made-up as usual, had made her entrance. Sherry, tomato juice with lemon wedges and the little sandwiches sans crusts had been served to a chatter of friends and relatives in the drawing room. Finally, we'd moved into the dining room. There were fourteen of us, and extra wings had been put in the table.

The dining room was the most elegant room at *Sucasa*, as large as the drawing room but brighter and more open, for its tall, west-facing windows lacked the heavy valances of the drawing room. Light also streamed in from the adjoining breakfast room, though the glass door between them was kept closed for Sunday dinner to mute the chirping of Bobby and Dicky. A Venetian sideboard on delicate legs, holding gleaming Oliver silver brought out from the safe, stood on one side of the room. On the opposite side, under the windows facing the great lawn, stood two matching tables made by the same Venetians and bearing the 1785 silver made by Thomas Shields, the Philadelphia silversmith whose son David married Eliza Leet and got us all going.

The dinner this Sunday was roast beef, which meant Simpson had rolled out the carving table and set out the silver carving set. There was bubbly conversation aided by wine, poured by the very British Simpson. I was seated next to Cousin Todd, who reminded me not of Beatrix Potter's Mr. Tod, who was a fox, but of Mr. Jeremy Fisher, a frog, to whom my rotund and avuncular cousin bore a certain resemblance. The youngest child of David Oliver, the longest-lived of the four brothers, Cousin Todd, whose given name was Charles, had never married and was a frequent Sunday guest at *Sucasa*. He lived in a handsome Georgian mansion on West Drive, just above the Edgeworth Club and always came to dinner alone. I suspect he was not so well off as Granny because Uncle Dave Oliver had sixteen children while his brother James, Granny's father, had but four, only two of whom survived.

Uncle Dave was the second of Dungannon Henry Oliver's nine children, and what drew my attention to him when a copy of the Oliver family tree eventually came into my hands was not just that he lived to be one hundred—rare for someone born in the nineteenth century (1834)—but that his closest siblings, sister Eliza Jane and brother William, died in their first year. Uncle Dave got one hundred years and Eliza Jane and William each got one.

Across the table from Cousin Todd and me, three down from Mother, sat my uncle, Jim Crittenden, who'd given me his captain's bars when he served in the Army and now was at the University of Pittsburgh medical school. Uncle Jim loved talking about blood, especially when roast beef was served. The Crittendens served it rare, and if you didn't like it that way, as I didn't, you asked Grandpa for an end piece (usually to be ignored) or used enough horseradish or hot English mustard so you didn't notice the blood so much.

We'd had consommé to start and were finishing the main course. Little salads had been brought in and all the fluted butterballs I'd watched Amanda roll that morning had disappeared from the butter plates. As usual, Grandpa had carved large slices of roast beef for everyone, save Granny, who nibbled more than ate. After carefully surveying the scene,

Granny had buzzed for Simpson, using the button under the table—different from the breakfast room, which had a foot buzzer under the carpet. It had been a long and leisurely dinner, and I'd started thinking about the vanilla ice cream with hot chocolate sauce and walnuts when Mother asked Grandpa for a second helping of roast beef.

Simpson, who'd just entered the room, stopped in his tracks. Grandpa motioned to him to keep coming.

"Daddy," said Mother again, "I'd like a second helping."

The conversation, which was buzzing, dropped a few decibels. Grandpa stared straight ahead, lifting his eyes from Granny to the portrait of Henry Crittenden, his grandfather, above the mantle behind her. The brother of Kentucky Senator John Jordan Crittenden, Henry was one of the handsomest men I'd ever seen. He died young and Grandpa's father, the governor, had largely been raised in Kentucky by the senator himself. What fascinated me about Henry were his curls, which came down in little ringlets over his forehead. I'd never before seen a grown man with curls.

"Simpson," intoned Grandpa.

"Daddy," insisted Mother.

The butler stood frozen, not even his mustache twitching, as motionless as Henry Crittenden in the picture frame. The drone of conversation fell off into silence, with not even the clank of a Shields fork on a Salviati plate.

"Caroline," said Granny, "really."

"No, Mother, I'd like a second helping of roast beef. I hardly had any."

Even for Mother, this was unusual. An exhibitionist, yes, but not one to make scenes when she was the object. Normally, she was the manipulator of other people's embarrassments. Sitting across the table, I could see her discomfort. It was an insouciant request for a second helping, like Oliver Twist at boarding school. Like Oliver, she hadn't expected the consequences. Fully committed now, she couldn't back down.

"Daddy," said Mother.

"Simpson," said Grandpa.

Standing with her plate, Mother advanced on the carving table. Spry for an eighty-one-year-old gentleman in suit, vest, tie and gold watch

Henry Crittenden, circa 1820. Artist unknown.

fob, who never went walking without a cane, Grandpa was on his feet in an instant. As Mother closed on the roast, Grandpa picked up the platter, spun on his heel and was out the door. With Mother, plate in hand, in pursuit, we heard him cross the entrance hall and head down the hallway toward his den. If he was quick enough, he could lock her out.

"Simpson," said Granny, composed as always, and the butler nodded and left the room. A few moments later, Mother reappeared, muttering how she'd never seen such a thing, that all she wanted was a second help-ing, what was wrong with Daddy, etc., etc. Edith and Amanda began clearing, and soon Grandpa re-entered, flushed and sans roast beef, which reappeared the next day as shepherd's pie. The meal resumed as if nothing had happened, with Granny asking the Reverend Browne to expand on a point from his sermon that morning. We waited for plates to be cleared and the home-made ice cream with chocolate sauce to be served.

It was a tragi-comic scene, one I failed to understand at the time. Those people carried baggage I would only unlock years later. There had to be a mountain of frustration built up for a man as normally composed as my grandfather to do something quite so ridiculous as punish Mother for the Twistian crime of soliciting a second helping. But Grandpa's frustrations were rooted only partly in Mother's contumely. On a deeper level, I suspect most of his discontent stemmed from having always been an outsider in Shields. It was what drew him to Dr. Browne, his closest friend, another outsider who, like Grandpa, arrived in Shields by accident.

A member of Shields Church vacationing in Nassau heard the Reverend Henry Robinson Browne preaching and wrote the trustees. There was an opening in Shields, an offer was made and Browne accepted. When Grandpa became church trustee and treasurer, the friendship between the two outsiders was sealed. Arriving in Shields from the cosmopolitan Bahamas in 1912 must have been as great a culture shock for Henry Browne as coming from Mexico had been for Grandpa, both men closing the books on what must have been considerably livelier former lives. Thinking back on things, I wonder why Grandpa's frustrations didn't boil over more often.

And the family frustrations went both ways. Mother's life was more than just a reaction to her parents—as I reacted to mine—it was a revolt. And while I have long understood my reaction, I failed to understand hers, at least for many years. The roast beef incident brought to the surface currents, rip tides even, I didn't know existed.

§

Why would anyone keep three baby books? Leafing through them, I find many of the same things repeated in each—baby's first word, first step, first lock, first laugh, baptism, guests, etc. etc. The only difference is the words Granny has written down beside the entries. On October 9, 1910, when Mother is four months old, Granny writes in "Baby's Biography":

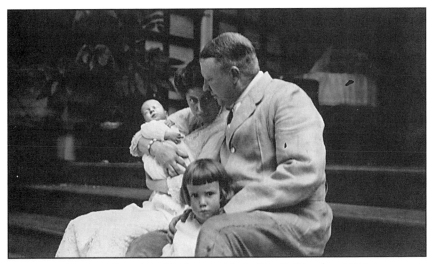

Granny, Grandpa, Mother, and baby Jim Crittenden, 1913.

Mother dressed her darling for the first time in short clothes and cried while doing it. She wore the gowns her Mother had made in Paris in 1908 for the baby sister who died.

I feel my own tears as I read that. Granny was pregnant with "the baby sister who died" (the second Caroline Jackson Crittenden, the governor's wife being the first and Mother the third) while in Paris. I am so curious. Where did they live, what did they do? How long were they there? I lived in Paris for thirteen years and want to know everything. They could have known Henry James, in and around Paris in those days. They were so like characters in *The Ambassadors*, Americans abroad, innocents abroad.

Plunging deeper into the baby books I find no further references to Paris. One cryptic entry in *Baby's Biography* is all I am entitled to know about their French *sejour*. Why did Granny never mention Paris to me? But then how could she know I would live there some day?

Eventually I read every page of the baby books, even those crumbling with a century of age, as though reading some forbidden diary, some hidden trove of feminine secrets not meant for prying masculine eyes. Why three books? It makes no sense other than that she was so ecstatic with motherhood that she had to write things down three times. What spills out from every page is Granny's love and considerable awe at becoming a mother, as though she had lost all hope after the miscarriage.

On a page titled "Secrets" in *Our Baby Book*, she writes:

> *Miss McCully (the nurse) says that 'when a baby smiles the angels are talking to her.' Our baby first smiled a few days after she was born, as she was nursing at mother's breast, and then mother knew that the angels were indeed whispering secrets to her little one.*

Reading this, I wonder: Would she want me to read this? Was anyone meant to read this? It is a story that Granny wrote down for someone to read—surely these words were not intended only for her. Who else would have read them over the past century? Granny meant these books to tell a story to someone, but not this story and certainly not to me. The story doesn't end quite the way she anticipated as she regarded the angelic Caroline in her crib. But does any family story?

The pages are full of warmth and wonder. There's a passage on Mother's fourth birthday, June 23, 1914—yes, Granny still keeps the books going after four years, long after most mothers would have moved on. Jim Crittenden would have turned one year by then, but still Granny dotes on Mother. She kept no baby books on Jim. It would have been too painful. He reminded her too much of Leet. The family is staying in East Hampton, New York, the summer home of Uncle Dave Oliver, the man of sixteen children, while *Sucasa* is in the early stages of construction:

> *I took her in my bed as I do every morning at a quarter past five, laid her tenderly on my body and told her that was the way she had laid four years ago this morning. Last night Daddy and I knelt by her crib and we all three thanked God for our baby, and throwing her arms around her Father she explained, Daddy I love you, God bless you, then saying to me, O, Mother, I do love you so!*

How do we get from these baby books to the roast beef scene? How do we get from a doting mother who filled up three baby books for her daughter to one who can no longer communicate with that daughter and has nothing to say about her to her children? These baby books speak of nothing but love and affection. An entry for June 23, 1911, Mother's first birthday, explains the mystery of the stuffed elephant I'd found under the covers in the ballroom. On the page "Baby's First

Page from Our Baby Book *by Fanny Cory, Bobbs-Merril Co., 1907.*

Birthday" under a heading, "Personages Present," I find a list of presents that includes, "an elephant from India from her Grandmother Oliver."

The baby books show a close and caring household. The Crittendens expected their children to take advantage of their extraordinary surroundings and grow up as loving, loyal and striving children, as they themselves had done. Do not all parents expect that? Are they not entitled to that? Granny and Grandpa had grown up to revere and emulate their parents and carried a great sense of obligation toward them.

There is no record anywhere of defiance. Today's youth makes a habit of revolting from parents, but until Mother came along, there'd been none of that in the Oliver and Crittenden clans as far back as I can trace. As for the very fecund Shields, all my research can turn up is the revolt of young Tom Shields, duly punished for it.

These families were close-knit, living as neighbors, working together and taking care of each other. Kentucky Senator Crittenden raised his nephew Tom, the future Missouri governor, when Tom's father, Henry, the man with the curls, died. Grandpa gave up his Kansas City business to accompany his father, the ex governor, to Mexico and serve as his vice counsel. On the Oliver side, the four brothers were like the musketeers, all for one and one for all. Henry may have been the business brains, but the brothers were side by side with him in affairs and left their own marks outside of business—George in newspapers and politics, David as the "father of Pittsburgh education" (fatherhood seems to have been strong in Uncle Dave's blood) and James as a land and low-cost housing philanthropist for steelworkers living in Leetsdale and Ambridge. These families were loyal to the end and expected the same from their children. Tradition was respected.

§

The industrialists of early twentieth century America became as rich as anyone had ever had been. Theodore Roosevelt tried to do something about it—which is why he was never popular in Pittsburgh—and so did the labor unions. By the time government regulation, income and inheritance taxes and labor unions created countervailing power, Pittsburgh's titans of industry already had made their fortunes. The formation of United States Steel by J. P. Morgan—a product of the merger of Carnegie and Oliver operations—made three dozen millionaires with the stroke of a pen. The great Pittsburgh industrial machine—created by families such as Carnegie, Chalfant, Childs, Dilworth, Frick, Heinz, Horne, Hunt, Jones, Laughlin, Oliver, Painter, Phipps, Rea, Robinson, Scaife, Snyder, Thaw, Westinghouse—was oiled by money from the Mellons, the Pittsburgh banking family of patriarch Thomas and his two banking sons, Richard and Andrew.

Mellon loans were behind most of the great Pittsburgh families, many of which, like the Mellons themselves, were of Scotch-Irish heritage and knew each other personally as well as professionally. By Andrew's time, Mellon success and banking acumen was sufficiently acclaimed across the nation for him to be named Secretary of the Treasury by President Harding, a position he retained under Coolidge and Hoover, all Republicans, not resigning until 1932. Leaving office, Andrew was blamed, more even than Hoover, for the deepening depression. His extraordinary conservatism had led to his advice to Hoover to do nothing to ease the great crisis. Letting the Depression run its course, Andrew argued, would "purge the rottenness out of the system."

Andrew's father would have been proud of that phrase: "Poverty," wrote Thomas Mellon in his extraordinary memoir, "may be a misfortune to the weaklings who are without courage or ability to overcome it, but it is a blessing to young men of ordinary force of character; it protects them from excesses, withholds unwise pleasures and indulgences, teaches the value of time and of wealth, and the necessity of well-doing to better their condition."

One need not agree on the virtues of poverty to understand that the great men of Pittsburgh rose on their own talents. Nothing was given to Andrew Carnegie or Henry Oliver, who both started as Pittsburgh messenger boys. They were, like Thomas Mellon, the children of immigrants, of strivers and achievers, tradesmen and farmers, dreamers and entrepreneurs, all seeking to better their lives and pass that spirit on to their children.

Sometimes, however, instead of passing on the spirit, they simply passed on the money, which led to the very excesses, unwise pleasures and indulgences against which Thomas Mellon believed poverty the inoculation.

The historian Allan Nevins summed up the life of Andrew Mellon this way: "With the misfortune of great wealth, he coped as conscientiously and efficiently as his training and tradition permitted."

Others, lacking the training or tradition, coped less successfully. If poverty is a blessing to young men (and women) of ordinary force of character, then great wealth, its opposite, must be a curse. If it did not prove a curse for those whose hard work produced the wealth and lifted them from poverty, the same thing cannot be said for those to whom they passed it on, their children, not all of whom proved able to surmount the curse.

Encounter in Rome

In flagrante at Francesca's wedding followed by an annulment in Tucson; Mother and the cold baby, followed by a short disquisition on what constitutes family rebellion.

Editta, Mother, Jim, and Jimmy Dusmet in Rome, 1929.

Mother and I didn't talk much. Our relations were tolerable because as much as she liked men and disliked women, she was bored by boys and mostly left me alone, which was fine. The fact is that throughout most of our lives we didn't really enjoy each other's company, didn't have a thing in common besides family and usually contrived one way or another to have someone else present when we had to spend time together. I blamed her for this state of affairs because she had no curiosity or conversation. She couldn't get outside her own skin to talk about things in general. She blamed me because she found me boring—"stuffy," to use her favorite world—too serious, too rational. She liked me better, she said, when I was drinking, and I should do more of it. Reflecting on it isn't painful for there's nothing either of us could have done about it. It's how it was.

Mother told Carol I'd been a "cold baby." Carol and I spent a lot of time over the years talking about Mother, most of it critically. Carol was always a dutiful daughter, especially when Mother got old and needed help, but basically disliked her. She said she was a mean person, though I think she was mostly just indifferent. Mother said she never cried, which struck me as strange because I cry at everything—movies, music, books, even horse races. Why would a non-crying mother have a crying son?

I think she couldn't cry because she couldn't live vicariously, couldn't put herself in another person's skin to feel the pain. She was a narcissist, pure and simple, born for personal pleasure, living a totally unexamined life. The good side of it was that she didn't cry about herself either. In ninety years of living I don't think she wasted a whimper on anyone or anything, including herself. "Don't whine," she would say.

She was the ultimate empiricist: Things existed—feelings and ideas did not. The thing that existed above all else was her own life, and events were good or bad to the degree that they affected it. For some, it's hard to understand people like that, people whose motives are selfish rather than principled, but you have to give them credit: They're not hypocrites and never waste any emotional energy. They don't lie because they have no reason to: They don't care about sparing somebody's feelings or covering up their own. They deal in raw, naked truth. They are remorseless, unsentimental and guilt free. They rarely embarrass and never blush. They are cruel without knowing or caring, and if you're thinking of retaliating, forget it. They won't notice.

When I was in college, I had a crush on a girl named Joan whom I'd met in biology class. I was looking for something special for a first date, like the Hollywood Palladium or Hollywood Bowl or Jack's at the Beach, which was still on a pier in Santa Monica in those days. Mother, I found out, was giving a pool party.

She was married to Burnie Adams by then, living on Rindge Avenue, her second Playa del Rey house. In all, she had three houses in her half century in Playa del Rey: Montreal Street with Dad, three children and Queenie; Rindge Avenue in the pink house with Burnie, Billy, me and Queenie; Rees Street as a widow with a cat named Tango.

The idea of an elegant Rindge Avenue party on the cliffs overlooking the Pacific struck me as a good way to make a first impression on Joan, though it posed the usual risks. I figured Mother would be high on something, and Joan and I could have a drink and be gone by the time she even knew we were there. I had a new suit from Bullock's Westwood, where I worked afternoons, and a snappy, black MGB convertible purchased with Oliver trust fund money I didn't need for college. Millie Oliver had assumed I would go to Yale like her son Leet and grandson Jim Crittenden, but UCLA, in those days, was free.

Joan was unforgettable 1950s perfect: petite, brunette, Debbie Reynolds if you remember her at age nineteen; pageboy hair, touch of the gamine, dress off the shoulders held by little straps that seemed they might give away at any moment. In those days, college couples still had romance and marriage on their minds more than sex, which always seemed more or less out of the question, at least with girls like Joan. Top down on a warm summer evening, we arrived at the pink house, went through to the pool patio in back and began mingling. I ordered a gin and tonic for me and a ginger ale for Joan, who didn't drink. Inside, Lester, the black piano player from Watts was doing what he could on the horrible Baldwin spinet with warped hammers and strings corroded by the salt air. Outside, people stood in clusters around the pool, refreshed by gentle breezes off the Pacific and not-so-gentle booze from the poolside bar, where one of Lester's Watts pals was presiding.

I could tell Joan wasn't having the best of times. We were the only young people there, and though the older gents in their red or yellow polyester pants and plaid blazers were enjoying themselves ogling her bare shoulders and talking about the good old college days, she didn't seem to be as titillated by the mood as I'd hoped. She was a science major who worked at the Los Angeles Museum of Natural History after class, which made things dicey because I was not strong in science. As I was contemplating my future with this delectable creature, Mother sneaked up and shoved me in the pool. I've always wondered why she didn't push Joan in, too, who was the one stealing attention from her. Something of the *Sucasa* social code remained to the end.

As I sloshed to the side and hauled my soaked self out, Mother stood by the pool smirking. To the credit of her friends, she didn't get the laughs she'd hoped, only a couple of nervous yuks from guys chattering to cover their embarrassment. We locked eyes as I stood oozing water over my tasseled loafers, and I could see her disappointment. But that was Mother, always searching for ways to shine, usually at someone else's expense. She'd found her parents too conventional and set out to be the life of every party. There was something pathetic about it, something of the little girl trying to steal attention from the smarter and prettier ones. "Perfect harmony with others," wrote Isaiah Berlin, "is incompatible with self-identity." Mother would have agreed.

Stuffy or not, I took the pool plunge well enough given that my future life with Joan had just been destroyed. I changed into some old clothes and offered dinner, but she wanted to go home. We didn't talk much as we drove back to Westwood. Science majors aren't used to people like Mother. It was our only date. I tried to catch up with her after class after that, but she was always with friends talking protozoa or something. It was painful, but I didn't really hold it against Mother, even came to think she might have spared me even worse pain. I had no future with a science major who worked at a museum and didn't drink. Looking back at it, I can almost laugh.

How do you become a cold baby? Are some babies born cold? Mother, as the baby books prove, clearly was not a cold baby. Nor was Granny a cold mother. If Mother had kept a baby book on me, I think I could prove I wasn't a cold baby. I'm sure I was just as warm as any other baby. But there is no baby book on me. There is a book of photos started after Carol was born, or rather the remnants of a book for some photos are mysteriously gone. Unlike Granny's baby books, Mother's photo book answers no questions. The pictures are mostly of Carol as a baby taken at *Sucasa*. There are some rare pictures of Dad, who hated having his picture taken, and only one picture of Mother and Dad together, on the boardwalk in Atlantic City, March, 1937. Mother has

Me and Mother at Sucasa, 1942.

written beside the picture, taken by a boardwalk photographer, "my new coat." It is a full-length mink, no doubt the gift of Millie Oliver, so is more the picture of a coat than a couple. Dad wears a long overcoat and a pulled-down fedora, looking like member of the mob. Why did he hate to have his picture taken? Did he have a premonition of the wasted life ahead of him? After 1937, I make my baby appearance in the book in various snow suits and sun suits, but, unlike in Granny's baby books, there are no comments with any of the photos.

There is only one snapshot in existence of Mother and me alone together, and we don't look happy. We are standing side-by-side on a summer's day under a large elm tree on the dirt path leading to the chicken pens and vegetable garden at *Sucasa*. I look to be about six and come up just above Mother's waist, which is made higher by her wearing high heels, which look strange on a dirt path. In short pants, I seem to be standing at attention although it is several years before Mother took me out of El Segundo grammar, which I loved, and put me in military school, which I hated. While I am at attention, Mother, waist squeezed by her perennial girdle, is at ease, arms clasped behind her. Not the hint of a smile can be detected on either face.

The photo book ends abruptly in 1938, when I am one year old. Why did she stop it? I am a smiling and happy baby in most of the photos, taken mostly at Larchmont, Westport, Rye and New Rochelle when Dad was working on Wall Street. It sounds odd to write, "when Dad was working," for he never worked very much, though he'd had the seat on the New York Stock Exchange since Millie Oliver's wedding gift in March, 1933, at the very bottom of the Depression, not the best time to be a broker. Wedding presents like that were one of the advantages of Oliver money, which also had disadvantages.

I have an idea what happened back there in the crib. Baby Jimmy reached for a nipple or finger or anything he could get his fat little hand around and got shoved off. Freud would say everything started there. Baby gets rebuffed, and the gray matter or whatever color it is in pink babies gets an imprint in the psychological goo. Imprints in the gray matter never get erased. Even if they could be erased with enough coaxing, as Freud thought, Mother never bothered to try. In my life I never saw her give a real hug of affection to anyone. She didn't like touching, and once when my daughter Kelly, who was ten, took her hand on a walk, Mother pulled back, saying, "I don't hold hands."

Of course, I never tried to erase the imprints either. At least not until now.

§

I had difficulty finding out about Mother's past. She didn't talk much and the grandparents didn't talk about her. Some of this is my fault, but there are limits to a boy's curiosity about his mother. It's different if she's a story teller and makes things interesting, but Mother didn't tell stories. If I asked something, she'd give a vague answer and fall silent. It's like she'd pressed the delete button on her memory and erased the past, living dimensionless, entirely in the present. She said she didn't dream, which is unusual and may explain why she had so little imagination. She didn't read and cared nothing about how the past might relate to the present. What was over was over. We were different that way, one of the reasons we could never connect.

I didn't find out about her elopement until I was thirty-one. For all I knew, Dad was her first husband. I might never have learned about it if I hadn't had the occasion during a visit to Rome in the mid-1960s to look up my Italian cousins—"the Italians," as we called them, the family of Granny's sister, Edith, who'd married the marchese.

I'd been working in Paris for the *New York Herald Tribune*, which had become the *International Herald Tribune*, and was sent to Italy to do some stories on the Italian economy, which had just passed the British economy in GDP and was closing in on the French. It was Italy's economic *miraculo*, and the Herald Tribune wanted me to write about it. I'd been to Rome once before, on a honeymoon with my French wife the previous year, 1967, but this was my first trip alone. It had occurred to me on the first trip to look up the Dusmets, but I didn't have any addresses. By the time I returned, I had Jimmy Dusmet's number.

Jimmy was Giacomo Dusmet de Smours, the first child of Great Aunt Edith and Great Uncle Alfredo who married in the Shields Church in 1904, a marriage I believe contributed to the union of Granny and Grandpa two years later and everything that followed. Jimmy and I had never met, but I'd heard something of his escapades around Sewickley in the late 1920s—still the "Roaring Twenties"—when "the Italians" came to Pittsburgh each summer to commune with their money, held in trust, like all Oliver money, by Mellon. Jimmy, five years older than Mother and eight years older than Jim Crittenden (we were all named after James Oliver), had been something of a rake, and the stories I'd heard about those summers were about parties, girls and speakeasies on the eve of the Depression.

He didn't sound at all surprised when I phoned him in Rome, saying he read the *Herald Tribune*, had seen my name and expected me to call. Everyone in the family wanted to meet me, he said, but it was the dead of summer and they were all either in the Italian lake country or in back in Sewickley. He invited me to lunch at his club, the *Circolo della Caccia*, the hunt club, just a pleasant walk, he said, down the hill from my hotel, the Hassler.

This was early August, 1968, and Europe, like America, was in Vietnam War-related turmoil. I'd spent most of the previous months covering European terrorism, the French student-workers revolt and the beginning of the Vietnam peace talks in Paris, so a few weeks in Rome was like a holiday—especially since August would end that year with the Soviet invasion of Czechoslovakia. Three years running I went to Italy for the *Herald Tribune*, staying at the Hassler when in Rome, sipping gin evenings on the Via Veneto, slipping around the corner to Piccolo Mondo for dinner or down to the Piazza Navona if I had company, sleeping late mornings.

Since my articles were for a supplement that ran in August, I faced no daily deadlines and arranged each day casually around interviews, taxi rides to the suburbs, train trips into countryside and occasional sessions with the typewriter in my elegant hotel room overlooking the Spanish Steps, gaining what little inspiration I needed from gazing on the house where Keats died, at the foot of the steps. When the weather was unbearable, I walked into the Villa Borghese for a swim or strolled in the shade of Via Condotti looking for gifts for my Parisian wife. After Rome came the Mezzogiorno and the Piedmont for more economic investigations. Life was good. As newspaper assignments go, they don't get any better. I appreciated life's refinements.

The *Circolo della Caccia* looked no different on the outside from any other villa, but step past the doorman and you entered eternal Rome. Jimmy Dusmet—*il marchese*, said the doorman—awaited me in the salon, which was off the marble hall. The villa dripped with Roman *grandezza*.

Jimmy was a man of more than medium height, ruddy, dressed in white summer linens and sporting a pencil mustache. He greeted me affectionately with a hug and two words: "Coco's boy." Half Italian or not, I saw the Oliver resemblance immediately, long nose, fine bones, same heart-shaped lips we all have. I could see him frolicking as a boy across the lawns of *Sucasa* with Mother and Jim. What a trove of secrets he held for someone who knew so little about his mother's past. He carried a snappy summer Panama as we mounted the cool marble stairs, the walls adorned with ancient tapestries and oils of the hunt. The dining room was done in dark oak and decorated with more scenes from the hunt, though sans gore, which might inhibit the appetite. Where and what did one hunt around Rome, I wondered? The maitre d'hotel bowed to the marchese and escorted us to our table.

In Rome one ponders the age of things, and the *Circolo* had the look of something that went back a few centuries and had survived a few wars. Chatty and spry at sixty-two, Jimmy was every bit the dapper Romano at his club, polite, elegant, civilized, a gay blade in the old sense of the word. A dozen tables around the room were occupied by elderly gents enjoying leisurely late lunches with wine, to be followed by naps. The room had a drowsy, late-summer hush. Somewhere off the dining room would be a reading room where these distinguished *signori* could repose themselves in deep leather chairs, nodding and letting newspapers slide from their grips as they drifted into cozy snoozes. My appointments didn't resume until 4:30, after the heat died, so I, too, would have time to return to the Hassler for a nap.

We ordered, and the waiter brought a bottle of chilled *Castelli Romani*, perfect in the un-air-conditioned *Circolo*. The fans turned slowly. Romans have managed for several millennia to get through hot summers without air conditioning, so why bother now? Like the *Californios*, the Romanos knew how to build buildings to keep out the summer heat. We sipped our wine and chatted easily about Paris and Rome, but it wasn't long before Jimmy got around to what I'd come to hear: Sewickley in the old days.

Yes, they'd had some wild times, he chuckled.

"We called it Sickly, you know. Prohibition and too much bad gin." He lifted his glass of *Castelli*. "In Rome, we stick to good wine."

He spoke without an accent, though he'd spent most of his life in Italy. A lover of languages, I wondered briefly if his mother, Aunt Edith, had learned Italian or like so many Americans was inoculated against foreign languages. At some point I intended to ask him about the war years, but understood that the subject was as delicate in Italy as in France or Germany. As the saying went, every Frenchman had been in the Resistance, and no German had ever been a Nazi. I wondered how it was in Italy.

How was Coco, he wanted to know? He'd always liked her. She had some Italian in her, he said, fun, wild, a bit *buffone*. Not made for Sewickley.

"That's why she ran off with the cowboy," he said off-handedly. "'I have to get out of here,' she used to say."

He saw my surprise and stopped abruptly, a look of shock on his face. He'd had no idea I didn't know the story—that a newspaper reporter son could reach my age and not know about his mother's elopement. He fell silent, and I could see he wouldn't continue without coaxing.

"I suppose you could call running off with a cowboy *buffone*," I said. "I don't think I know that story."

"It should come from Coco," he said softly. "I'm sorry if I've been indiscreet."

"Mother doesn't talk about family. . . at least not to me. I have to depend on others to find out anything."

He was weighing the matter, sipping his *Castelli*, fiddling with the stem, glancing around the room, pondering. A gentleman, he naturally would hate gossip. Yet he also would recognize my right to know about the family and his right to pass on information to me if others wouldn't.

"Yes, that was not *buffone*," he said, making up his mind. "That was plain crazy. It was in all the papers, a very big scandal. It was just after the Crittendens came here for Francesca's marriage. Coco created a scandal here, too, you know."

He was getting warmed up, and it turned out Jimmy didn't hate gossip after all. I was going to learn more than I'd bargained for.

His younger sister, Francesca, named after Fanny, Granny's sister who died in childbirth, had married Francesco, Conto di Campello, on June 8, 1929. Mother had been expelled the previous year from Westover, a girls' school in Connecticut, for taking a bath with another girl. Grandpa, whom Jimmy called "Uncle Will," had fetched her from Westover and taken her to New York, where she was enrolled in Miss Spence's finishing school. That summer, faced with the choice of graduating from Spence or sailing with the family to Europe for Francesca's wedding, she sailed and never did graduate from Spence or anywhere else. Francesca and Francesco's first daughter would be the beautiful Donatella whom I would meet at *Sucasa* and fall madly in love with when I was 12, the same summer Jane Shape came into my life.

Various photos survive from Francesca's wedding, four months before the Great Crash, photos rescued from the yellowing plastic bag Mother kept under her bed, along with the *Sucasa* photo album, when she died in the Palm Desert nursing home. Like the baby books in her

Crossing Saint Peter's Square after Francesca's wedding, 1929. Mother is to the left of the bride, Maria Ciano, in the rear.

Playa del Rey attic, the family's photo past was kept well hidden. Why were these pictures dumped in a plastic bag instead of being put in albums on bookshelves to be appreciated by all? Carol and I spent days going through the photos trying to identify people. By then, no one was left to help us.

In one riveting picture, the towering Conto di Campello, in full royal regalia with plumed hat and sword, and Francesca, in her wedding dress, sans train, are leading the wedding party across Saint Peter's Square on their way to the basilica where the marriage is to be blessed. Mother, aged eighteen but looking ten years older, is in the front line of this large group spread out across the sunny piazza, escorted by a distinguished, balding gentleman who may have been the cause of the incident with the potted palm, which I will come to. Mother and the Roman are surrounded by a group of mostly Americans and Italians, many identified in the photo and looking festive in the Roman summer. Toward the rear is Maria Ciano, sister of the Fascist Count Galeazzo Ciano, who was to become Mussolini's foreign minister and end up with a bullet in the back delivered by his father-in-law's friends, who didn't trust him. The Cianos and Dusmets were friends.

It is June, 1929, Mussolini has been in power for a decade, asserting his power over Italy and the Vatican and sending troops to slaughter North Africans. Hitler is on the rise in Germany. The insouciant people in Francesca's wedding party on Saint Peter's Square have no idea of the storm about to break over them. How many of them survived the catastrophe? Had I known about the photos that day at the *Circolo della Caccia*, I would have asked Jimmy the question that burns in me: Were you Fascists? I know the answer, of course, but would like to have asked him anyway.

The photos show Mother in various poses around Rome, always with Jimmy nearby. In one in photo, taken on a hill with Saint Peter's in the background, Mother, a second young woman who looks like her clone—it must be Editta, Jimmy's other sister, named for her mother, Edith—and Jim Crittenden are seated on a low wall on a hill. Jimmy, arms folded, stands to the side, under a lamp, looking like a chaperone. From the angle of Saint Peter's, I'm guessing they're on the Monte Mario. The young women—Mother was 18, Editta, 21—are wearing those bell hats to the eyebrows fashionable with the flapper set; skirts over the knees and high heels. Jim Crittenden is dressed in knickers, coat and tie. In the photo-style of the times, they all look monumentally bored.

In other pictures, I finally find someone who is smiling: It is Grandpa, looking jauntily Henry Jamesian in knickers, snap-brim and bow-tie, clearly in his element—as comfortable in Rome as in Mexico City. This was the summer of 1929. Wall Street was still roaring ahead just three months before the crash during the period economists whimsically refer to as—after the popular Broadway Eddie Cantor show—*Makin' Whoopee*. One reason Grandpa was smiling is that he was enjoying Rome. Another reason was that with the stock market setting record highs in volume and value every day, he knew his blue-chip portfolio would easily pay for the wedding.

"Coco was engaged in Sewickley to a young man I'd met," said Jimmy, getting to the heart of the matter. "Bobby or Billy something. . . very respectable Pittsburgh family. . . blast furnaces, I think. Anyway, the summer after Francesca's wedding, so it would have been 1930, Uncle Will took the family to a dude ranch near Tucson. . . still the Wild West

Grandpa (left) Mother (middle) with Italian cousins in Rome, 1929.

in those days. She met this cowboy and eloped with him. . . disappeared without word for days. Uncle Will was beside himself. He hired a detective to track them down and got an annulment before they left town."

If I'd wondered about the roots of hostility between Mother and her parents, this would do for starters. Jimmy diverted his attention momentarily as the waiter brought our orders. I'd ordered smoked trout and cold pasta salad which was laid out with a flourish. Jimmy had lamb chops and string beans, tame fare for a hunt club. The waiter tarried while the marchese took a nibble, pronouncing it *squisito*.

"How did he manage to get an annulment?" I asked.

"You're asking an Italian how to get an annulment?" He chuckled. "I'll tell you how: You need a name, influence and money. We—the Olivers, that is—had big holdings in Arizona—both Calumet & Arizona and Phelps Dodge. Copper was Henry Oliver's idea because of long distance telephones. When Henry bought something so did all the brothers. We still have too much copper in the portfolio in my opinion."

He paused to eat and sip some wine. The room was stiller now, the *signori* finishing up and conversation slower. The waiters slipped silently about.

"Uncle Will knew some people and made some calls. You don't have the Pope out there, you know. Probably a justice-of-the-peace could arrange the annulment... maybe the same one who married them. It was probably a civil ceremony, and I wouldn't be surprised if money changed hands."

"Why would she do it?"

"You're a newspaper reporter," he said. "You want facts? I'll tell you. If it was prohibited, Coco wanted it. That's why Prohibition was so bad, and not just for her. It was the same when she was over here. We had to watch her all the time. You've heard the story about Uncle Will catching her *in flagrante* during Francesca's wedding and locking her in a room at Mother's house, where she had to pee in a potted palm."

Dumbfounded, I shook my head.

He was wound up now. "So I've opened by big mouth again. I'm surprised she hasn't told you that one because she loves it. That story is Coco. Ask her about it some time. If she'd gotten pregnant during that wedding, Mother would have killed me. I was her guardian."

"But why...?"

He finished a lamb chop. Across the room I spied two elderly gentlemen ogling the dessert cart. "She felt confined at *Sucasa* and in those girls' schools. When we were visiting she complained all the time. Always trying to sneak away... climbing out of windows."

It didn't add up. "It couldn't have been that bad," I said. "You know *Sucasa*. People do what they want."

"It wasn't that bad. Coco rebelled. It happens. How can we know really? It was more in her than in them."

Mother and Jim Crittenden at Sucasa, *1929.*

"Rebelled against what? There's nothing to rebel against. Look at our family. . . they settled the land. . . fought the wars. . . built the industries. How do you rebel against that? That's history itself."

His mustache twitched into a smile. "You know about Edward VIII?"

The question stopped me. "You're not. . . "

"I'm only saying that people who are both willful and frivolous do strange things. . . whatever the family."

"Edward's family rejected him, not vice versa."

"No, no, not at all. He made a choice... and accepted the consequences. Look, we all rebel in one way or another, don't we? Haven't you? It was the good life but Coco was bored. She wanted out. Not the way most of us would do it but her own way. So she grabbed a cowboy. Uncle Will got her out of it, probably by threatening to cut her off. Money talks..."

"There's the difference with the Duke of Windsor. He couldn't be bribed out of rebellion."

"Let's say Coco was making a statement. In coming back to the fold, she showed she didn't want to make it too loudly."

It was exhausting. I gazed around the room while the waiter cleared our plates and took orders for espresso. Jimmy offered me a Partagas and we both lit up. Most of the tables were empty. I'd been so involved I hadn't seen one person leave the room. The *signori* of the hunting circle had been on time for their naps.

"What happened to Bobby or Billy?"

He laughed. "I believe marrying another man is grounds for breaking an engagement."

Exhausting... also a little depressing. The two of us might have spent the afternoon talking about Mussolini, de Gaulle, the *grande politique*, the Cold War, Italy's *miraculo economico*, which brought me to Rome. It was my fault I'd side-tracked this debonair Roman onto the subject of Mother. Or rather, like so much, it was her fault, wasn't it? Had she told me what a son needs to know, I wouldn't be searching for lost time over lunch with my Italian cousin. I would already have seen the photo on Saint Peter's Square, noted the presence of Maria Ciano, inquired what she, from the noted Fascist family, was doing at Francesca's wedding, heard the story of Mussolini himself calling on Aunt Great Edith and Uncle Alfredo, the Marchese Dusmet de Smours, sitting in the very room with the potted palm.

"I don't get it. Why didn't Jim Crittenden rebel? Boys rebel, not girls."

He looked surprised. "In his way, Jim did rebel, just like Coco."

"What do you mean, in his way?"

"The opposite of Coco: He became a workaholic, went to medical school, became a doctor. He never takes a day off."

Jim Crittenden and Grandpa at Sucasa, *1932.*

"He takes vacations. He visits me in Paris."

"Even on vacations he's working. He visits the French clinics, right? He does the same thing when he's in Rome. It's smart, he deducts the trips that way, but it's also his nature. And you've seen him at home. No days off, not even weekends."

"But why?"

He searched for the words. "Jim heard too many people say Uncle Will married Aunt Amelia for her money—that he lived off Oliver money. He hated that."

"That never bothered Mother."

He shrugged. "They were different."

I didn't buy it. Mother was no prisoner in Sewickley. After Westover she went to Spence—Spence, that's New York City, not exactly a convent. She was kicked out of Westover for taking a bath with another girl —another story that didn't make sense. If ever a woman had nothing of Lesbos in her, it was Mother. I assume they had a no-bath-sharing policy at Westover just in case and Mother, reckless as always, said the hell with it and ended up at Spence, which obviously was a great deal easier to get into in 1927 than it is today. In any case, her life at *Sucasa* wasn't so bad. She had every opportunity to make something of her life. She just wasn't interested.

As for Jim Crittenden, I think Jimmy was wrong there, too. Jim knew it was Leet's death that brought his father back to Sewickley. Grandpa didn't want to live off Oliver money, he was going back to Mexico where he had his business. His insistence on returning to Mexico had delayed his marriage for a decade. He didn't know Leet would be killed. Grandpa had no choice. What's more, after coming back to Pittsburgh, he had great success managing Oliver affairs, and Jim knew it. Coming out of the Depression with great fortunes intact was not something achieved by all families.

In Granny's eyes, Jim Crittenden, her only son, was the reincarnation of her brother Leet, who died seven years before Jim was born. Leet's death permanently traumatized her—she could never stop talking of it—but also brought her back to Shields and gave her the chance to raise her son in the image of the brother she'd lost. The children's pictures of Jim and Mother together around *Sucasa* eerily mirror the childhood pictures of Leet and Edith together—as if Granny asked the photographer to duplicate the poses. Jim even looked like his lost Uncle Leet—had the same eyes, light complexion and mischievousness smile. As a young man, Jim attended Yale and even took classes in Leet Oliver Memorial Hall, where he probably was the only person to know that LOM, as it's called, was endowed with funds provided by Millie Oliver after her only son's death in the car accident, which may have been the first ever automobile fatality at Yale.

Jim continued the family tradition, didn't rebel from it. Not that there's anything wrong with rebellion. America is not an Asian or Arab culture where the individual owes more to his family than to himself. America is the land of individuality. But the true rebel—*l'homme revolté*—asks himself what he is rebelling against and why, and whether he's likely to achieve something more by his act or diminish both himself and his cause.

Jim Crittenden didn't rebel. He built a house one hundred yards from *Sucasa*, set up his medical practice in Sewickley, built a medical center and became a pioneer at Sewickley Valley Hospital in the field of radioisotopes, which may have contributed to his own death from cancer. He sent his children to the Sewickley Academy. He stayed in Sewickley until he retired in 1976, long after Granny and Grandpa were dead, becoming a surrogate father to me when Dad was too far gone to matter anymore. Unlike in Mother's case, Grandpa gave Jim control over his Oliver trust funds because he trusted his judgment. As a professional man, Jim Crittenden had so little use for his inherited wealth that he turned it over to his sons long before his death—just as Thomas Mellon had turned everything over to Andrew. Jim understood something about the "misfortune of great wealth" and never let it affect his life.

In a prickly sort of way, Mother and Jim remained close to each other all their lives. Different in every possible way, they connected in what they had shared—their childhoods, growing up together at *Sucasa*, the only ones to have spent their entire youth in that rarefied atmosphere. It was not different genes, environments, nor Sewickley's constraints on women that gave them such different characters and values. It was the "X factor," our own specificity, that part of each one of us that is unique.

The X factor is the greatest variable, capable of overwhelming all else. Nothing ordains that two individuals be alike, even when they grow up with the same parents in the same house at the same time with the same amount of love and care. But the Crittenden siblings were alike in this one way: Jim never let wealth interfere with what he wanted to accomplish. Neither did his sister.

WAR AND CHANGE

An embezzlement with a tragic outcome, how the trials of wartime help to build character, and our departure for California.

War is not all bad. Baby Billy in front of our house in Wichita, 1943.

I was born in New York City in the middle of the Depression, the only member of the clan besides my grandfather, Will Crittenden, of Kansas City, not born in Pittsburgh. Granny, Mother, Dad, Uncle Jim, Carol, Billy and most all the Olivers and Shields are Pittsburghers. As much as I love Pittsburgh, I've enjoyed the unique family distinction of being born in Manhattan, at Bellevue Hospital, America's oldest public hospital, a lineal descendent of the infirmary for soldiers established in New Amsterdam in 1658. In a sense, I was born into history.

I was technically a "Depression baby," though with all that Oliver steel money carefully tended and preserved thanks to Grandpa, the term didn't really apply. Dad was still working on Wall Street in 1936, the year I was born, and we were living in Larchmont, hardly a working-class community. With the markets depressed—the Dow bottomed at one hundred in 1938, well less than one percent what it is today—and the economy stagnant, I'm not sure how much work there actually was. We lived in four places during those New York years—Larchmont, New Rochelle, Rye and Westport, Connecticut—none of which I remember too well, though I do have a distinct memory of the family crowded around the radio in Westport after Pearl Harbor listening to Roosevelt's "day of infamy" speech. We had a dachshund named Adolf who executed himself several years before *Der Fuhrer* by chewing through an electrical wire. Perhaps it was an omen.

For all the Oliver money, my parents never owned a house during their sixteen years of marriage, unusual in a nation of homeowners in an era when land and houses, like everything else, were cheap. I understand why they never bought in Wichita during the war years, but how to explain eight years of rentals in New York or renting five more years after we arrived in California. The fathers of my best friends in Playa del Rey, Bobby Taylor and Ronnie McKee, were, respectively, a milkman and a fireman, and they both owned houses. But the heirs to the Oliver fortune were always renters, a sign, I suspect, that they really didn't believe in their future together. At any rate, whatever capital came into Dad's hands went for more exotic uses than home mortgages.

The war turned things upside down for everyone, but before that there was an incident that rattled the family and widened the rift between Dad and Grandpa. From the photos saved from under Mother's Palm Desert bed I see pictures of Dad at *Sucasa* as late as March, 1936, seven months before I was born. Something happened after that to wreck relations between the two men and cause Dad never to return to Sewickley, and I know what it was.

Millie Oliver had given Dad the New York Stock Exchange seat as a wedding present, and he found a partner in Frank Bliss, a Wall Street denizen known as the "Silver Fox" thanks to his silver locks and maybe also because he was a bit craftier than your average broker. The Silver Fox knew an accountant named Otto Berndt, a German Jew who'd come to America during the great immigration wave of 1900-1920. Berndt had worked for several Wall Street firms in the Twenties and lost his job in the crash. When Dad found Bliss, Bliss remembered Berndt and hired him to keep the books. The year Dad got his seat, 1933, was the year Hitler came to power, not an auspicious omen.

Berndt was good at numbers, but so was Dad. I remember him years later at the race tracks when he was trying out a crazy system of betting on every horse in the race, varying the wagers according the odds. He'd put, say, five dollars on each longshot, twenty dollars on the favorite and ten on the others. He'd watch the tote board before the race, making calculations in his neat fountain pen script, working as fast as with a slide rule. At the window it took him a while to get all the bets down. He did a lot of figuring in his head, but with ten horses going, he had to write it down. Even after leaving Princeton, he could easily have found a career in accounting or finance if he'd been more disciplined. It wasn't in his nature.

If Otto Berndt had known Dad was that good with numbers he might not have started raking money off the books. The cause, getting Jews out of Germany, was a good one, but embezzling money to pay their way wasn't the best of ideas. It must have been hard for Berndt to see what was happening to Germany, a country he loved. Like Viktor Klemperer, whose diaries from the Nazi period would become best-sellers when they were discovered, Berndt came from one of those old Jewish families assimilated into German life and converted to Christianity for centuries. "I am German and am waiting for the Germans to come back; they have gone to ground somewhere," Klemperer wrote. That's how it was for Berndt.

"I'll never forget," Dad said one night at Tom Morris' when I finally heard the Berndt story. "Otto marches into the office in March, 1938— it was *Anschluss*, the day Hitler invaded Austria—and announces 'we just took Austria.'" Dad laughed. "He's a Jew, he's stealing money from me to get Jews out of Germany, and he says we took Austria. . . we—! It didn't figure."

Thanks mainly to Bliss, the firm was making a small profit by 1938. Berndt kept the books but Dad wrote the checks to pay the bills and the checks started bouncing. Going over the books, Dad found that deposits matched invoices, but that the invoices themselves had been altered. An auditor was brought in, and it was clear Berndt was embezzling. Some $40,000 had been skimmed over time. Confronted with documents altered in his own handwriting, Berndt confessed. He'd used the money to help bring dozens of Jews from Germany to America.

Unless the firm came up with $40,000 it faced bankruptcy, but punishing Berndt wouldn't change the situation. Knowing what we know now about Hitler and the Jews, it's easy to say Dad should have let him off. The moral corruption of the era was so deep that Berndt's humanitarianism might have been rewarded instead of punished. But exonerating embezzlement would only have deepened the moral collapse. The greed of the 1920s plus the criminality that underlay Prohibition made the Crash look like God's vengeance on America. Next came the 1930s, which brought the Depression, Japan's invasion of China and Korea and the rise of the Nazis. Hitler's war in September, 1939, following his invasions of Austria and Czechoslovakia, was a fitting end to what W. H. Auden called in a stirring poem, a "low dishonest decade."

The main issue for Dad was not Berndt, but coming up with $40,000 to prevent bankruptcy and loss of his stock exchange membership. He had to turn to Shields, but how to do it? In the meantime, Berndt was arrested, charged with embezzlement and freed on bail. Dropping the charges was never considered. As far as Dad was concerned, in everything I ever heard about the affair, Berndt was a crook who tried to bring him down and that was that. He might have thought differently had he known what we know now, but this was still pre-war 1938. He may have rationalized that the Jews Berndt helped leave Germany already were safe in America. The legal process went forward.

"Mother pawned all her jewelry."

Carol told me about it years later. I was skeptical, but Carol had gone with her to the New York pawnshops. Mother's jewelry had been passed to her from Millie through Granny, who wore only pearls. She got what she could for it, but apparently it didn't make much of a dent in the debt. What puzzles me is why Mother would have bothered to hock her stuff. She would have hated approaching Grandpa for money, but there was always Millie.

Dad should have gone directly to Grandpa. He should have gotten on the train to Pittsburgh and gone down to *Sucasa*, his Canossa perhaps, but a necessary journey. Will Crittenden could be gruff, but underneath the gruffness was a good man. I don't think he disliked Dad, just didn't have a great deal of respect for him. That respect would have increased had Dad sat across from him in his den and made his peace. Berndt's action was criminal, but those were unique times. Any number of people in his situation might have acted similarly, putting their firms in jeopardy. Grandpa would have had his say, but he would have helped. This was his daughter's husband, father of his only grandchildren, appealing for help. The matter had to be addressed.

But Dad sent Mother in his place, and not to Grandpa but to Millie, who gave her the $40,000 plus something extra, which Dad used to buy Beech Aircraft stock. Millie had already set Dad up with the stock exchange membership, provided Mother with trust funds in perpetuity and passed on the family jewels to her through Granny. For Dad to turn to her for money to avoid bankruptcy could only have shamed him, which is why he stayed in New York and let Mother do the work.

When Grandpa found out they'd gone behind his back he must have been outraged. Visiting *Sucasa* after that would have been difficult for a man like Dad, so he stayed away—permanently. But if he figured he didn't need Grandpa as long as he had Millie in his corner, it was a bad bet. Grandpa would be around far longer than Millie, already in her tenth decade.

§

Germany's war reached my family, like that of every other American, in December, 1941, when Hitler made the incomprehensible mistake of declaring war on us following Japan's attack on Pearl Harbor. Isolationists like Charles Lindbergh and the Republicans in Congress who had limited both the nation's preparation for war and President Roosevelt's margin of maneuver for nearly a decade were pushed aside as the nation mobilized for a war on two fronts.

With Hitler's conquest of France in 1940, Congress had passed the nation's first peacetime conscription act, but conscripts, age twenty-one to thirty-five, were required to serve only one year, an absurd limitation in those perilous times. In August, 1941, the one-year limitation was removed—the measure passing the House of Representatives by a single vote, 203-202, showing the power of the isolationists even as war raged in both Europe and Asia. Four months later, following Pearl Harbor, the draft was widened to include men ages eighteen to thirty-eight. Unlike during the Vietnam War, there were no college or father-hood deferments. Exemptions were allowed only for jobs in the war industry, agriculture and certain "hardship" cases. Like every other able-bodied American male of draft age, Dad, age thirty-one, faced military service.

But Millie Oliver's generosity during the embezzlement had enabled him to buy Beech Aircraft stock. As a broker, he'd touted Beech to clients, which brought him in touch with Olive Beech, who ran the business side of Walter Beech's aircraft company in Wichita. When Millie took pity and slipped Mother an extra $15,000, Dad took a position in Beech himself, putting him back in touch with Olive.

Olive Beech beat Uncle Sam to Dad by a few weeks, maybe even days. In January, 1942, barely a month after Pearl Harbor, she offered him a job, which kept him out of the draft and took us to Wichita, home of Beech Aircraft. I've often wondered if it wasn't Dad's name as much as his talents that attracted Olive's attention. An aviator named Brice Herbert Goldsborough had been a close friend and colleague of Walter Beech in the 1920s, winning several air races with him (Brice would die in 1927 trying to cross the Atlantic). An Iowan and no relation to Dad, Brice had helped develop Beech Aircraft's first all-instrument plane, something used to great advantage in the war.

In any case, Olive's offer meant that for the third time Dad had been rescued by Oliver money, helping him avoid what most men did not seek to avoid. Ten million Americans were drafted and another six million volunteered to serve in World War II. Each of those three times, the Oliver gift seemed to be a stroke of almost celestial good luck for Dad. In reality, each time, he would have been better off without it.

But Millie Oliver, Dad's soft touch, wasn't getting any younger. In May, 1943, she died in her house down the red brick path from *Sucasa*, the house where Granny, sisters Edith and Fanny and brother Leet had grown up and where Millie and Granny had entertained Harry Thaw before he became a killer. Millie was ninety-six and left Mother several more trust funds, all of which, at Grandpa's urging, were held in safe-keeping by Mellon and denied her the use of the principal. After Millie's

Millie Oliver, 1940.

death, to get to the principal, Dad would have to pass through Grandpa, and the two men no longer spoke.

Wichita was good for Mother—good for all of us. She never would say so, always insisting she hated it, but Sewickley hadn't done much for her and in Wichita she came into her own as a mother, which probably is why she hated it. We went to Pittsburgh for Billy's birth in July 1942, and then it was on to our new life in the aircraft industry. Granny sent a nurse from Pittsburgh to take care of Billy, but the nurse, a good woman used to the woods and streams of upstate Pennsylvania, hated dry, flat, bare Kansas and went home again. No one came to take her place.

In Wichita, for the first time Oliver money didn't make any difference because everything was rationed or unavailable. A million dollars in cash wouldn't have mattered because there was nothing to buy. Dad never would have bought a house in Wichita, and, as for the other things money buys—cars, boats, clothes, jewelry, vacations—forget it. It was wartime. We didn't miss what we didn't have and learned to enjoy the little things—radio programs, movies, gardening, ice cream at Gessler's drug store, trips to the Clyde Beatty circus when it hit town. Wartime imposed the first limits my parents couldn't break. They suffered none of the privations of those who actually went to war, but forced by circumstances to live in a place they didn't like and do things they wouldn't have done, both were better for it, though neither ever recognized it.

Photos from this period show happy children, though Mother still wears her perpetual frown and Dad is present in none of them. There are no photos of him in existence after 1936. He shunned the camera as though he were a guy on a most-wanted poster. Carol and I have good memories of our two years in a rented house at 4348 East English Street, corner of Crestway, one of those numbers that remains indelible on my mind, like *Sucasa*'s phone number, Sewickley 12, which isn't too hard. A half century later, Carol returned to Wichita and found the neighborhood unchanged, unthinkable in California.

We lived in a white, framed, two-story house with steps to a front veranda under an overhanging gable and a screen door into a large Midwestern living room. We had a front lawn, and in the back was a two-car garage with a trap door leading to an attic where the owner had stored stuff meant to be hidden from nosy children. Turned out the owner was a Shriner, and when my pals and I got into his costumes we held some secret meetings of our own. He also had a collection of matchbooks, which we burned, managing, however, not to set the garage on fire. He later sued us, winning a $1,000 settlement in a Los Angeles court.

I was in the second and third grades in Wichita, Carol the fifth and sixth, and we walked to school and stopped on the way home at Gessler's if we had a nickel for ice cream or a dime for a comic book. When Dad and Mother went out, they slipped comic books under the bedroom door for us. Saturdays, we took the bus to the local movie house where we spent the afternoon with cartoons, Movietone newsreels about the war and double features, sometimes even some kind of "talent" show on stage between the movies. It was life off a Norman Rockwell *Post* cover. There were plenty of kids in the neighborhood, I had my first crush on

Jim and Carol G. with Granny, at the Oliver farm, 1939.

a second-grader named Charlotte, and the little sister of Carol's friend Diane across the street, whose name was Kay, gave me my first soppy kiss in their backyard, with Carol and Diane holding me down.

For the first and only time we led ordinary lives. There were no maids, nannies, cooks or chauffeurs. Mother raised Billy alone, which is probably why she was always closer to him than to Carol or me. If I was a cold baby maybe it's because with all the nannies around I hadn't recognized her as my mother: Billy had no choice. Dad drove to work in our still snazzy '41 Buick convertible with the gas-rationing sticker affixed to the windshield and sometimes on weekends took me to the plant and gave me 11 cents, the price of the movies, for sweeping up steel shavings. Beech was turning out planes for both the Army Air Force and the Navy, different versions of Twin Beeches called "Kansans" used to train bombardiers. Along with another trainer called the "Wichita," Beech turned out some 7,400 planes during the war, which meant that even if Dad didn't do any fighting, he at least had a role in the war industry.

I can't say Dad completely deprived himself, for if there were no bars or liquor stores in bone-dry Kansas, nor any race tracks or casinos, there were bootleggers. Except for the hooch, we led a Spartan life in a Spartan place, not by choice but necessity. For the first and only time in my parents' life, they showed how things might have been if they'd been on their own. We were thrown together as a family for the first time because there was nothing else. That didn't mean Dad turned into a regular father because I have no recollection of any family outings with him along. Mother took us swimming and to the circus, and Carol and I sang in an Episcopal Church children's choir—Episcopalians and Presbyterians being the same thing in Mother's view, which would have horrified Granny. Carol remembers Mother jumping up at a movie, rushing out and heading straight to the doctor's. She was bleeding, the after-effects of an abortion. Billy had been an accident, and there would be no more of them. She joined a country club and played a little golf, and I was expelled for a week for swimming in the club pool during a storm by someone who came running out shouting that I would be electrocuted.

Dad found the local bootlegger thanks to his new Beech buddy, Jim Collins, and we'd take the Buick periodically into the cornfields to pick up the hootch. I made the trip countless times, stopping outside a concrete bunker where a guy came out to pass the brown bags. For me, at seven, visits to the bootlegger were a chance to take a ride, which because of gas rationing we didn't do very often. As I think back on it, Dad might have had an ulterior motive in taking me along, but I was still happy for it. Not many seven-year-olds have a chance to visit bootleggers.

We were responsible for part of a "victory garden" in the vacant lot across East English on Crestway. We planted dandelion greens, which none of us had ever heard of eating before, but it was all part of the war effort. I doubt that anyone in Shields ate dandelions during the war, but I developed a lifelong affinity for greens. Dandelions today are a gourmet item, but in those days were still sharecropper food. All the neighbors were responsible for parts of the garden, raising different vegetables and swapping them at something like a weekly farmers' market. Each day after work, the families came pouring out, women in bandanas, kids in shorts, elderly men in overalls, everyone on his knees weeding or hoeing away. Dad never set foot in the garden and hated greens anyway. Carol and I shared a room for the first time and lay on our beds after dinner listening to radio shows like Superman and the Lone Ranger.

There were none of the parental fights that started after we moved to California, maybe because war was such a dominant theme that people had their fill of fighting. Though Wichita was about as far from any front as you could get, the war was with us constantly—in school, movies and on the radio; in the games we played, in rationing, shortages and the victory garden. Boys dressed like soldiers or pilots, and a prize birthday present for me was a leather coat with a furry collar like pilots wear and one of those soft-helmets with chin straps and goggles.

Wichita was good for us, but Dad had used Oliver money to buy his way out of the draft every bit as much as the well-heeled had bought their way out of the Civil War. I can't help thinking how his life might have changed—as Jim Crittenden's was changed (and mine, too, at a much later date)—had he gone into the Army. Of course, it depends on the war you're fighting, but the war in '41 was not like recent wars. No one had any doubt about World War II.

§

It was the fall of '44, the Allies were marching into Germany and it looked like the war was over, though Hitler had other ideas. Mother and Dad found someone to stay with us, drove to California, and Mother came back on one of those twin-engine Douglas DC-2's with the throw-up bags I would learn to hate. Dad stayed on the coast, leaving the work of moving to Mother.

"We're going to California," she announced over a Spam dinner at the East English kitchen table as I read the Heinz ketchup label for the umpteenth time. After two years at that table, I knew the label by heart and have never forgotten it: "red ripe tomatoes, distilled vinegar, corn syrup, salt, spices, onion powder." The war took away a lot of things, but not Heinz ketchup, made in Pittsburgh. If you eat Spam with dandelions, don't forget the ketchup.

"We've found a house. Jimmy, your room, which you'll share with Billy, has a secret room in it. Carol. . . you'll have your own room."

We complained, as change makes children do. I'd made good friends with a kid down Crestway named Clifford and was invited to Charlotte's house sometimes after school. Carol was best friends with Diane across the street, though I would not miss her soppy sister, Kay.

Mother was never much for talking people into things. She announced what she wanted and you either did it with her or didn't, depending on how she wanted things. But knowing how we children had been moved around—Wichita was already our sixth house and I'd just turned eight—she at least made an effort to dress things up. Carol would get her own bedroom, and the secret room was definitely an enticement.

Secret things were big during the war. I had a ring with a secret compartment and sent away for a secret decoding set.

"What kind of secret room?" I asked.

I'll never forget the answer. She could have pulled her punches, but gave it straight, which made it all the more exciting.

"In case of a Japanese invasion," she said. "You can hide in there. They'll never find you."

California was Dad's idea and I thank him for it, but it's clear he was running. Returning to Pittsburgh was out of the question because he didn't like being around family and had made up his mind Wall Street wasn't for him. Frank Bliss had taken over his stock exchange seat, and Dad was collecting the rent. There was no question of staying in Wichita, but Beech had introduced him to airplanes and though he made the mistake of selling his Beech stock, he kept a keen interest in aviation. He was right in sensing that the nation's center of gravity was shifting westward. The war was ending, and the income from Millie Oliver's wedding gift and Mother's trust funds gave him what most Americans didn't have coming out of the war—a grub stake to build a new life in a new place.

He was right about Wall Street. The Dow Jones highs of 1929 would not be topped until 1954, a decade after we moved to California. I have no idea how he got out of his war industry commitment to Beech eight months before the war ended, especially since it might have gone on for years without the atomic bombs, and who knew about atomic bombs in December, 1944? But when we left Wichita that fall, Carol was the only one ever to return. We hit California two weeks before Christmas of 1944, moved into the Wilshire Motel in Santa Monica and took our meals at a place called the Toad Inn while waiting to move into our new house in Playa del Rey. We became, like millions of other Americans moving westward after the war—Californians.

But we got there first, before the war was over. Dad had given us a head start. Would he know how to take advantage of it?

Adventures at *Sucasa*

*Contradictions, the truth about Jesse James
and a meeting with a new kind of woman.*

*Governor Thomas T. Crittenden, 1882.
Reproduced from* The Crittenden Memoirs, *Henry Huston Crittenden, 1939.*

We were Californians except for the summers. If Mother rebelled against her parents and Sewickley, the rebellion stopped when our school was out. Come mid-June, we boarded the Super Chief and were off for ten weeks of living like royalty in the castle. A three-day train trip took us from Playa del Rey proletarianism—T-shirts, buses, bare feet and messy beach burgers—to the elegant world of the Oliver baronets. I developed a lobe for each life. Summers I lived like a little lord in his manor, but in Playa del Rey was just one more kid waiting for the bus in a city filling up with kids as fast as parents could buy tickets out of Newark, Chillicothe and Paducah. In Playa del Rey, I dreamed constantly of Sewickley and in Sewickley constantly of Playa del Rey. Mother tried to merge my two lives, one of order, one of disorder, by putting me in military school in the sixth grade—the dreaded California Military Academy—but it didn't take.

She loved Playa del Rey, was always more comfortable with its rough beach egalitarianism than in staid Sewickley, which brought out all her insecurities. Ostracized by the Junior League in Pittsburgh after her elopement with the cowboy, she was embraced by the League in Los Angeles where they don't care about your previous life. That's why people go west, isn't it? She got back in the Blue Book on the strength of a 1932 certificate showing membership in the Daughters of the American Revolution, which was the work of Granny, a DAR regent. Mother might reject her parents and be banned by the Pittsburgh Junior League, but direct lineage to Revolutionary War Majors Henry Crittenden and Daniel Leet counts for more in Blue Book Los Angeles than an escapade in Tucson. In Los Angeles, escapades are no big deal.

With the name Goldsborough unfamiliar in the West, Mother used the same DAR certificate to prove she wasn't Jewish and gain admission to the Westport Beach Club—beach clubs substituting for country clubs along the coast. Anti-Semitism was arriving on the West Coast along with the new Eastern immigrants. Hating clubs as always, Dad never set foot in Westport, which foretold problems because that's where Mother spent most of her social life. Free of war, victory gardens and children—even Billy was in nursery school—she was back in her element, clubs, shopping, friends, fun, sun.

Playa del Rey was different from anything we'd known—casual beach chic. It wasn't fashionable chic like Santa Monica where you lunched at the Jonathan or Uplifters or elegant chic like Santa Barbara where you stayed at the Biltmore. It was down-home, bohemian chic in sandals

Carol, Mother, Jim and Bill at Westport Beach Club, 1947.

and sand between your toes. Dad, with his common Welsh tastes, loved the ocean. He didn't love it like Mother, for lunches, parties and square dances at Westport, but loved it existentially, because it was there. Years later, reading the poems and stories of Dylan Thomas, I would think of Dad—red hair, reckless, searching, boozing, a Welshman's innate love of the sea. Until we arrived in Playa del Rey, I hadn't realized how much he hated waterless and boozeless Wichita. Until we arrived in Playa del Rey, I didn't even know he knew how to swim.

The happiest I ever saw him was riding the waves during our first years in Playa del Rey. Because of his red hair and fair complexion he couldn't stay long in the sun, but he'd ride the breakers for an hour without leaving the water and then it was straight home. Later, after the divorce and before drinking completely destroyed him, he bought a little red frame beach house in Manhattan Beach—on the strand, not far from Bunny Warren's. Like everything he touched, the house was a mess inside, but I remember some good times with him, stepping out the front door to plunge in the ocean and ride the waves. The ocean freed him from his demons.

Our little beach community was egalitarian in a California kind of way. It was hard to be more egalitarian than wartime Wichita with rationing and victory gardens, but Wichita was egalitarian because nobody had anything. Playa del Rey was more exotic egalitarianism. My dad was unemployed (he would have said self-employed), my friend Bobby Taylor's father was a milkman and Ronnie McKee's dad a fireman, but up the road lived the movie director Cecil B. DeMille and across from him the actor Charles Bickford and over the hill the comic Mel Blanc, whose son Noel and I became fast friends during the horrible year at the California Military Academy. Down a wooden path that ran across the sand and iceplant below our house lived Wally Westmore, makeup man for the stars at MGM and Paramount, who nagged me to quit using his path as a speedway for the soapbox car Bobby and I built.

Different as we all were, everyone dropped into Charlie's Market and Dolson's Drugs in shorts and sandals; everyone stopped for burgers at the Dutch Village by the jetty, and the biggest event in years was the opening of a hardware store next to Charlie's Market. Famous or obscure, descendants of the Founding Fathers or fatherless, we were all friends and equals in our sandy little village. The postwar masses hadn't yet arrived.

Unlike our neighbors, we packed up each summer and set out for the East. Rebel or not, Mother knew where the money was and wanted to escape Dad, for they'd started fighting. Once arrived at *Sucasa*, Mother would disappear, and I'd spend the days mostly hanging out with the workmen on the estate. The more we made these summer trips, the more trouble I had assimilating the contrasts between my two lives—east and west, grass and sand, rivers and oceans, sobriety and drunkenness, order and disorder. I was becoming a creature of contradictions—a bourgeois proletarian, an elitist meritocrat, a white revolutionary. The struggle started in boyhood and never stopped during a forty-year newspaper career. Something hard-wired in my system said that status and wealth—called class in other countries—must never take precedence over merit. I began to understand what inherited status had done to Mother and gifted money done to Dad.

With their stories, Granny and Grandpa never let me forget what our family had achieved, and those stories, compared to the lives of my parents, had the intended effect. They were determined to make sure I didn't follow the path of my father. Granny's stories were long on morals—and they stuck. Though, like Grandpa, my interest in church was never religious (his was social, mine aesthetic), from those mornings in Granny's bed I can still recite the *Twenty-third Psalm* and the prayers she taught me. Grandpa's stories were full of action, drama, up from the bootstraps, courage in the face of danger, victory over long odds, moral and physical perseverance. He knew the Civil War and could lay out the battles of Chicamauga and Murfreesboro yard by yard. Little Big Horn, where Lieutenant J. J. Crittenden Jr., his first cousin, was killed, was another of his favorites.

He first told me about Jesse James on one of our walks to the river.

Our walks normally started out the same way, around eleven on mornings when he didn't go to Pittsburgh. He was a little over seventy years older than I, so most of our walks took place when he was into his eighties and only going downtown to his office once or twice a week. He'd catch up with me somewhere after breakfast, ask if I was interested, grab a walking stick from the rack near the front door and we'd be off. Our favorite walk was down the hill, crossing Beaver Road and up Church Lane to the Ohio. He dressed mostly the same whether he was walking or going to work—jacket, vest, tie and hat. Even his shoes were the same, tending to light brown Oxfords with pointy toes and heels that made a click on the sidewalk. The gold chain always dangled from the watch in his vest pocket. Because we normally stopped for tea with the Brownes on the way back, I guess he felt he couldn't be too casual. He did most of the talking on our walks and one day asked if I knew the story of his father, the governor, and Jesse James.

Thomas T. Crittenden, a pro-Union Democrat in a state where most Democrats had sided with the Confederates, took office as governor January 1, 1881, when Grandpa was fourteen, having promised the people of Missouri to rid them of the James brothers and their gang of bushwhackers who'd been rampaging across the state for a decade. One of the governor's first acts was to issue a proclamation offering $5,000 apiece for the arrest of Jesse and Frank, and another $5,000 upon their conviction. The proclamation was posted across the state.

"Their father, Robert James was a minister," said Grandpa. "He was a Baptist, an educated and courteous man, but he had been a slaveholder."

We were striding along Church Lane, shaded from the morning sun by elms and sycamores, just passing the lawn of white chapel, as it was called, and coming up to Shields Presbyterian. Across from the church was the Adams' house, with its wide front veranda, where Sam Adams, who would become Carol's first husband, and his younger sister, Margaret Jane, who would become my friend, lived. "It is an astonishing thing," said Grandpa. "The Jameses were the worst criminals in the history of Missouri, and their father was a preacher."

It was my first lesson in the X factor.

Grandpa could be intimidating. He'd always been a horseman, and there's something about people who get on with horses that gives them an air of authority. Maybe it's that just as you communicate with horses with little tugs and nudges more than with brute force, the same techniques work with people. It was the way he carried himself, a mixture of vigor, self-confidence and courtesy, which gave the impression this was a man worth listening to. Some of it came from his parents, but I suspect most of it was just his nature. I don't think he took himself too seriously, for he was a companionable man, even to a little kid, and had what all kids like best in an adult: he knew how to laugh. He also had an exotic side to him from his years in Mexico.

We passed by the Shields mausoleum. Next came the Brownes' house, and Grandpa greeted Mrs. Browne, who was sweeping the porch.

"Half an hour, Will," she called.

"But Reverend James died," he said. "Jesse's mother took up with a man named Samuels who was sympathetic to the South. Some people, you know, were still fighting the Civil War."

He looked at me, but knew I knew about the Civil War.

"The Unionists hunted down Samuels and hanged him, but his wife cut him down. Jesse and Frank were mad enough about it to go off with Will Quantrill's gang and 'Bloody Bill' Anderson and the Younger brothers and they started murdering and robbing across the state. In one town, Centralia, they stopped a train, robbed the passengers and shot in cold blood twenty-six unarmed Union soldiers. Lined them up and shot them down. Can you imagine anything worse?"

We were halfway to the river, walking briskly for Grandpa was no slouch. On the right we passed the house that had belonged to the Shields sisters, Hannah and Rebecca, Eliza's daughters, now residing in the mausoleum. On the left was the red brick house where two Scotties, white and black named Salt and Pepper, recognized us and barked a friendly hello. I waved at them. They would greet me for decades to come on my returns to Church Lane in dreams.

"After Anderson was killed, the James' took over parts of Missouri just like the Confederates would have done if they'd won. The citizens were fed up and elected the governor to clean up the state. He was a Democrat, but they knew he was the nephew of Senator Crittenden of Kentucky who had sided with Lincoln and tried to prevent the war."

"I saw the movie about Jesse James," I said. "He was the hero."

"It wasn't like that at all," said Grandpa, quickly. "All myth. There was a newspaper man named Edwards, another pro-slaver. He called Jesse a Robin Hood, giving back to the poor who'd been robbed by the Yankees. All lies. Jesse never gave anything back. He was a mean, cold-blooded killer. I was there, just a little older than you are now."

I listened to the taps of his cane and clicks of his shoes. The river was in clear view, and we could see a coal barge coming downriver and approaching the locks on the far side. It gave a toot.

"You probably know there were two other brothers in the story— Bob and Charlie Ford. Charlie was a member of Jesse's gang, and Bob met up with him and said they should bring Jesse in and collect the reward. Charlie thought about it a while and agreed and asked Jesse if Bob could join up with the gang, and Jesse said, sure, bring him down. The gang was living in Saint Joseph, Missouri, with Jesse and his wife and two children while they planned another bank job. They say there's honor among thieves, but not that bunch. They were looking for a way to get the drop on Jesse."

"Did you learn this from the governor?" I asked.

"Yes, from the governor and from the newspapers. And from the trial. It all came out in the trial."

We'd reached the end of the sidewalk and went down metal-tipped steps into the flinty tunnel under the tracks, climbing the stairs at the far end up to the old Shields station, where Grandpa had detrained the first time he came to Shields but which now was abandoned, for the trains didn't stop there anymore. In front of us stretched the broad Ohio, with the low Dashields dam, named for the first David Shields, running the width of the river to the locks on the far side and to the woods sweeping up into the hills beyond. I never came to this place without thinking that this was about where George Washington powwowed with the Indians when the French still held Fort Duquesne. The trees I was looking at were the same ones he saw. There was a place upriver called Washington's Landing. But that was Granny's story.

We took in the roar and the rush of the river. A bit winded, Grandpa sat on a bench a while. Across the river, the barge entered the locks and disappeared as the water level dropped.

"Jesse never took off his guns," he said, shouting over the crashing of the dam. "He wore two .45s: one Colt, one Smith and Wesson. Even took them to bed with him. The Fords lived with him a week and couldn't get the drop because of those guns. Then one day—it was a sweltering Missouri day, nothing like you see around here—Jesse came in from the yard, took off his hat and guns and dropped them on a bed. He climbed up on a chair to dust off a picture. Charlie gave a sign, Bob popped in the room and shot him in the back."

The doors of the lower locks swung open and the barge began heading downriver on the swift current. Except for Grandpa's voice, the only sound was the pounding water.

"Well," shouted Grandpa over the roar of the dam, "you can imagine the consternation. The governor's proclamation didn't say 'dead or alive.' It said—and I've got it at home to show you—reward for 'arrest and conviction.' People said the governor had authorized the Fords to shoot Jesse in the back in his own home in front of his wife and children, but it wasn't true. There was a huge outcry, some people even demanded his resignation."

He fell silent. It was a good story, and he knew just when to pause.

Across the river, the lower locks started closing again.

"The newspapers tried to set things right. They pointed out that the governor had offered twice the money for conviction, proving he wanted Jesse brought in, not murdered. They said the Fords took things in their own hands, and that anyway Jesse got what he deserved. They said Missouri should be cheering."

He stared across the river, watching the barge drift away, listening to the surge over the dam. Another barge was approaching from the Pittsburgh side and gave a toot for the master to open the upper locks.

"... but the people blamed the governor."

"What did he do?"

Governor Crittenden proclamation.
Reproduced from The Crittenden Memoirs, *Henry Huston Crittenden, 1939.*

Grandpa stood up. "We don't want to be late for the Brownes."

We crossed the platform and started down the sooty stairs into the tunnel.

He was shouting now, trying to be heard over the river's roar echoing through the tunnel. "President Cleveland named him counsel general to Mexico, and he took me with him. That's where I met your grandmother. That's why you're here today."

§

That summer—I was eleven-and-a-half—I had a big surprise.

Her name was Jane Shape, and she'd been hired out of nursing school to take care of Jamie, Jim Crittenden's toddler. We'd just arrived from California, but I hadn't been back to the nursery or into the kitchen at the right time and so I had no idea. One morning I'd drifted into the kitchen to do morning Jumbles with Viola, the cook. The kitchen in Sucasa was in its own two-story wing, cut off from the main part of the house by the butler's pantry and swinging doors at the end of the main hallway leading past the dining room to the breakfast room at the end. You didn't just stumble into the kitchen by accident, you had to be heading there, and over the years its isolation had turned it into a kind of sanctuary, first for Carol, then for me.

I cannot ever remember seeing Granny, Grandpa or Mother in the kitchen. Granny, of course, must have been there a lot, but by my time the main communications with the kitchen were done through an intercom system that reached into every upstairs room. One could call down for breakfast in bed if so inclined, though I never actually tried it. Viola, a large Italian woman from Ambridge whose cooking skills were vast and unique—if blissfully ignorant of what passes today for "healthy cuisine"—always welcomed me, and sometimes I stayed for lunch in the servants' dining room.

I'd been sitting at the white metal-topped kitchen table, hunched over the newspaper in deep concentration while unscrambling words. Behind me the door to the back service stairs opened and shut. Viola looked up from the sink, her hammy hands red from the water.

"Jimmy have you met Jane? Jimmy, get up."

Fresh from a year at the California Military Academy, I sprang to my feet almost expecting to see Major McLaren's icy blue orbs riveted down on me for some unknown infraction. Instead, I turned to see to see a young woman a couple of inches taller than me and dressed in nurse's white except for bare legs, which for some reason got my attention. I tried to stand a little straighter. She put out her hand and we shook.

I would spend all summer with this young woman, the first time I ever spent social time with a female not of my clan. But it was those first few minutes in the kitchen that sealed our friendship. Viola stood watching, tap water still running.

"So you're Jimmy."

She was still holding my hand, which, though she was a girl, I did not object to for some reason. I was pleased. We hadn't met, but already she'd heard of me.

"I hear you're a baseball player. I hear you're pretty good."

"I am the best," I said.

She was still holding my hand.

"Are you being facetious?"

Facetious was not a word I could have precisely defined, but I got the idea that Jane was not someone on whom my almost-12-year-old superciliousness was going to work. A year later, I would have a personal meeting in New York with Joe DiMaggio. Had I known then, dumbstruck in Granny's kitchen, of my coming celebrity I would at least have had a retort, a defense against puerility. Instead, I stood speechless, agape, ears burning. Who was this person? Was she a girl or a woman?

Jane was nineteen, a female age new to my world. She had thick auburn hair down to her shoulders pulled back by barrettes, rosy cheeks and blue eyes that fixed on you like you were the only one in the world. She stood straight and talked straight as I found out nurses were trained to do. She was warm and outgoing and the prettiest girl I'd ever seen. Maybe others were just as pretty, but the thing is, I hadn't really noticed girls up to then. They were like the paintings on Sucasa's walls: I was aware of them, occasionally glanced at them, heard people talk about them, but they never really entered my world.

The most incredible thing about Jane, totally unbelievable really, was that she knew more about baseball than I did.

Jane knew the name of every player on the Pittsburgh Pirates, even guys in the farm system. We would sit in the servants' dining room going over box scores in the *Post-Gazette*. If an afternoon game was being played—in those days they had day games during the week—we'd turn on the radio and listen to Rosey Rosewell and Bob Prince call the game. She knew arcane statistics I didn't even know existed, knew who was good in the clutch and understood how great Ralph Kiner was. He would go into the Hall of Fame, she said. In the early 1950s, nobody cared that the Pirates finished last. Pittsburgh was used to the Pirates finishing last, after all, weren't they the Pirates? Jane didn't care about that. It was the game that mattered. She could talk about Rip Sewell's blooper pitch and why the Pirates were smart to get Tiny Bonham from the Yankees and why Stan Rojek and Danny Murtaugh were right behind Brooklyn's Reese and Robinson as the best double-play combo in the National League.

But it was that first morning, as I stood there at attention in Granny's kitchen with Viola grinning—she knew what was happening—that Jane did the unthinkable.

"You want to catch a Pirates game with me tonight?"

And so it went that summer. We saw ballgames and movies and drove up to Sewickley just to hang out. Over the years Sewickley village hasn't changed much. I've seen photos that show the buildings the same as a century ago, same two-story affairs clustered along the same two long blocks on Beaver Road, or Beaver Street as it's called in the village. My favorite places were the Sewickley Theater and Isely's across the street, where we went for ice cream after the movies. Next to Isely's was the Penguin Book Store, which is still there, and across the street Knapp's Drugs and Hegner's Hardware, where between the two of them you could find just about everything you needed. Down the street, next to the People's Bank on the corner of Blackburn Road, was Carroll's Music Store, where I took clarinet lessons for a while, and next to it Murphy's five and dime. Over one hundred years, the only thing that's changed along Beaver between Broad and Blackburn is the names on the shops.

We saw a half dozen games that summer, walking down to Beaver Road to catch the Pittsburgh-East Liverpool bus downtown, then onto the Fifth Avenue trolley to Oakland and Forbes Field. Hot dogs were still a quarter loaded with onions, mustard and relish, and I collected pennants of all the teams. Since Jane was employed by the Crittendens, and since Mother was disappeared as usual, Jane and I could go off any time she wasn't needed. She came from "someplace up-state" like Franklin or Warren where there's nothing but rivers, farms and woods

Jane Shape, 1948.

and where Granny periodically voyaged in her chauffeured black Buick searching for household help among the farm girls. She'd found Jane at a nursing school where the girls were ready for summer break and hired her to take care of Jamie. Jane spoke in that mellifluous Western Pennsylvania accent that is the product of so many Poles, Czechs, Irish, Italians, Scotch, Germans, Serbs and a dozen other peoples merging their native accents into American English.

Rural girl, new in town, surrounded by comfort and wealth, temporarily employed in a strange family, she saw in me a little guy to take under her wing, to relax and joke with, to be her surrogate little brother and accompany her to places she wanted to go so she didn't have to go alone. She loved baseball, and it's not like they have big league games in Franklin or Warren. And since I was a kid, there'd be no complications.

Except that, for me, there were. Jane didn't know I was going to confuse her with the mother I didn't have and the girl friends that were still years away.

We were sitting one day at the Edgeworth Club after I'd done some diving from the high board. Jamie dozed in his pram. Jane and I were together all the time and, looking back, I suspect people thought she was taking care of both Jamie and me—though that thought at the time would have mortified me. I was sure everybody, just like Jane, saw me as her boyfriend. Yes, I was almost twelve, but everyone said I was mature for my age. Seven years is not a big difference. When I was twenty-one, she'd only be twenty-eight, and from my almost twelve-year-old vantage point those two ages were practically the same thing.

I'd toweled off and was sitting in my bathing suit uncomfortably aware of the skinniness of my body, though I reached 100 pounds that summer. Jane complimented my dives, admired my courage off the high board. She'd never gone off a high board she said. I asked if she knew the Cardinals were in town the coming weekend.

There was a long pause. I listened to the floc-floc of tennis balls on the green clay courts behind us.

She said that she knew that.

"Do you want to go?" I asked. "Friday night game. . . Saturday, day."

She was wearing a white blouse and blue shorts, her red hair just brushing the collar of her blouse, sapphire eyes deeper than the blue of the Edgeworth pool. I had it bad. She stared at me, wordless. I felt a chill.

"I'm already going to the game," she said after a moment. She spoke softly, almost sorrowfully. "Someone I met bowling. He has tickets Friday."

He?. . . bowling? I didn't even know she went bowling. When could she have gone bowling?

Jane had no idea what had happened. How could she? How could she know that the kid she was palling around with would fall in love with her? How could she know I would transfer to her the feelings I could not transfer to my mother? I know now why Nickie and Florence came into the lifeguard house at the Fort Sill Officers' Club twelve years later

Edgeworth Club circa 1950.

and hugged me as I was leaving the Army. Those girls were my age when I was with Jane, though maybe a bit more mature, and I took their affection seriously and let them hold on. I could remember how I'd felt the day Jane told me she had another boyfriend, a real boyfriend.

It was as pure and sweet a relationship as I've ever had. Months later, when I was back in Playa del Rey, we corresponded for a while. Once she sent me a framed photo of her taken outside a house near Sucasa with nothing but grass and trees in the background, her auburn hair and blue eyes leaping out of a sea of green. Looking at the picture a half century later—I still keep it on my desk—I see her in pastel shorts, a plain white T-shirt with her shoulders back, white socks and sneakers, a watch, no jewelry, light lipstick, rosy cheeks, hair down to her shoulders, the don't-mess-with-me look in her eye. I've studied the photo a million times. As I look at it today, I see a fine nineteen-year-old figure and think how wonderful it would be to put my arms around her and lift up that T-shirt.

In those days, I didn't see things like that. She was my friend, my companion, my confidante, my admirer, the girl who knew more about baseball than any girl I'd ever known or ever would, someone who liked me the way I was. I knew there could be more to it some day. She was seven years older, but she'd wait. I was sure of that. I was a Shields, an Oliver, a Crittenden. That's why she'd sent the picture, wasn't it?

I'd not known that girls like Jane existed. She would have a radical and permanent influence on my thinking about the opposite sex, which had been mostly influenced up to that point by Mother.

EAST MEETS WEST

Fifty years after the railroad, Will Crittenden goes to California in hopes of completing an airline connection to Mexico.

Douglas DC-3 aircraft, circa 1950. Courtesy Jaysen Snow.

Will and Amelia settled back on the banquette as the train pulled out of Chicago Union Station. They admired the wood paneling of the drawing room that would be their home for the next forty hours and watched the Chicago suburbs slip away. They were tired but excited. The hardest part of the trip was over—the Pittsburgh-Chicago stretch that started with a 5:30 a.m. awakening at *Sucasa*, the thirteen-mile drive downtown with Stewart at the wheel and an 8 o'clock departure from Pittsburgh. They'd had a light lunch as they crossed the Ohio-Indiana border, and the train pulled into Chicago just after 5 p.m., only a few minutes behind schedule.

The Super Chief was scheduled to pull out at seven sharp, and they were on board with time to spare. They had a day-and-a-half of cross-country America ahead of them, Dickens to read, a comfortable drawing room, a gourmet dining room and were looking forward to their first train trip together since before the war. Caroline and the children had raved about the Super Chief since moving to California, but it was a new train for them. Streamliners, they were called, silver and sleek like their name, and they cut the travel time to the coast by a third.

They sat quietly, enjoying the scenery as the train pulled through the suburbs and picked up speed through towns and fields on its way toward Joliet. It had been a hot day, the second of September, the day after Labor Day, and outside they watched the towns just beginning to cool off in the sultry early evening. In one place they saw people swimming in a town pool, with boys lined up on the ladder leading to the high board. Just a quiet, Midwestern, end-of-summer evening, almost in still-life. A few cars, pre-war models, moved noiselessly about nearly empty streets. They watched closely, searching for signs of how their country had changed since the last time they crossed it. There were very few. The Depression and war had frozen the country in place.

Beyond Joliet, the train entered the countryside, and they saw tractors chugging in from the loamy Illinois fields. The farmers likely had a long lunch and nap so they could work into the cooler evening. It was a peaceful and bucolic sight, far from the problems one reads about in the newspapers. The war was not long over, and in Middle America if you stayed away from radios and newspapers you might think there had never been a war and would never be another one.

They'd signed up for the first dinner seating and past Joliet heard the steward coming with his chimes. They started toward the dining car, moving slowly as the elderly tend to do, passing through the lounge car, noisy with passengers celebrating the start of the voyage, nodding here and there at people who smiled at them, as they do to the elderly, people they might get to know over the next forty hours. The lounge car was the gathering spot on this cruise, though not for them on their first night when a hard day's travel had put them in mind of a good meal and sleep. Most people, Will noticed, were less than half his age, healthy-looking young men and women heading west. He'd expected to see more children, but with the new school year just days away couples with children had no doubt already arrived wherever they were going.

Leaving the lounge car, he pulled open the heavy steel door to the vestibule and held Amelia's arm as she went through. The train gave a sharp jolt as it began a turn, and Will caught his wife's arm as she rolled against the grinding metal sleeves where the cars were joined. He looked closely at the sleeves. Knowing steel as he did, he knew the new lightweight alloy used in the cars was one of the things that made the Super Chief so fast.

They took window seats, and Will ordered a glass of sherry and tomato juice. The long, hot day was ending and outside the first signs of dusk approached. Watching him gaze dreamily at the passing fields, Amelia thought he had rarely looked so content. Blissful fatigue, she thought. As much traveling as they'd done in the past, they'd not slept on a train since taking the old Santa Fe Chief, the Super Chief's predecessor, on their way to Tucson in 1932. How could they ever forget that trip, which ended in Caroline's elopement—first elopement? There was no comparing the Chief with the streamliners. It was exciting to be back on the road again.

The trip was Will's idea, and she was entirely in agreement: A comfortable trip to the West Coast was a perfect way to end the summer. Except for a three-day excursion to Valley Forge the previous year to show me Major Daniel Leet's name on General Washington's roster, she hadn't been away from Western Pennsylvania since before the war. Trips to Europe and Asia were out of the question. And where would they have gone? Asia was off-limits and Europe still in turmoil. Even if they'd been able to find a quiet spot in Britain or Normandy, they were a bit old for ships, trunks, hotels, country trains, endless taxis. Will had just turned eighty-one, and she, though six years younger, had more trouble getting around than he did. Why not visit Caroline and the grandchildren? Flying was not for them, but Will had always loved trains. How often he talked of his venture with the Mexicans. This trip would mix business with pleasure, though he'd been quiet about his business intentions.

The steward brought the drinks and left menus.

"A penny for your thoughts," she said.

"Cost you a dime."

She smiled.

"There's the fact that this train is going to pass through Arizona, which will remind me of Tucson, which will remind me of our daughter's folly the last time we were there." She could tell he was in a good mood, but there was no hint of a smile as he mentioned Arizona.

She held his gaze. "Caroline's been married now for fourteen years, Will. Give her some credit."

"If she's married, how is it we never see her husband?"

They fell silent, enjoying the easy roll of the train.

"Speaking of trains, there was the one to Mexico," said Amelia, watching her husband.

How strange that she would say that. Yes, he knew she thought of it often. . . always. . . had never forgotten it, was reminded of it each time she looked upon her son, who looked so much like Leet. But, as though repressing pain was easier than expressing it, she never mentioned it. The train had brought it back and though he said nothing—what could he say—the thought of that dreadful day forty years earlier returned to him, just as it had returned to her: His wife, swooned in his arms in the fading Dallas light, lost in a gloom from which would never fully recover, the telegram at their feet.

Every life is a series of accidents, some good, some bad. For Leet Oliver, that June day of 1906 marked the end of a short life filled with great promise. For Leet's sister and her new husband, it was the day that turned their world upside down. Without that day, everything would be different: They would not be on this train, there would be no *Sucasa*, no Caroline, no Tucson, no trip to California to discuss an airline to Mexico. Without that day, they might be on a different train, their own train, the Kansas City, Mexico and Orient Railway, on a trip into the Barranca del Cobre, where the Mexicans were working to finish the railroad started by Will and others a half-century before.

The car hit a nail, blew a tire and flipped, tossing Leet onto his head. Whose car was it? How did the nail come to be lying in that place at that time in New Haven? What trick of fate caused it to lie in the precise spot it had to be to blow the tire?

They began the meal in silence, lost in thought, gazing at each other from time to time or turning to watch the countryside race by in the fading twilight.

"Will," she said after a while, and he could tell she had moved on, "you haven't told me what you have in mind with this airline of Red's."

He did not answer immediately.

"Not bad steak," he said, finally. "Tastes like Kansas City." He was pulling his mind back from where it had been. He laid down the knife and fork. "You know, the governor used to take us to a place down by the stockyards—Gus's, it was called. . . wouldn't be surprised if it was still there. . . best steaks in the world. It's not just the beef, you know, it's how it's cooked."

"You'll have to take me some time," she said.

"What do you think?" he asked, watching her.

"But I've never been to Gus's. . . "

They both smiled. "About the airline. I mean. I believe that's what you were asking about."

"I have no idea. Red. You know Red. . . "

"I know Red."

"You perked up the moment you heard about this airline of his. I saw it in your eyes that morning in the breakfast room.'

"I thought mostly it was a good excuse for a trip."

"That's not all you thought. Mexico! That's what you thought. Admit it."

Looking outside as it grew darker, he began to see his wife's reflection in the window. Though traveling westward with the sun, the train was too slow to delay the approach of night. Airplanes, that was the thing. He'd read about ideas for jet propulsion that could keep a plane's speed up with the earth's rotation so you didn't lose time as you went west. You might leave Chicago and arrive in Los Angeles before you left. What a strange thought! Of course, you'd lose it back again on the return.

"How long has it been since we've seen Red, Amelia? When was the last time? Do you remember?"

"I do remember. It was soon after the Saint Patrick's Day Flood. I remember because the trains had just started running again. We had the Goldsboroughs down for Sunday dinner. Caroline was pregnant with Jimmy. Red was there that day."

"Jimmy was born in '36."

"He was."

"Eleven years. . . you don't find that strange?"

"You know I do."

"He hasn't wanted to face me since the embezzlement business."

"I understand."

"He won't come and see us so we'll go and see him."

"You're interested in this idea of his, aren't you?"

"The truth is, Amelia, I'd like to go back to Mexico before I die. There's so much I'd like to see again—and do again—and this time with you. We didn't make it the first time, did we?"

Amelia studied him. "We didn't make it."

"If Red has a good idea, I'll listen."

§

"Where's Dad, I'm starving."

We were in the living room, Carol at the piano, Billy and me horsing around on the floor while Mother fixed dinner. My watch and stomach said 7:30, half an hour after we normally ate when Dad was home, as he was supposed to be, and still no sign of him. Emotionally, all of us were still back at *Sucasa* where we usually were the first week in September, only returning after Labor Day.

This year we'd come back early to greet Granny and Grandpa. Because of Jane, it had been tougher than usual to leave *Sucasa*, but the long drive in the pre-war, baby-blue Plymouth Grandpa bought for Mother made it easier to deal with my first love hangover. We spent the first night in a hotel in Terra Haute, where I slipped down to the lobby to call Jane, but by the second night, in Hannibal, Missouri, I was already starting to forget. I might have learned something about Mark Twain in Hannibal, but Mother was anxious to press on to the Broadmoor in

Colorado Springs, more elegant than our dowdy inn in Tom Sawyer's home town. Poor Mother, never much of a driver but forced to endure 2,500 miles with three whining children—insisting each day that Carol, age fourteen, take the wheel, though Carol didn't know how to drive, which added to the excitement. The last day, we stopped in Las Vegas, still a one-horse town, for lunch at the Flamingo and to buy a water bag to cool the radiator so we wouldn't add to the dried bones of the desert.

I still couldn't imagine the grandparents in California, cut off from their roots. I couldn't imagine *Sucasa* without them or them without *Sucasa*.

Dad was nowhere to be found when we arrived home. Mother called Mrs. Wire, the woman from up the hill who was supposed to take care of things while we were gone, but she had gone to Sacramento to be with a daughter having a baby. Dad had lived in the house for days without cleaning, washing or taking out the garbage, and cockroaches and ants had invaded everywhere. It was too much even for Queenie, who'd taken up residence at Bobby Taylor's, a few sandy lots down the street. We'd hardly stepped in the house when Mother had us cleaning up. What a difference from *Sucasa*, where you'd just press the buzzer, and Rose, Mabel or Edith would arrive.

Dad had called at some point to say he was still in Del Mar. The last big race was on Labor Day, and he was supposed to be back, but still hadn't shown. At least the house was clean. We had everything spic and span in two days and then Mother let us go down to the beach club, which was jumping with kids, the last week before school. The best weather, you learn when you've lived in Los Angeles a while, is in September.

Carol stopped whatever she was playing and flopped on the couch. She'd been restless all summer or maybe anxious is a better word. Just as Mother had experimented by sending Billy and me to military school the year before, an experiment that flopped badly, she'd decided to send Carol to the Marlborough (girls) School this year, though that meant losing all her friends in El Segundo. It also meant taking three buses to get downtown everyday, which seemed silly since El Segundo was only 15 minutes away on one bus.

Mother had a thing about private schools even though everyone said that El Segundo, because of Standard Oil, was just like a private school. I only found out later that Millie Oliver had set up trust funds for our education. Not only did Carol and I have to attend schools miles away that we didn't like, but we paid for them with our own money. What's more, Dad, who had no money and no trusts, had been listed as one of the dozen "patrons" of the California Military Academy, which meant that not only was our education money used for tuition at a school I detested, but another $1,000 was donated out of sheer magnanimity. Dad couldn't have cared less about our military education, and I imagine Mother donated the money in his name so as not to embarrass him, surely the only time his philanthropy helped support anything but race tracks and casinos. Billy, too, had to pay up. He'd been a kindergarten soldier at CMA, as it was known (founded in 1936 and located in Baldwin Hills, the school was razed in the 1990s). He wore a military hat twice the size of his head, a ridiculous sight.

"All right, children, we'll start anyway."

She was standing in the living room doorway, hair in a bandana, reminding me of the victory garden. "He probably stayed another day at the races."

"There are no races today," Carol said.

"How do you know that?"

"There aren't any races on Tuesdays."

Mother looked befuddled. "Then I have no idea where he is. Let's start."

Montreal Street was a nice house. One thing I have to say about all the rented houses we lived in over the years is that they were all big comfortable houses. Too bad we never owned one, which would have been a good investment in those days, especially in California. The best thing about Montreal Street, of course, was the secret room behind the bookcase in my room. What puzzled me about the secret room was that to get in it you had to remove books, shelves and the wall board behind the shelves so that if you were to hide in there, you'd have to have someone on the outside put everything back, which meant you couldn't all hide in there together. In other words, if Billy and I wanted to hide from the Japs or Mother or anyone else they'd know where we were because all the books and shelves would be out. It wasn't at all like the secret rooms in movies where the books and shelves together swing out controlled by a hidden button behind one of the books and then swing back in place again.

The secret room wasn't all I liked about the house. It had a large back patio overlooking the ocean, a side patio big enough for a ping-pong table, which Bobby Taylor and I used for cover when we slept outside, and a big living room. We had a baby grand player-piano on which both Carol and I practiced and on which we'd get the piano-roll going when we were fed up with our own limitations. We both took lessons from Mrs. Acosta, who lived up Vista del Mar about a half-mile away, just past Captain Stone's house, where we dropped off the hundred dollar monthly rent check on the way to lessons.

The dining room was past the front door and down the hallway to the left, with the den and Mother and Dad's room to the right, everything done in walnut paneling and broad exposed beams, no plaster showing anywhere. The outside was brown wood shingle, perfect for a mountain retreat as long as no one dropped a match. Upstairs was for Carol, Billy and me, so we not only had our own rooms, but our own floor. Past the dining room was the kitchen and the back door leading out to vacant lots of sand and iceplant where Queenie mostly hung out. Queenie was not an indoors kind of dog.

Mother put plates of meatloaf, potatoes and string beans on the table, and came out with her own plate. It was Wichita fare with string beans instead of dandelions, meat loaf instead of Spam and tomato sauce instead of Heinz ketchup, definitely an improvement but hardly up to *Sucasa* standards.

"Are Granny and Grandpa coming over?" asked Carol.

"Yes, they'll come over for dinner," said Mother. "I hope Mrs. Wire gets back."

"Her daughter's had her baby?"

"Yes, last week. She'll be back this week."

"Are you picking Granny and Grandpa up?" I asked.

"I'll let your father pick them up in the new car," said Mother.

"Speaking of cars," said Carol. "One just stopped outside."

We couldn't see the street, but had no doubt who it was. We heard the Buick door slam and soon saw Dad through the window on the brick path leading to the house. He was dressed in his usual race track attire—slacks and a Hawaiian shirt. He was sunburned and had had a few drinks. Even as a boy, I could always tell.

"Hullo," he said.

"Yours is in the oven, Billy," said Mother, curtly.

None of us had seen him since June, but our parents weren't big on displays of affection. Dad didn't look quite right, even quite right for him after a few drinks. Win or lose, he usually came back from the track in reasonable spirits. Gamblers are like ballplayers: however bad the day, there's another game tomorrow. Mother looked mad and didn't hide it, which spelled trouble. There was no doubt that in the nearly three years we'd been in California, the parents had been growing apart. In Wichita, they'd spent some time together, but here they lived separate lives, which would be easier now with two cars. Having dinner *en famille* was not a common occurrence.

Dad fixed a drink and brought his plate in from the oven. "How was Sewickley?" he asked.

"You know Mother and Daddy arrive Thursday," said Mother.

"That's why I'm here," he said. "Are you meeting them?"

"Why don't you?" said Mother. "You can take the new car."

"I like my car. Anyway, they'd rather see you."

"Where have you been, Billy? You said you'd be back this afternoon." Mother was really sore about something.

"I stayed for today's races."

He knew that we knew it was a lie the minute he said it, for we all stared at him in disbelief.

"There are no races on Tuesday," said Mother.

"Okay, so I was taking care of business."

Carol says Mother knew about Bunny Warren, whose name came out during the divorce. I didn't know anything at the time. Why didn't Mother confront him that time over dinner? I asked Carol years later. With her quick temper, it was not in her nature to keep things quiet, even with children around—especially with children around. If she could embarrass someone, she didn't normally miss the chance, and she liked an audience. Because, said Carol, what do you think Mother was doing every summer in Sewickley? Why do you think we went back every summer even when Mother was barely speaking to Granny and Grandpa? She went to see her old boyfriends. Everyone knew about it, she said.

A few years later, Carol, nineteen, would marry Sam Adams who grew up in the house across Church Lane from Shields Presbyterian and the mausoleum. Mother went back for the wedding, which I missed because school wasn't out. Prior to the wedding, Mother offered her some advice about sex. Like me, Carol had learned at an early age never to tell Mother anything because it would be used against you, so they'd never had a real heart-to-heart, girl-to-girl, birds-and bees gabble. A day before the wedding, Mother decided it was time to offer some motherly advice.

"Never go anywhere without your diaphragm," she said. "I don't even go to lunch without mine."

In the history of advice to daughters on their wedding eve, that may have been unique. My first thought was—wouldn't it depend on with whom you're lunching? Finally I understood why Mother had gone missing at all those lunches in Sewickley. Did the Crittendens know about it? They'd lived in that community for a half century, and it's unlikely they wouldn't have known about their daughter's lunch habits. It would be part of the explanation for the ice storms between daughter and parents during *Sucasa* summers and for their often bizarre behavior together.

I broke the silence. "They're coming to talk about Ramsa, aren't they?"

"What have you done about Ramsa since we left?" said Mother, ignoring me.

"What is this, the third degree?" Dad looked sullen. "I only walked in the house five minutes ago."

"It isn't the third degree, Daddy," said Carol, exasperation in her voice. "We haven't seen you all summer. We're asking questions. It's natural."

Dad looked at her and took a long swallow of his highball. "I don't have answers. We're trying to start a company. There are problems. It's hard."

"If this airline is such a great idea," snapped Mother, "how come someone hasn't already done it. . . someone smart. . . like Howard Hughes?"

Howard Hughes was a big name at the time. His airfield and the Spruce Goose were down the hill a mile or so from our house, and he'd just made a movie called "The Outlaw," with Jane Russell's lipstick sneer and bulging blouse plastered on billboards around town.

"Goddamit, Howard Hughes is not the only one with ideas."

"I'd like to go to Mexico," I said.

"Sure," said Dad, "why not?"

"You'll be in school," said Mother. "Eat your string beans."

"Are you going to take Granny and Grandpa to Mexico?" Billy asked.

"I don't know," said Dad. "We'll see."

"Finish your milk, Billy," said Mother.

Thursday morning, before the rest of us were up, Mother drove downtown to meet the grandparents at Union Station. I've always wondered how she felt about their only visit to Playa del Rey, where she'd moved to escape them, to start a new life. Her feelings would have been confused not just because of her always awkward relations with her parents, but because they were coming to look into Dad's Ramsa project at the very moment she was getting ready to leave Dad for her new boyfriend, Burnie Adams, though none of us knew it at the time. It's one of the things I would like to have asked her about. But I didn't, and she wouldn't have had much to say about it anyway because she operated on instinct, not introspection.

From Union Station, she drove them to the Del Mar Beach Club in Santa Monica, where they'd booked rooms. The Del Mar is a large red brick structure on the beach and boardwalk between Ocean Park and Santa Monica, built as a hotel for the stars in the 1920s and having nothing to do with the Del Mar race track, which is near San Diego. Dad should have gone with her to meet the train. After all, the Crittendens were coming to California largely to see him. It would have been a nice gesture, but Dad wasn't big on gestures.

He could have gone with her, for he sat in the patio reading the newspaper that morning before heading to E. F. Hutton, a stone's throw from the beach club. Though he wasn't a mean man—he never laid a hand on any of us children even when in his cups—like Mother, he didn't pay much attention to the feelings of others. Booze numbed his emotional reflexes—probably even was meant to numb them. Either that or he didn't have the kind of punishing conscience that keeps most of us from doing hurtful things.

One afternoon, about a year after we'd arrived in Playa del Rey, he took me to the movies in Ocean Park, the beach village between Venice and Santa Monica. The movie was Roy Rogers, my favorite, we were early and Dad wanted a drink. He told me to meet him in front of the movie in half an hour. I wandered out on the amusement pier, watched the roller-coaster and kids playing games, thinking Dad and I might be doing that. I was back at the theater ahead of time, but no sign of Dad. I checked the clock in the ticket booth, but after a half hour he still hadn't appeared. I was nine years old, had no money and no way home. I checked where we'd parked, and the car was still there. I started checking the bars—at nine, I was used to checking bars—dashing back between times to check the movie entrance. Frustration set in, or maybe it was anger. I knew the movie had begun. I planted myself at the entrance. I could think of nothing else to do. After an hour or so of mounting desperation, I checked the car again. After two hours, I was ready to panic. Something was wrong.

Then he walked out of the movie.

"Where were you?" he asked.

"You went to the movies. . . ?"

"You were late," he said.

"I was not," I said, fighting back tears. "I was here on time."

"If you'd been here," he said, "I wouldn't have gone in alone."

It was a puzzling answer, a Roshomonian lesson in relativity. But whether Dad was right or I was right—and I had checked the clock—I knew he was wrong to go in without me. Why didn't he know that? It takes a particular level of *sans-gêne* to do something like that, but that was Dad. On reflection, I'm glad he didn't stay for the second feature, but he needed a drink.

It wasn't meanness, just indifference. He couldn't feel for a nine-year-old left alone outside a movie for two hours, wasn't in touch enough with himself to remember when he was nine and how it felt. Most of us can't imagine going to the movies, much less enjoying them, with a child gone missing in a place like Ocean Park. But Dad didn't imagine things, he just did them. Like Mother, he didn't suffer a lot from remorse. He was physical with her, but never with us. Mother, on the other hand, had no trouble administering slaps and pinches to her brood, not so much as chastisements for bad behavior but out of her frequent frustration and anger. Because Dad basically floated through life, unengaged, she had reason to feel frustrated and angry.

The Crittendens came for dinner the next day. Dad, who'd been in a sour mood since returning from Del Mar, put on a jacket over his Hawaiian shirt and picked them up in the dilapidated '41 convertible, which would have been an embarrassing car except that almost everyone drove dilapidated cars in those days. I suppose he didn't drive Mother's Plymouth because it had been Grandpa's gift. A few postwar cars had begun to appear in 1947—the Ford Sportsman with wood panels is the one I remember—but the car industry didn't really start going again until 1948. Even after '48 there were still few enough cars around that kids knew them all by heart. There was *the* Ford and *the* Chevy and *the* Chrysler, and they didn't all look alike as cars do today. Some really strange ones came along, like the Studebaker, the Tucker, the Kaiser, the Frazer. Kids knew all about all those cars. Besides their black Buick, the grandparents kept a green Nash at *Sucasa*, funny car with the gearshift on the dashboard where the radio should have been. I never saw one of those in California.

Dad had got the Buick's raggy top up despite its metal braces being completely corroded by salt air and drove the grandparents back along the coast road with everybody in the front seat. It was only two weeks since we'd seen them at *Sucasa*, but we hugged like it had been years. It felt good to hug. We took them on a tour of the downstairs and the patios, with Dad opening the swinging redwood shutters in the patio fence to show off our view of the ocean. Queenie seemed content to be back in a normal house and nuzzled up to Grandpa when we invaded her patio space. Grandpa, dressed in his usual three-piece suit, was enjoying himself at our beach house. A Missouri and Pennsylvania man, he knew his lakes and rivers, but had not spent much time around oceans.

Dad fixed drinks, and we gathered in the living room while Mrs. Wire took care of the dinner preparations. Granny wanted to hear us play, so Carol played *The Donkey Serenade*, which she was learning for Mrs. Acosta's recital, and I played something. The grandparents had to arrive from Sewickley for anyone to ask us to play anything, but that's how it was in the family. For Mother, piano lessons were to keep children out of the way. The only reaction I ever had from Mother during a lifetime of piano-playing was when I hit a bad note. Wherever she was, in whatever house we lived in at whatever time, she heard only the bad notes. She was constitutionally unable to give compliments. With her intuition for it, she probably heard my bad notes even when I was playing in some faraway place. I still think of her when I hit a clunker. She lives on that way.

Dinner was correct, without sparks. Mrs. Wire's presence meant Mother didn't have to do the cooking, and Carol and I didn't have to do the cleaning up. Dad and Mother were at the head and foot of the table as usual, with Carol and Granny flanking Mother; Grandpa and me flanking Dad, and Billy between Granny and me. That left Mother to talk mostly to Carol and Granny while Grandpa had me and Dad as partners. Dinner was roast beef with roast potatoes and succotash. Hot mustard and horseradish sauce was set in little pots around the table. Nobody asked for second helpings. Mrs. Wire served through the swinging door into the kitchen, and if she didn't wear the shiny black uniforms with white aprons the maids wore at *Sucasa*, she did the job.

I'd never seen my father and grandfather together because they'd never been together in my lifetime, and I spent most of the evening watching them and listening. They seemed friendly enough. Dad had his usual highball glass at the table, but was being careful. Mother and Grandpa also took a drink. Nobody drank wine in those days. Now that Dad had said I could go to Mexico with him, I kept waiting for them to start talking about Mexico, but the word was not mentioned either at dinner or afterward, for I kept my ears open.

I was too young to understand anything of their complicated relationship, but even as a boy, it tantalized me. These were two of the three most important men in my life (the third was Uncle Jim), and yet as far as I knew they were complete strangers to each other. Dad had never accompanied us to *Sucasa*, and of course the grandparents had never visited us in California. My parents had been married for fourteen years in 1947, yet, to my knowledge, my father didn't even know my grandfather, something that seemed more than a little strange. The dinner that night was correct, leaving few traces on my memory. If there's one meal I could return to today to study the things I missed at the time (the roast beef dinner at *Sucasa* would be a close second), it would be that night at Playa del Rey. There must have been a great deal going on under the surface, unseen by me but detectable to a trained eye. Both Mother and Dad had difficult relations with the grandparents, who resented it, and by this time the parents had their own disintegrating relationship to deal with as well. Things were at the breaking point all around, though I understood none of it at the time.

They used us, the children—as adults often do—to avoid talking to each other. There was some chit-chat about California at dinner, and everyone seemed courteous, but also serious and edgy, more like strangers than family. I'd never thought much before why Dad never went to *Sucasa*, but the grandparents' presence in California set me to thinking about it. I still knew nothing about the cowboy or Bunny Warren. I'd never heard of Otto Berndt or the embezzlement or how Millie Oliver had saved the day. I'd only heard about the Kansas City, Mexico and Orient Railway a few weeks before and knew nothing about Ramsa except the name. I had a lot to learn over the next few days.

Families and Money

Opportunity in California doesn't mean everyone succeeds; details of Dad's life throw light on the effects of gifts and inheritance.

Dad and Mother at Atlantic City, March 1937.

Dad and I never had much conversation until after the divorce. I don't find this odd because long years in Europe exposed me to cultures that leave the education of children primarily to professionals, with decent enough results. That's not the American way, but the truth is that Dad, like Mother, didn't have a lot of interest in family or children. His main interest was money, not for what it would buy, for he was a man of common tastes, but as proof of success, proof he was smarter than the next guy. He didn't need to show off, there was nothing ostentatious about him, but he wanted the satisfaction of knowing what someone making money meant to others: that there goes a guy who made it, there goes a sharp operator. It's called reputation. His appetite for money was natural, but whetted by coming of age during the Depression and nourished by his marriage into a family that had known how to make money for a century, back to the time of Andrew Carnegie and Thomas Mellon.

I think what Dad disliked about *Sucasa* was that for him it was a symbol of money. He didn't need symbols, even disdained them. What he needed was the existential success that symbols represent, inner feelings not outer ones. His dream of dreams, I suspect, was to sit with Grandpa in his den at *Sucasa*, good whiskeys in hand, talking about business not as a supplicant, not as a son-in-law living off his wife, but as a man who had made it the hard way, on his own, up from the bottom like Henry Oliver, not through inheritance, and that everyone understood.

Dad abandoned his NYSE seat in part because whatever success he had on Wall Street would always be put down to Oliver largesse, not to his own acumen. Wall Street also was work, which he never liked. All his later deals and schemes were undertaken to show he could make it on his own and at his own pace. If any of his ideas—Ramsa above all—had worked, he could have sat down with Grandpa, man-to-man, and had that drink and talk. His base problem was a lack of discipline. He was too lazy to use hard work to create the kind of success he sought—as Carnegie, Mellon and Oliver had done. He had ideas, but needed others to realize them. He saw himself as the architect, not the engineer, believing his native smarts plus lady luck and a little seed money would sooner or later lead to the jackpot, and minions could be found to take care of the details.

He'd had a regular enough life growing up. His family came to Pittsburgh from Maryland's Eastern Shore—where the name Goldsborough

is familiar thanks to various governors and senators—around the time
the Olivers were arriving from Ireland, the middle 1800s. Dad's father,
William West Goldsborough, was a broker on the Pittsburgh Stock
Exchange in the days when there were regional stock exchanges from
Boston to San Francisco, with Saint Louis, Chicago, Detroit, Philadelphia, Cincinnati, Detroit, Cleveland and Pittsburgh in between. Only
a few regionals survive today, the others wounded by the invention of
the telegraph—which connected the country to the big exchanges—
and given the *coup de grace* by the Depression. Bill Goldsborough, Sr.,
who earned every cent he ever had, did well enough on the Pittsburgh
exchange for his family to live in the fashionable Squirrel Hill district,
near Schenley Park. Bill Jr., known as Red, attended Pittsburgh's best
private school, the Shadyside Academy, went on to Exeter, an elite New
Hampshire boy's school, and then entered Princeton.

The Depression was worse for Pittsburgh than for many cities
because of its strong industrial base. A famous editorial in the *New
York Daily News* the day after "Bloody Tuesday," October 29, 1929,
pointed out that "the sagging of stocks has not destroyed a single fac-
tory, wiped out a single farm or city lot or real estate development,
decreased the productive powers of a single workman or machine in
the United States." The market's crash, said the newspaper, had nothing to do with the United States economy, which was still as strong as
the week before.

But it wasn't. The market dragged industry down with it. On September 3, 1929, U.S. Steel, the Morgan conglomerate put together from
the Carnegie and Oliver companies, closed at 262. That same day, the
Dow Jones Industrial Average hit 386, an all-time high. Three years
later, with Pittsburgh mills producing at ten percent capacity, U.S.
Steel was at twenty-two and the Dow would not surpass its September 3, 1929 level until 1954—from Hoover to Eisenhower. Pittsburgh
industry was dead and so was the Pittsburgh stock exchange. Only one
would recover.

I didn't find out much about Dad's past until after the divorce, which
took place when I was twelve, so I must jump briefly ahead.

Seeking to keep some contact with his children after Mother remar-
ried, Dad began taking me on gambling and racing trips to Las Vegas
and Del Mar. Mostly, however, we went to Santa Anita and Hollywood
Park, closer to home. By this time, in the early 1950s, he was addicted

to gambling and the races, just as he was to booze. Why a man as clever with numbers didn't understand that Las Vegas, like the tracks, was a mug's game, I don't know. When I went into the Army in 1958 I got to know some professional gamblers from New York—like me, draftees—and they swore a smart guy could make a living at the tracks. I don't know if they were kidding me or themselves, but Dad had that attitude. A smart guy could beat the odds at anything. Plus he liked the gambler's life—not much work, some numbers, thrills, booze, travel. By the 1950s, with his chances for the Big Time fading, gambling was all he had.

He didn't do a lot of chit-chatting when playing—which was also one of the few times he wasn't drinking much—but the trips helped create a closer bond between us. We also saw some movies together—he never had a television—and he came to a few baseball games when my high school team played at Rancho Playground in Los Angeles while he was living in the La Brea apartments across the street. By the time I was at UCLA, he'd sold his beach house in Manhattan Beach and moved into a succession of rooms across town, ending up in one of those West Hollywood stucco triplexes built in the 1930s for the growing movie crowd and popping up in just about any Ross MacDonald or Raymond Chandler thriller. We'd get together from time to time for dinner or a drink, usually at Tom Morris's house, for Dad stayed close to Tom. Perhaps because I could have a drink with him by then (with a phony ID), he looked on me as an adult of sorts and began to open up.

He was kind of a mess. He'd gone quickly through the money from his house, and his only income was from Millie Oliver's wedding present, the stock exchange seat. Drinking was wasting him, and when he switched to beer-only for a while he ballooned up and soon was back on the hard stuff. I liked meeting him at Tom's because I liked Tom, always dapper and friendly, and liked his house. Despite his key limitations, Tom was an entertaining piano player and I knew some piano myself. He was more than willing to lend his house for cocktails so I didn't have to go to Dad's rooms, always a bigger mess than the college frat room I shared with three other guys. I think Dad was gabby by then because he was trying to figure out where things had gone wrong. Tom was still as curious about Dad's past as ever. For a descendant of the *Californios*, a guy who didn't know Pittsburgh from Toledo and rarely went East, Tom Morris never seemed to tire of the Oliver-Crittenden fable.

You had to get Dad on a good day, or more specifically at the right time on a good day. Sober or hung-over, he didn't socialize much. Drunk he was a slob and you wanted to get away. But catch him in between, say before the fourth or fifth drink, and he was an entertaining guy who'd done some living and could open up and enjoy the give-and-take of conversation. If he'd learned to stop after the third drink, he might have had a different life: The story of every drunk.

I never saw him drunk at Tom's. Tom was self-made, smart, still hob-nobbed with the Hollywood crowd, and Dad wasn't about to embarrass him at his house. On a good day, Dad still was the sharp East Coast operator with a seat on the exchange, a relaxed, flame-haired guy who didn't agonize over things and had an easy smile. On a good day, he was still like he'd been when we arrived in California, snappy in high-belted slacks, a Hawaiian shirt and a good after-shave, a guy with a touch of the Princeton preppie gone west. But there weren't many good days any-more.

There was one at Tom's on a warm spring evening in '58, my senior year at UCLA. It was rare for Dad to open up about his past, but it wasn't entirely his fault. Unlike Mother, Dad liked a good gabble and the evenings at Tom's were always interesting, but he'd learned along the line—as all of us had—that conversation with Mother went nowhere. Mother and Dad never talked about their early years much, and I didn't get curious about his past until I was in college. Like Mother, non-introspective, he tended to avoid reminisces, preferring to talk about horses, planes, stocks, gambling, a little politics—the things he cared about. Dredging up his youth must have pained him as he got older, not because it was sad, which it wasn't, but because it was wasted.

"I dropped out of college in 1930," he told us over drinks.

The piano playing had been fun that night—simple, two-handed blues riffing which was about the only thing I could manage in F sharp. Tom and I were through playing and ready to drink and be entertained. It was the spring of my last semester, and I had the world on a string. I'd have a degree in economics in a few weeks, was thinking of going on for a graduate degree and had asked Dad what he did during the Depression. Studying economics had led to my interest in the Depression, which made me curious about his past. I'd begun to realize how little I knew about him. He would have been twenty when the markets crashed in 1929, which was exactly my age.

"The brokerage business went sour like everything else, and Dad couldn't pay the bills," he said. "I went to work for a Pittsburgh bootlegger named Heinie—guy who made this stuff." He held up his glass. "Only not as good. I was one of his muscles."

I could see it. He wasn't big but was thick and feisty and before the booze got him hard as nails. When we first moved to Playa del Rey after the war, he'd go out to the patio behind the house and stand with his back to the slatted wood fence enclosing it. He'd hook his arms backwards over the top board, about six feet off the ground, and raise his legs straight out at ninety degrees. He'd do that a dozen times, rest and do a dozen more. Then he'd tell me to punch him in the stomach, and it was hard as rock. He told me the story of how Harry Houdini died from a punch in the stomach and said he knew how to control it. He'd put me up on that fence, and I couldn't do one pull-up.

"Pittsburgh wasn't Chicago," he said. "There were some guys knocked off—a family named Volpe gunned down in a coffee shop—but it was rare. The money was good, but you could see the end of Prohibition coming. The country turned against it. Bootleggers were making all the money. The Feds didn't like that."

He never talked about Princeton. In his life, I never heard him mention the word. Mother once told me he'd won the maypole contest as a freshman, which had something to do with climbing a pole to fetch a piglet. I don't think he was too broken up over leaving college because he always was more interested in money than study. Like Mother, Dad was no scholar. Growing up, I only saw him read three things: financial pages, racing pages and the *Saturday Evening Post*—three things more than I ever saw Mother read. There were no books in our houses. The boozing didn't help. You can't blame everything on Prohibition, but there's no question that the habit of drinking, especially around affluent places like Sewickley, grew from the illegality of it. They passed Prohibition to get rid of alcohol and produced a generation of alcoholics. Speakeasies and bootleggers added a thrill you don't get in the corner pub, and while you might have a few beers in the pub, Prohibition's main product was blood-cell destroying gin.

"I met your mother at a party in Shadyside. She liked a good time. We went out a few times and after one long weekend decided to get married. Drove to West Virginia. . . a place called New Cumberland. . . not even a one-horse town. . . no horses in New Cumberland."

Everybody laughed.

"But there was a justice of the peace. Will Crittenden was not happy when we got back. . . downhill with him after that."

If he'd mentioned Mother and the cowboy that night I wouldn't have had to wait another decade to find out. Of course he knew about it. Mother told Carol it was in Walter Winchell's syndicated column, which ran in the *Pittsburgh Dispatch*. Mother basically eloped twice, but the second time Grandpa had to accept it because she was legally an adult. Mother also told Carol she thought she was pregnant, which she wasn't. In any case, the Goldsboroughs were not cowboys but a respectable Pittsburgh family reduced to shabby gentile like a lot of people, but still respectable. Grandpa Goldsborough was a long-time member of the Duquesne Club, restricted to Pittsburgh's WASP elite in those days. Any hopes the Crittendens might have had for an elegant wedding in Shields Presbyterian had been dashed by the cowboy business anyway.

"The seat on the exchange was a present from Crittenden, right?" asked Tom.

"No, no, never," he said. "It came from Millie Oliver. I told her I liked numbers and the next thing I know she buys the seat as a wedding present. They'd gone for $600,000 before the crash, but were down to $90,000 in '33. That's how bad the markets were. The Dow hit forty-one in '31. Forty-one."

"How come you didn't keep the seat?" I asked.

Fingering his glass, he stared at me. Usually ready with a smile, when he sensed a challenge any trace of smile disappeared. Strangely, despite his boozing and reputation for a quick temper, I don't remember ever quarreling with Dad. He and Mother had big fights, but he left us kids alone. I don't think we interested him that much except as occasional company to fight off lonesomeness. He didn't identify with us any more than did Mother. I don't remember him ever asking me anything about my life.

"What do you mean I didn't keep it?" he growled. "I own it, don't I?"

"You lease it out," I said.

He didn't like that. "You want it, smart guy, it's yours. You're getting a degree in economics. It could be arranged. . . call it a graduation present."

"Hey, Red," said Tom, laughing, "take it easy. You still have to eat. Not to mention drink."

"How come you didn't keep the seat?" I persisted.

"Okay. . . look, I was your age. I was new to New York. I did what anyone would do: Found a guy who worked the floor—Frank Bliss, the Silver Fox—and we set up a partnership. It was the bottom of the Depression. It made sense to let a pro like Frank take the floor. I worked the office."

We fell silent, the only sound the clinks of ice in our glasses and the low hum of the overhead fan. I looked at my father, who was staring blankly at the rubber tree outside. For the first time I asked myself— was Dad a drunk? Had the Depression created wounds, scars—depressions—that people like me with happy pasts and bright futures could never understand? Dashed dreams, smashed lives, divorces, the bottle, clinging to vain hopes of a killing at the track or in the casino that would reverse everything, provide the stake for the big come-back. That's all he ever wanted, the break that would lift him into the big time, get him on the wagon, get the flab off those stomach muscles, make him a lean, tough operator again instead of a flushed, soft has-been living off his wedding present. He'd come close with Ramsa, hadn't he?

The amazing thing was that Dad was only forty-eight that year, the prime of life.

What Tom and I were hearing was not just nostalgia, it was regret, maybe even shame. Whatever his rationale for giving up the seat, turning it over to the Silver Fox to finance a mythical bonanza in California hadn't turned out so well. Introspective or not, he couldn't duck the truth anymore, and it ate at him. He'd taken the easy way. What irony! Millie Oliver sets up her granddaughter's husband with work for life, and he uses the money to create a life without work.

He broke the silence.

"We kept waiting for the markets to turn around, but the economy was dead until the war. People were killing themselves. Jesse Livermore—Frank introduced me to him, the 'boy plunger' they called him—walks into the men's room at the Sherry-Netherland and shoots himself. Leaves a note to his wife at the bar. . . at the bar!. . . 'my life has been a failure.'"

The words hung in the air.

"They call suicides cowards because they can't face life," he said. "Cowards are people who can't face death."

I watched a fly ride the air waves under the fan.

"Otto wasn't a coward either. You know about Otto, don't you?"

"The guy who embezzled from your firm?"

He stood and went to the bar. The Hawaiian shirt, which used to hang straight over iron-tight muscles, now bulged over a spreading paunch.

"You know what happened. . . ?"

"How would I know?"

He refilled his drink. "I never told you. . . ?"

I stared at him, puzzled.

"Put it this way: The firm was saved, not Otto."

"He went to jail. . . ?"

"No, he avoided jail."

"How?"

"The Dutch Act."

"The what?"

"The Dutch Act. Four years in college and you don't know what the Dutch Act is? Tom, enlighten the kid."

"Killed himself," said Tom. "Shot himself through the head. Just like Jesse Livermore."

Two kinds of investors came out of the Depression more or less whole, the alphas and the betas. Joe Kennedy was an alpha, someone smart enough or lucky enough to get out in time and not be closed out by margin calls. The alpha index measures the investor's skill, the money he makes (or doesn't lose) above and beyond the market averages. Kennedy's skills helped him ride out the Depression and kept his children in school instead of dropping out—like Dad—to look for work. The rest is history.

Will Crittenden was a beta, someone who owned stocks outright, not on margin, and was content to ride up and down with the averages and never be closed out. Dad said of his father-in-law—"all Will Crittenden ever did was never sell"—his voice full of derision. Dad was a born speculator, gambler, risk-taker; a trader who changed stocks on the exchange as often as he changed horses at the track. Will Crittenden, though he didn't create wealth like the Olivers, Mellons and Carnegie, knew the recipe for protecting it—even during the Depression: invest prudently, diversify, stay in blue-chips, never buy on margin and never sell short. Take care of your money, and maybe when you go you'll have enough left over for philanthropy or your children.

Will Crittenden saw the value of U. S. Steel fall to a low of twenty-two during the Depression, but never faced a margin call. He still held his blue chips when World War II started and by war's end was already getting well. When Dad was launching Ramsa, Grandpa's prudence during the Depression had made him wealthy and secure enough to consider a flyer on Mexico. If not railroads, why not airlines?

Some in Sewickley said Will Crittenden married Amelia Oliver for her money, but their correspondence during the long courtship proves it wasn't so. Some in Sewickley said Red Goldsborough married Caroline Crittenden for her trust funds, but that also wasn't so. That's not to say Dad didn't enjoy spending Oliver money or that if he'd gotten his hands on the principal he wouldn't have spent it as fast as he spent the income. Put Dad in Will Crittenden's place during the Depression and he would have ended up like all the speculators—sold out, bankrupt and maybe in the men's room at the Sherry-Netherland. Dad hated real work and was always looking for a soft angle involving somebody else's money. Growing up, I never saw him do any known household chore—wash a car, dry a dish, mow a lawn, make a bed. He had no practical skills. He preferred hatching schemes with buddies over drinks.

In many ways, Mother and Dad were birds of a feather when they ran off to West Virginia together—lazy, spoiled, selfish, reckless, ignorant, rebellious. She'd run off once before so why not do it again? They were twenty-three, Prohibition was on the way out, they had some money, no jobs and liked the sex. The Oliver money didn't hurt, but I see them doing the same thing if the Olivers and Crittendens had lost as much in the Depression as the Goldsboroughs. Their marriage wasn't for love, it was a lark. Why not? They stayed married for sixteen years, and I never saw one sign of affection between them. Love? Mother would have laughed at the word.

For Dad it was more complex.

A few months after that night of confession at Tom's, I drove down to Del Mar in my black MGB convertible with friend Win Yandell to

Henry Huston Crittenden, author of The Crittenden Memoirs, *and Grandpa at Sucasa, 1950.*

join Dad for a few days at the track. I'd graduated from UCLA in June and been greeted with a draft notice from Uncle Sam for October. It was August, and we were hanging out in Dad's room at the Solana Beach motel where he'd become a track pal of the motel owner. The owner and his wife, transplants from Oklahoma, had cute, twin teenage daughters whom Win and I had been escorting about, and one night we were invited to the family's rooms at the front of the motel for a spaghetti dinner.

Dad was already looking worse than he'd been at Tom's. He'd tried and quickly abandoned the beer-only regime for it took too much beer to satisfy his body's need for alcohol, and he'd bloated up. Like most redheads, he was sun-sensitive, and afternoons at the track followed by booze had turned his skin the color of his hair. He never went near the ocean anymore, having abandoned any form of exercise except walking from paddock to window to rail at the track. Win and I were having a beer in his room while Dad drank gin and tonic. He'd had a bad day at the track, and I'd asked him, as I occasionally did, why he didn't get a job.

I did it with a smile.

He didn't smile back. "What do you want me to do, sell shoes?"

"Why not? It's honest work."

He gave me a nasty look, but no more was said. My timing was bad.

At dinner, it got worse. Maybe it was the twins, silky brunettes who looked too much like photos of Mother at that age. Maybe it was the sun and booze. Maybe it was the bad run he'd had at the track or my nagging about a job. Maybe it was all of that, but Dad was losing it. As the conversation moved east—from California to Oklahoma to Sewickley—he'd gotten sullen. I'd forgotten how he hated talking about Sewickley. Win and I were trying to get away with the girls, an idea that their parents, glass for glass with Dad, didn't seem to mind, but Dad wouldn't let me go. Sloshing his gin, he pulled me out on the porch, the screen door slamming shut behind us. He was sunburned, unshaven, sloppy, drunk and for some reason the day's losses were eating at him. It was a gentle California twilight, the planet not in phase with human emotions. I felt the warm ocean breeze wash over us.

"Why'd she do it?" he sputtered.

"Who. . . what. . . ?"

"Your mother. . . why'd she do it? You're the smart guy. You tell me. There was no reason. . . after sixteen years? No reason."

I looked at him and for the first time saw a broken man. Maybe I should have seen it before, but I'd been too wrapped up in my own life. He'd always been able to bounce back, but now I was seeing something different. I'd never heard self-pity from him before. I'd never heard him talk about Mother before. I felt like putting my arm around him but, like Mother, Dad didn't like touching. He wiped his eyes with the back of his hand, and I looked away.

He tried to get a grip. "Tough on you kids, wasn't it?"

What could I say? That it had been good for everyone but him. . . that at heart he was a selfish, affectionless loner who'd never needed a family at all. . . that Mother dumped him because he was a loser?

"Get a job, you said. . . sell shoes. Why the hell should I sell shoes?"

"You need something."

He was leaning on the porch rail. Inside the twins were saying something about Oklahoma that made Win and the parents laugh. If there are two states that have nothing in common they are Oklahoma, where I would spend some of my Army career, and California. Up and down the driveway, a few cars were parked, but most of the guests were still at dinner—good or bad ones depending on how they'd done at the track. The sky grew darker as the sun slipped behind some marine clouds at the horizon.

The tone softened. "I missed the boat, didn't I?"

"You're not even fifty years old."

"Fifty-year-old shoe salesman. . . that how you see me?"

"Why not? I sold suits at Bullocks. I liked it. . . liked the routine, the discipline."

He gave a nasty little laugh. "You can do better than selling suits. You're an Oliver. . . a Crittenden. . . Your grandfather wouldn't approve."

"I liked selling suits. I liked the people. . . I liked the friendship."

"You're going in the army as a private. Your grandfather wouldn't like that either. You should be a general like the Crittendens."

It was one of the few times he mentioned the military. He never talked about the Wichita years.

A car pulled off the coast highway and nosed in toward the rooms. A middle-aged couple emerged, man in long-sleeved white shirt, woman bulging out of her dress like a sausage. I tried to make out the license plates. . . definitely not California in those clothes. They disappeared laughing into their room. Time to celebrate a good day at the track with a little dessert. Dad couldn't take his eyes off her. I thought of Bunny Warren, nice Manhattan Beach woman who got tired of his boozing.

"My fault," he said, staring into a sky gone deep purple.

I didn't answer.

"Don't clam up. . . It was my fault, wasn't it?"

"I don't think so."

"It's like the track. You get lucky, the world's good. But sometimes it's not your day. . . or your week. . . or your month. You can have all the answers but without a little luck. . . "

"What if you have a lot of bad weeks and months?"

"You sure as hell don't give up. That what you're saying? Quit?"

"Try something else."

It was hopeless. Dad thought that if he'd gotten a break during the Depression, hit it big just one time, he'd be up there with the big shot—like Billy Durant, Sam Insull Charley Mitchell—operators who never walked away from a good deal, who knew how to win because they weren't afraid of losing. They made fortunes and lost them back but were always players and became legends. That was the life worth living in his eyes, not that of a coupon-clipping, dividend-collecting pensioner like Will Crittenden.

Dad never got it: These men made money, lost it, made it back again, but it was always their money. They didn't spend time at the track and the local E. F. Hutton office living off income from a wedding present. In a sense, the whales of Wall Street were no different from the whales of Pittsburgh—the Carnegies, Mellons, Fricks, Heinzes, Olivers. The rails on their rides to the top were greased with their own sweat, their own money, which, even borrowed, was backed by their own assets and reputations. He might have learned a lesson from the fates of people like Livermore, but thought he could succeed where they failed. Always looking for a sweet deal, he missed the real opportunities that came along and there were several, including the Ramsa airline in 1947. When Ramsa came along so did Will Crittenden, who was in a position to help.

At the time, Dad had been married to Will Crittenden's daughter for fourteen years. Had he been cultivating his father-in-law during those years so that at the crucial moment he might turn to him? The business opportunities in Mexico, which had been opening up to foreign investment following decades of protectionist nationalism, were enormous in 1947, but required capital. By then, however, Dad hadn't spoken to

Grandpa since before the war, had not set foot in *Sucasa* since the mid-1930s. He had an excuse: it was acceptable practice in those days for women to take their children home to their parents on summer holidays, leaving the men at the job.

But Dad had no job, and Grandpa knew it. Dad had no excuse for his permanent boycott of his wife's family and homestead. He had not even bothered to stay in contact with his own parents in Pittsburgh, and now his marriage was heading for the rocks. In every sense, Dad's family life had collapsed.

Grandpa's emotional ties to Mexico, ties reaching back to his youth, piqued his interest in the Ramsa project and brought him to California that summer of '47. But the two men had never been close, and it would take all Dad's (sober) charms and diplomatic skills to close a deal with his father-in-law. At eleven years old, I didn't yet know the details of their complicated relationship, but I know what happened to Ramsa.

Ramsa

The fledgling airline faces its moment of truth,
and a problem is encountered with the books.

Del Mar Racetrack, summer, 1937. Courtesy Del Mar Thoroughbred Club.

I suppose it couldn't have turned out differently. The seeds of failure were sown deep and had been growing too long.

Following the first night's dinner with the grandparents, Dad dropped us off at the Del Mar Beach Club the next day on his way to the E. F. Hutton office. The visitors from *Sucasa* had a suite of rooms on the top floor, with their bedroom giving onto a large sitting room overlooking beach and ocean. Dad promised to have a swim with me when he came to meet us later. The Del Mar Club is at the foot of Pico in Santa Monica, only a mile or so from the Hutton office on Wilshire, but since the New York markets closed at noon California time, I suspect he spent the afternoon at the track.

After lunch, I took Billy out to the beach while Granny, Grandpa, Mother and Carol returned to their rooms. It was only the grandparents' second day in town, but I was getting used to them in California. Later, I dropped Billy off and went back to prowl the hotel, the first grand hotel I'd been in. I poked around each floor as though it were *Sucasa* itself, questioned by no one and stopped only by locked doors.

Dad and I had our swim, though it was a short one. The best time for us together was always in the water, and it's too bad over the course of his life we didn't do more of it. He was thirty-eight years old that year, 1947, still in good shape and loved body surfing, not fearing even the biggest waves that sent you smashing face-down into the hard sand. Not a clubby sort of man—he had never gone to Pittsburgh's Duquesne Club where his father was a member and never set foot in the Westport, our own Playa del Rey beach club—for him the Del Mar was a hotel, not the club that gave it its name in the 1920s. We body-surfed, laughing when one of us was wiped out, but serious about our surfing and doing little talking. Dad had not been himself since coming back from the races after Labor Day, but maybe having the grandparents around unsettled him. The water was perfect, having warmed up as Santa Monica Bay does by the end of summer, but he wanted to get back to the room. He didn't want to keep Grandpa waiting.

Joining the others in the living room after showering, his mood picked up. The windows were open, the sheer white curtains billowing in breezes off the ocean, perfect ending to a late-summer, Santa Monica day. Carol was telling Granny about Marlborough and pretending to be happy about it when I knew how anxious she was to be starting a new school. She'd counted up the schools she'd attended so far, and Marlborough made eight as she entered the tenth grade. Dad and Grandpa had pulled two chairs over by the open windows, and I sprawled on the floor not far away. They seemed more comfortable than the night before.

For two days I'd been listening for the magic word, and, finally, I heard it.

"You know about our railroad to Mexico, I suppose," said Grandpa.

Dad nodded and said he'd heard something about it.

So Grandpa told him about the mighty Kansas City, Mexico and Orient Railway, some of which I knew from *Sucasa*.

He took his time, speaking deliberately as the elderly tend to do, and it was a long story. Dad didn't interrupt, and when Grandpa finished, they fell silent. Dad looked more relaxed than he'd been earlier. Grandpa's stories had a way of doing that to people, and I wondered again why I'd never seen these two men together at *Sucasa*. Dad's curly red hair was slicked back from the shower, and he looked content, as he usually did over drinks before dinner and after a swim, the time of day he most enjoyed. Grandpa was comfortable in an easy chair, breathing softly and gazing outside.

Pretending to read a *National Geographic* magazine, I was tantalized. The women were chattering away. Why were the men so slow, so quiet? What was taking them so long?

"The opportunities are still there," said Dad, finally, staring into his glass.

More silence. "That's what I hear," said Grandpa.

Dad shook the ice in his drink.

"Coco's told you something about Ramsa. . . ?"

Grandpa's gaze came back in from outside.

"Mentioned the name is all. . . "

Dad raised his eyebrows.

"What do you think. . . ?"

Grandpa didn't answer straightaway. After the long railroad story, I was surprised at how quiet he'd become.

"Don't know a thing about it, Red. . . hard to have an opinion."

The pace of the conversation was maddening. Why didn't they lay it all out, get up, shake hands and sign the Ramsa deal with me as witness?

"Mexico gets in your blood, doesn't it, Mr. Crittenden?"

"*Mr. Crittenden. . .*" Strange, I thought.

Afternoon zephyrs carried salt smells in from the ocean. With the Santa Monica pier so close, the day's catch was riding the air as well. Grandpa had shed his jacket, but still looked Eastern formal in vest, long sleeves and tie. From the floor, I saw his cufflinks plainly, gold squares with horses. He nursed his drink, ginger ale, the same thing I was drinking. Dad's was gin and tonic.

"It's been in my blood for more than fifty years, Red," he said, "since President Cleveland sent the governor down there as consul general and I went along. Eighteen hundred and ninety-four is when I first set foot in Mexico. More than half a century. . . long time to have something in your blood."

"Why don't we get together this weekend and talk. . . ?"

The pace was quickening. "What can you show me?"

"Show you?"

"I'd like to see your books?"

Dad stared blankly at Grandpa, then looked away. I didn't know what "books" were, but clearly Dad hadn't counted on that. Or maybe he had and that's why he'd been nervous.

He recovered quickly enough. "I can do better than that. How would you like to see one of our planes? Clover Field is ten minutes from here."

"How many planes do you have?"

"Two for now—one at Clover, another on the way. Others are in negotiation."

"What are they?"

"DC-3s."

I rolled over to face them. "Can I come?"

Dad was ready with a negative, but Grandpa laughed. "Of course," he said. "Red, you mean you haven't shown this boy your airline? Boys live

Clover Field, camouflaged, 1943. Courtesy Santa Monica Public Library Images Archives / Museum of Flying Collection.

for something like that. Right, Jimmy? What time will you fellows pick me up tomorrow?"

I knew something about Clover Field. I'd entered the third grade at Florence Nightingale grammar school in Venice—Venice because Playa del Rey didn't have any schools. We'd only been in California two weeks and were still living in the motel on Wilshire Boulevard when a kid came up at school and asked me if I could keep a secret. Naturally, I said. In wartime you kept secrets, we all knew that, even at eight years old. He told me there was a secret airfield a couple of miles away that you couldn't even see if you drove past it. It was camouflaged so that from the air it looked like houses and trees just like the rest of the area. Under the camouflage, he said, planes were being built that were bombing the Japs. The government was afraid Tokyo would find out and bomb us back so it camouflaged the plant and the airfield.

If it was such a secret, how did he know about it, I asked, and he said his dad worked there and that's why it was a secret, which made sense, though his telling me didn't.

And he was right—mostly right. The thing was that you could see some of the airfield if you drove past it. The city buses I took to school from the motel each day—probably the only eight-year-old in Santa Monica commuting to school with two transfers from a motel—went right by it. If you looked hard, you could see chicken wire stretched over what looked like hundreds of telephone poles, and you could even see some of the fake stuff on top, like trees and houses. If you knew where to look you could see it, and so maybe the Japanese knew about it, too. Maybe they had spies around.

The chicken wire, telephone polls and fake houses came down the summer of '45 when the war ended, but that's where Douglas had made the bombers, like B-18s, that were used in the war. The DC-3s Dad bought for Ramsa had been made in that same formerly camouflaged place, the Douglas Aircraft plant.

We set out after breakfast Saturday morning, zipping along the coast road with the Buick top down through Venice and Ocean Park, heading for Santa Monica. Dad had been quiet since talking with Grandpa the day before, and when we got home that evening went into his den, shut the door and told Mother to leave a plate for him in the oven. We heard him on the telephone, but when we went to bed he still hadn't come out, not even for a drink, which was unusual.

Billy and I, who shared a room, were up early and went down to fix breakfast. The door to the den was shut so apparently Dad was sleeping in there. I saw empty plates and a glass that smelled of whiskey on the counter so at least he'd eaten before going to bed. There were ants around because he hadn't rinsed anything, so I cleaned up, fed Queenie, fixed orange juice, made toast and scrambled eggs with Heinz ketchup for Billy and me and washed up. Then we grabbed baseball mitts and a ball and with Queenie headed for the vacant sand lot next door. From there I could survey everything. I wasn't about to let Dad slip away without me, which he could easily have done.

Grandpa was reading his newspaper in the lobby when we got there, and I fetched him while Dad waited in the car. He was in his usual three-piece suit and carrying a hat, but it was a light-colored suit so he looked summery enough even if it was a Pittsburgh kind of summery. To me, Grandpa always looked like the pictures of President Truman in the newspapers, the same square ruddy face, rimless glasses, jaunty way of walking and dressed about the same. Two men from Kansas City. I couldn't imagine Grandpa, like the president, dressed any other way but in a suit, even in California.

I squeezed in the cracked rear seat with Grandpa in front, and Dad headed the car toward Ocean Park Boulevard, turning east toward Clover Field. They were talking, Grandpa saying something about palm trees and gesturing at the trees along the street, but with the top down I couldn't hear everything. In Playa del Rey we were surrounded by palms, but I'd never heard Dad comment on them one way or another. At *Sucasa*, on the other hand, there were no palms. I still was not used to seeing them together and watched the back of their heads, Dad's curly flame locks fixed in place, smelling of the Kreml hair tonic he used, Grandpa's wispy tufts fluttering out beneath his hat. Unlike Californians, Grandpa was never without a hat, but it was more a matter of generations than of states.

From outside the Clover Field gates, I saw the planes gleaming bright in the sunlight. My God, they were beautiful! Two years before—the last time I'd passed this place—everything was camouflaged and hidden, and now you could see plants, hangars, planes and a vast airfield. No more netting, stilts and fake houses. Dad showed a pass and we drove onto the tarmac and down a row of hangars where men were working on planes. We went past them, around a corner and into a kind of aircraft storage site, a dozen or so planes of different makes and sizes sitting together like on a used car lot. He pointed, and there it was: Ramsa's first plane, bright as a steel mirror in the sunshine, nose pointing upward, propellers ready, crouching back on its haunches like a lion ready to pounce. We circled the plane and stopped in the shade of a hangar. On one side was painted, "Ramsa Airlines;" on the other "Aeronaves de Ramsa."

We walked around the plane and then back toward the hangar where Dad explained how they were sharing facilities, but that Ramsa eventually would have its own service crews. There was nothing left to do but head back for the car. It was nearly noon, the sun was high and despite his hat and the shade Grandpa looked like he needed to cool off.

"When do you fellows start operating?" Grandpa asked.

"Frankly," Dad said, "there are some problems. More than we anticipated." He took out a handkerchief and wiped his brow. I knew that look. He was thirsty. Time for a roast beef sandwich and highball.

I slipped in the rear seat, which I was skinny enough to do without moving the front seat forward, and they climbed in after me. Dad didn't start the car.

"On the Mexican side. . . ?" asked Grandpa.

Dad turned on the cracked seat toward him. "On our side."

Grandpa was staring at the plane. "With the railroad it was the opposite," he mused. . . trouble with the Mexicans."

"They've been fine so far. The problems are here."

"What kind of problems?"

"Planes, airports, cash flow. . . lots of little things."

"I thought you had planes lined up."

"We need four to start. Minimum. We bought two, and I'd hoped to lease two Beeches, but I can't find any. We need cash to buy them."

"How much cash. . . ?"

"Probably $20,000. . . and that's just for the planes."

"So you need more. . . ?"

"I'd say we need another $50,000 to get this business up and running."

Grandpa fell silent as he stared at the plane. Then I heard him reading the words, *Aeronaves de Ramsa*, rolling the rrs in the Spanish style and savoring the sound. I could see he was impressed—a railroad man playing with the idea of investing in an airline. "What's the problem with airports?"

"Los Angeles is moving its airport from Burbank to Mines Field, near us on Sepulveda, by El Segundo. They say they only have space for existing airlines. I think someone's looking for a *mordida*."

Grandpa turned to face him. "I didn't know you had *mordidas* in California."

"I didn't either."

I had no idea what a *mordida* was, but wasn't going to interrupt. They'd forgotten about me, which was fine.

"What's the cash flow problem?"

"We can't make money until we start flying, and we can't start flying until we have an airport and customers."

"You mentioned Burbank. . . "

"It's a possibility. So is Ontario. But we'd rather be in on the ground when the new airport opens."

Grandpa fell quiet again, his eyes back on the gleaming plane in front of us. In the distance, I saw a plane taxiing for takeoff that looked like another DC-3.

"Sounds to me like you're cash short," said Grandpa.

Grandpa must have been thinking of the railway. Hadn't he said the KCMOR failed because it was "cash short?"

Dad was silent, waiting, watching.

"Maybe I can help you there," said Grandpa, finally.

Dad cleared his throat. "How do you mean?"

"I looked into this a bit," said Grandpa. "I've followed Mexico, you know, and it looks like they're ready for changes. They still had Diaz when I was there and then came the revolution and a lot of killing and in the thirties they got that damned fool Cárdenas who thought he did his countrymen a favor by taking over the oil companies. Truth is he scared everyone away. Since then they've gotten some decent people who know that the way you lift up a poor country is by bringing in investment."

Still Dad waited. The key dangled in the ignition. It's a good thing we were parked in the shade, for it was hot on the tarmac.

"What I'm saying," said Grandpa, who looked ready to go, "is that your project interests me. If it's sound and you need help, I'll see what I can do."

I held my breath. This is what Dad was waiting for, what had brought Grandpa to California. How exhilarating it was, but Dad sat staring at his plane, saying nothing. I scrunched to see his face in the mirror, but could read no expression. I wanted to shout at him, but made no sound, fearing interruption. Surely he had to say something. Grandpa had just given him what he wanted, and he had to acknowledge it. Still, nothing but silence in the car.

"You're right about Mexico opening up," he said at length. "The problem is not the idea. . . it's that we don't have enough money to do it right. We've gotten as much as the banks will give us before we have income. We need two more planes and enough to cover expenses."

Grandpa took out a handkerchief to mop his brow. "Fifty thousand dollars. . . ?"

"Yes."

"That's why banks are not the best source for new ventures."

"We're too small to go public."

"You need private investment."

Dad, who claimed all his life that Grandpa never offered him anything, was wrong. I was right there in the car, and heard it all.

"What can you do?" he asked.

"Well, Red, we'll see. . . first I have to see the books."

There it was again, and Dad's reaction was the same. His shoulders stiffened, and his voice was piqued. "Yes, you said that at the hotel," he said. "May I ask why?"

"Why a potential investor wants to see the books before he writes a check. . . ?"

"We're not exactly Pan Am. I can tell you what's on the balance sheet. It's my balance sheet."

"You're keeping the books? I didn't know. . . "

"That I knew how to keep books? I know how to keep books."

Grandpa was clearly uncomfortable. "Red, what I'm asking is not unreasonable. Even if you have the figures in your head, I need to see the books. That's how I do business."

With that, Dad started the car. I knew him too well. Whatever the "books" were, he didn't want to show them to Grandpa, and he wasn't one for changing his mind.

These two men, the main male adults in my life, had gone from chatty agreement to sullen discord in the space of a few seconds. I wanted to speak up, break the silence, get them back on track again, but they would have ignored me. There was not another word said about Ramsa on the way back to the hotel. Driving home after dropping Grandpa off, I asked Dad what the "books" were. He pretended not to hear.

"Why can't Grandpa see them?" I tried.

Still no answer.

I tried again. "Dad, what's a *mordida*?"

This time he heard me. "It's a bribe."

§

Sunday night, the grandparents came back to the house for dinner and this time came upstairs with us to see our bedrooms and, most importantly, the secret room behind the bookcase, which I invited Granny and Grandpa to enter, but they declined. Despite the disagreement over the "books," I learned at dinner that Dad planned to take Grandpa up in the plane the next day, and that they would fly over Catalina. I asked to go, but Mother reminded me—as if I didn't know—that school started the next day.

"Let him come, Caroline," said Grandpa.

"No, Daddy, he goes to school."

She squelched the plane ride, but I found out everything from Grandpa.

Jim Collins was leaning out the cockpit window when they arrived at Clover Field the next day, and the rolling stairs were in place. Aboard, Collins came back to greet them and led them to the cockpit to meet the co-pilot. Telling me later about his first plane ride, Grandpa could not hide his glee, which I remembered from my own first time up, the flight out from Wichita—all glee ending when I started throwing up. They took seats at the rear, on opposite sides, behind the wings and engines to have a clear view of things. Dad was a veteran flier by then, having flown in Beech planes in Wichita and to Mexico in DC-3s. For Grandpa, at age eighty-one, it was a true adventure.

Air travel was still rare in 1947. I didn't know any other kids who had flown, though everyone was dying for a chance. Mother was talking about taking flying lessons at Mines Field, but never got around to it. She didn't want me to go up that day because of school, but I'm surprised she didn't go herself, probably because she wanted to stay with Granny. As poorly as they'd always gotten along at *Sucasa*, Mother was working to make the visit go smoothly. She had things to prove. Playa del Rey was her turf.

Aloft, they were soon over the ocean and could see up close the Santa Monica Mountains past Malibu we saw daily from our Playa del Rey patio. The plane veered left, and onshore they saw the Venice oil derricks that had turned a cozy little beach town into a mucky cesspool before it had a chance to replicate its namesake. They might have seen our brown shingle house on Montreal Street, standing alone on its sandy bluff. Then came the beach towns—Manhattan, Hermosa and Redondo. Passing the Palos Verdes peninsula, they were immediately over the channel with Catalina Island dead ahead.

The ride was choppy, and Collins came on the intercom to say he would stay under 10,000 feet so they could see everything. He circled the island and came in from the south, telling them Catalina was ninety-nine percent uninhabited except for a cluster of houses around Avalon. There were more boats, he said, than houses.

"The round building in the harbor is called the casino," he said, "but you can't gamble there. It's strictly for dancing." I already knew about Avalon for Mother had taken us over on the ferry soon after we'd arrived in Playa del Rey. Collins pointed out the baseball field, owned by the Chicago Cubs, which I remembered from our visit. The Cubs owned the Los Angeles Angels, my favorite Pacific Coast League team.

"Phil Wrigley owns the island," said Collins. "Shows what you can do when you're rich: buy your own island."

"Wrigley owns the island," said Grandpa, "but I wonder if he makes any money."

"He built the water system and hotels," said Dad. "I hear he's finally getting something back."

"Takes money to make money," said Grandpa, "but with all that vacant land in Los Angeles, why would anyone invest in a bone-dry island?"

"More exotic, like Mexico."

But Grandpa was right. You didn't have to be a chewing gum millionaire and buy an arid island twenty miles off the coast to make a killing in southern Calaifornia. And you didn't need to start an airline to the Yucatán, either. The land and the possibilities were all around us. In Playa del Rey, I would go into empty lots of sand and iceplant to hit fly balls and play catch with my friends. The lots all had signs on them we took down to use as bases:

> T. O. McCoy
> Realtor
> 111 Culver Blvd.
> Playa del Rey

T.O. McCoy's office was sandwiched between Doc Dolson's drug store and Charlie's Market. Like the Olivers in Pittsburgh, McCoy looked to the future and saw people. Where we kids saw vacant lots, he saw houses. Every one of those vacant lots has a house on it today. Across the vast, nearly-empty basin of Los Angeles, reaching far up into the canyons of the Santa Monica and San Gabriel mountains, tens of thousands of other lots also had signs on them—signs belonging to people with lots to sell.

Californians were investing in vacant lots because they knew they would soon fill up. Los Angeles already was bringing in water from far-away sources like the Colorado and Owens Rivers—the Owens water stolen from that unsuspecting rural valley. Add to that the huge aqueduct from Northern California's rivers soon to be built, and Southern California would have enough water to irrigate arid land reaching from the San Fernando Valley to San Bernardino, eventually supporting a population of well over ten million people—more people than populated the entire state in 1947.

It had been the same in Pittsburgh a half century earlier. Negotiating in 1902 to buy a large tract of land along Smithfield Street, Henry Oliver, on his way to becoming downtown Pittsburgh's largest landowner, told the City Council:

> *I stood on Fifth Avenue and looked down over a hurrying mass of people that made the streets black as far as the eye could see. I stopped to think of something I had learned only a short time before; that the vast business interests of this city of ours were centered in an area of less than fifty acres. Think of it! Crowding our interests into space of that size! As I looked, I saw skyscrapers going up on every side of me, harboring their thousands of toilers, and I asked myself what our narrow streets would do if these thousands kept on growing. I saw then the necessity of more thoroughfares and I made up my mind to do what I could.*

Soon that tract of land along Smithfield, between Oliver and Sixth Avenues, was home to two theaters, three department stores, an expanded Duquesne Club and several office buildings, including the Henry W. Oliver Building, finished in 1910 and to this day one of Pittsburgh's finest buildings. Downtown Pittsburgh was renovated, and old Uncle Henry got a street and building named after him in the bargain.

Looking back on Dad's pathetic life, I see he had three, maybe four, chances to achieve his dream of business success. The first was when he was given a seat on the New York Stock Exchange by Millie Oliver. The second was when he used the extra money Millie gave him to cover Otto Berndt's embezzlement to buy Beech Aircraft stock—stock he sold because he thought the war's end would depress aircraft prices. The third was coming to Los Angeles just as the real estate boom began. Just as Henry Oliver had understood the real estate future of Pittsburgh, Dad might have seen the future of Los Angeles. T.O. McCoy made a fortune as a broker, which was also Dad's occasional profession.

If there was a fourth opportunity—and how many of us have four such opportunities?—it was when Grandpa came to Playa del Rey with the express purpose of helping him launch Ramsa Airlines.

§

Granny and Grandpa came over Wednesday to say good-bye. Mother picked them up in the Plymouth and they were waiting in the living room when Billy and I walked up the hill from the bus stop. Carol was still not home from her three-bus trek to Marlborough, but came in soon after. Dad was not there.

So used to them seeing us off from *Sucasa*, it was a new experience to see them off from Playa del Rey. They'd had a fine time and looked forward to seeing us again next summer, they said—or even at Christmas if we wanted to come back. There'd be a new sled for me, said Grandpa. We sat together on the couch, looking out over the ocean, and he filled me in on everything about the Catalina trip.

So I know what happened—or mostly know what happened. I know what Grandpa told me, and more of it came out that evening after Mother took them back to the Del Mar Club and Dad finally came home. Mother was dressed for square dancing at Westport and was giving us an early supper of cold beef left over from the roast we'd served for the Crittendens. Roast beef may be the curse of our family dinners. She looked nice in a frilly skirt and a peasant blouse, the kind of thing she always wore for square dancing. We hadn't expected Dad back, and he'd been drinking

"Where's the English mustard?" he said, after fixing himself a drink and sitting down with his plate.

"There's horseradish," said Mother.

Henry W. Oliver building and One Oliver Plaza, Pittsburgh, Pennsylvania, 2006.

"You know I take Coleman's with roast beef. You've known it for fourteen years."

"We finished it the other night."

"Didn't you go to the store today?"

"I didn't know you'd be home."

"Why are you dressed like that?" he said.

"It's square dance night at Westport. You know that."

"Who're you going with?"

"Burnie Adams is my partner tonight."

"Are you sleeping with Burnie Adams."

"Go to Hell, Billy. Are you sleeping with that woman in Manhattan Beach?'

When they got started it was as though we children didn't exist. I had no clue what they were talking about but could see that Carol was shocked.

"Why weren't you here to say good-bye to Mother and Daddy?"

"I was working."

"Daddy says he's not interested in Ramsa. He came all the way out here for nothing."

"I thought he came out to see his daughter and grandchildren."

"He saw them all summer. What happened?"

"None of your business."

"It is my business. His business is my business more than it's yours."

"Lay off, Coco. . . not the time for that."

"He said you wouldn't show him your books. Why not for God's sake?"

Dad slammed his fork down, sending horseradish flying. "Because they're my books, goddammit it, and it's my company, and Will Crittenden can go to Hell."

We looked back and forth at them at opposite ends of the table like spectators at a tennis match. "Why wouldn't you show Daddy the books? You were trying to get money from him, weren't you? Why couldn't he see the books?"

"Drop it, Coco, I said."

Already depressed from the good-byes, we sat in stunned but intrigued silence. It was an ugly scene, but one with an air of mystery: None of us had a clue what the "books" were or what secrets they contained.

"Why wouldn't you show him the books, Billy?"

"Why don't you shut up and go dancing."

When she had her claws out, Mother never let up until there was blood on the floor. With Dad she'd continue until he got violent. With us, she'd continue until she inflicted maximum emotional pain.

"Why wouldn't you show him the books?

Dad was on the edge. "Don't ask me that again."

"Why wouldn't you... good God! It's that, isn't it? It's that!"

Dad had been ready to get up, but stopped and stared motionless at her, fork poised in midair with a piece of roast beef on it.

"My God, Billy! That's why you stayed at the races."

Outside, we saw Burnie Adams' large frame passing the window, and Mother got quickly up.

"Good night, children. Carol *and* Jimmy, please clean up."

§

She must have been right, though I have no proof. If Dad took money from Ramsa to play the horses and lost, he was caught in a dilemma: If Grandpa found the money gone missing from the books, he would have refused to help. And if Dad didn't open the books, Grandpa would also refuse to help. And Dad couldn't alter the books because that was a crime.

Any way you looked at it, Dad lost, and in losing sacrificed the company's only hopes for obtaining money it needed to survive. If Dad did lose the money, he must have found a way to pay it back, for I never heard another word about it. Maybe he used the money from the Oliver silver he took when Mother told him she was getting a divorce.

Dad's failures can't entirely be blamed on family money. Receiving the same gifts of money, others went on to achieve something with it or in spite of it. Thomas Mellon's reflection on poverty—"a misfortune to the weaklings who are without courage or ability to overcome it but a blessing to young men of ordinary force of character"—makes just as much sense if one substitutes the word "wealth." Family money was the worst possible gift for both Mother and Dad, and had they not received one penny in their lives they didn't earn themselves, they could not have done any worse.

Picking Up the Pieces

*Divorces followed by marriages followed
by more divorces and exotic new ways found
for the use of inherited money.*

*Jim and Jan Crittenden marriage, Shields Church,
1939. Carol as flower girl, in the background.*

I can't say that Ramsa killed their marriage, for the signs of disintegration were everywhere. Carol was more aware of things than I and says she knew Mother and Burnie weren't just square-dancing. And Dad had his friend in Manhattan Beach. But they'd already been married fifteen years and who's to say it couldn't have gone on another fifteen? Marriages generate a kind of inertia that sometimes makes it easier to go forward than call it off. And divorce in those days was hard, especially if contested. In California, it took a year, and it was another year before a divorced person could remarry.

Jim Crittenden, an Army doctor at the time, had been posted to Lompoc, north of Santa Barbara, after the war, and he and Jan drove to Playa del Rey that fall to spend a few days with Mother and Dad at Rosarito Beach, across the border in Mexico. I'd been lying on the living room floor listening to them talk about their trip, still wondering when I'd get my first Ramsa flight into the jungles, when Jim suddenly said "let's take Jimmy along." Mother naturally opposed it, but Jim, who liked having either a dog or child along on trips, insisted. He normally won arguments with Mother because she was always impressed by doctors, even one who happened to be her little brother. Finally, I was going to Mexico, though not in a shiny Ramsa DC-3. It would be my first (and only) trip with the four of them anytime, anywhere.

Mother had a different kind of relationship with Jim than with anyone else. He was one man she couldn't seduce. Though sharing genes and the same childhood environment, they had few interests in common and could be prickly with each other, especially when drinking. Jim, as with most doctors I've known, had a broad range of interests beyond his profession, including family, photography, writing and tinkering, while Mother had no hobbies beyond dancing. One thing that always surprised me is that they never talked about growing up at *Sucasa*. Carol, Billy and I talk all the time about growing up, but if Mother and Jim ever talked about their childhood, I never heard it.

Being so different, one might have thought they wouldn't choose to spend much time together, but as he got older, Jim, always more sociable than Mother, sought her out and might have done more of it if Mother and Jan had gotten along. Jan grew to detest Mother—or maybe always had and just hadn't shown it—and when Mother died, didn't even come to her funeral. As a boy, I didn't notice the dislike between them, which Mother probably didn't notice either because she didn't bother with that sort of thing. She was used to women disliking her.

One summer, a few years after my own divorce, I was visiting Playa del Rey from Paris with my two young children. Jim had retired from medicine by then and moved from Shields to Playa del Rey to be near his son, Jamie, and his granddaughters. Mother, a widow, had moved into her third Playa del Rey house, on Rees Street. She was on one part of the hill, Jim on another, near Jamie, about a half-mile apart. The Missouri-Kentucky Crittendens had abandoned Shields and Sewickley, where they were always outsiders, leaving behind the hundreds of Shields, Oliver, Craig, Chaplin, Neville etc. cousins who truly belonged there. The *Sucasa* siblings settled on the same Playa del Rey sand dunes Mother had discovered forty years earlier on her first trip out from Wichita. As near neighbors, Jim walked over to Mother's every day, saying he liked climbing the steep hills for his health, but really just looking to schmooze with his sister.

One night, four of us, Jim, Jan, Mother and I, went to Jack's at the Beach—which by then had moved from the Ocean Park beach to Wilshire Boulevard—and were chatting before dinner over martinis. The tables were buzzing, actor Robert Stack was seated across the room surrounded by beautiful women dripping jewels and décolletage, and waiters were pirouetting with platters about the room. Mother's old Arthur Murray studio was just down Wilshire from Jack's, and the subject had gotten onto her dance lessons, which were running about $60,000 a year, a handsome sum at the time and not just for dancing. The lessons were a sore point with all of us. Jim told her it was a waste of money, reflecting my views exactly.

Mother's main interest during the last four decades of her life was her dance studios, and she hated criticisms of it. If she wanted to lavish Oliver money on her Arthur Murray friends, it was her business, she said. Though, thanks to Grandpa, she couldn't get at the capital, she'd found that Mellon tolerated a certain amount of borrowing against capital, which, added to her income (about $140,000 at the time), meant she had no trouble paying bills. She'd gotten to the point where if people asked her what she did in life, she answered she was a "dancer." It was a stretch, but I guess for the money she was entitled to say that.

She reacted to Jim's criticism that night with a sneer. It was good exercise, she said, worth every penny and none of his business anyway.

By that time she had dropped her Santa Monica studio and was driving to the San Fernando Valley, a forty-five-minute drive from Playa del Rey in her cream Cadillac, a drive she would continue to make until she was eighty-five and walked with a cane. The studio owner, we found out later, was monstrously over-charging her, which was how two lessons a week amounted to $60,000 a year.

"You'd get more exercise on walks with me," said Jim.

"And save money," I chimed in.

"Get off it," said Mother. "It's my money."

"It's not your money," said Jim.

"Of course it is."

"It's Oliver money," he said. "Family money."

Mother pursed her lips in a monkey-like gesture that signified something nasty was coming.

"Arthur Murray is the only family I have."

Maybe it was the martinis talking and maybe not. Dismissed into insignificance, each wounded in his way, the three of us stared at her as she gazed blissfully out over the room, pleased with her sally. Jim wore a quizzical look on his face that didn't mask the hurt. Family was important to him. Jan looked away. The look on my face, if I could have seen it, would have been one of disgust.

"That's the way it is," Mother would have said. "Quit whining."

Growing older, she clung to her dance studios as though they alone could roll back time for her, stave off the inevitable. It was an expensive diversion, but what she lived for. She might have chosen something more illuminating to fill her declining years, but Mother wasn't interested in illumination.

The evening at Jack's was forty years after the '47 Rosarito Beach trip, when we were still one big, occasionally happy family. We drove down Highway 101 in Jim's red, prewar Ford roadster, ocean breezes gushing through the windows, the first of dozens of times I would make that exhilarating drive along the coast. With Mother and Jan in the rear and me scrunched between Dad and Jim in the front, we stopped at La Jolla for lunch, still little more than a picturesque San Diego village, then crossed the wide-open border at Tijuana with a wave to the guards and entered Mexico.

For people used to today's endless waits in stifling traffic with armed police and drug-sniffing dogs circulating in a miasma of fetid fumes, it's hard to imagine the relaxed border of a half-century ago. But that's what California was like before one out of eight Americans lived there. The border was as invisible as it had been in the days when California was part of Mexico and Baja part of California. The Rosarito Beach Hotel was still a fashionable place, not antiquated as it is today, and I stayed up that night until the wee hours watching my father and uncle shoot pool. They had an easy camaraderie together, which made all the more strange their final contact seventeen years later.

Despite Grandpa's defection, Dad still had high hopes for Ramsa and discussed it with Jim as we drove along. He said nothing about Grandpa's visit, though Mother had surely told her brother how Grandpa had pulled back, and perhaps Grandpa himself had talked to him about it, though I never had the feeling those two talked much about business. Jim had the touch of the gambler in him that Grandpa lacked and later would lose some Oliver money on oil wildcatting around Bakersfield. But he had nothing of Dad's recklessness and was far too practical a medical man to get involved in something as exotic as Ramsa.

It was rare to take trips with my parents, but with Jim and Jan along they acted like a normal couple. Jim and Jan actually liked children. Mother did things with us out of duty, and Dad not even out of duty, but prior to having their own children, Jim and Jan often took me along on trips with them, though whether out of duty, pity or for the company I can't say. Two years after Rosarito, while I was spending the fall of 1949 at *Sucasa* during the divorce, they took me on a drive with them to New York, where I met Joe DiMaggio. It was just after the World Series, he was staying one floor up from us at the Elysee Palace hotel off Fifth Avenue and the hotel doorman passed word to him that there was this kid downstairs. Joe said just come on up.

I have no idea why DiMaggio was staying at the Elysee Palace. The Yankees had just begun their incredible run of ten straight World Series appearances, and Joe was the star of the team, still two years away from retirement and three years from meeting Marilyn Monroe. Why he made time for a twelve-year-old kid, I have no idea, but I knocked on the door, he asked me in, we sat down and had a chat. He was genuinely curious, asking me about schools and positions and batting averages, and I left with an autographed ball, miniature bat and a 45 record called "Joltin' Joe DiMaggio."

If only I'd known about that coming meeting when I met Jane Shape in the kitchen at *Sucasa*! Fifty years later, in March, 1999, Joe DiMaggio died and I had a chance in a newspaper column to set the record straight. Some obituaries described him as cold and aloof, even to his family. They told how he shunned the public in later years and sold his autographs. So I had to tell what I knew about Joe and kids.

§

The summer after the Rosarito trip, 1949, we caught the Super Chief as usual for Chicago. Granny was there on the porch as Stewart pulled the Buick up the long gravel driveway from Beaver Road, with Grandpa in the background. It was the first time we'd seen them since Playa del Rey the previous September, and nothing hinted this summer would be any different.

It started normally enough with my days spent hanging out with the hands learning useful things like how to play craps and drive a truck (I was twelve), and evenings spent romping the lawns with the fireflies. One morning, I was sitting in the kitchen doing Jumbles with Viola while awaiting a late morning walk with Grandpa when Edith, hairnet in place and feather-duster in hand, came in to announce that Mother wished to see me in the drawing room.

She looked fine that morning. She'd just turned thirty-nine, which was middle-aged to me at the time and now seems hardly beyond girl-hood. She was dressed in a summery dress and high heels and had gone heavy on the makeup. I knew she'd been driving to Pittsburgh a lot, which she normally never did. Normally fidgety, she sat motionless on the Victorian velvet couch Granny used to serve tea, hands folded in her lap. I sat in the velvet rocker across from her, my legs finally long enough for a good rock.

She cleared her throat, that long, gargley morning sound I was used to.

"There's something I have to tell you," she said. Hesitation and more throat clearing: "I'm leaving your father."

I rocked back and forth several times, waiting. That was it. She was silent, watching me for reaction, unsure how to proceed.

"What do you mean, leaving?" I asked after a while.

She was not the least embarrassed about it, her brown eyes boring into me, looking rather content. "I mean I'm getting a divorce."

Sucasa drawing room.

Later I found out that everyone in the house knew about it but me, even the servants. Either Mother figured I didn't matter or wouldn't care, which is more or less true. As I sat rocking, I was aware that I had no emotional reaction at all.

"Burnie and I are going to be married." She smiled.

This, too, failed to register high on my e-meter. Mother was divorcing Dad and marrying Burnie. Looking back on it, I wonder why I wasn't saddened or even shocked at the news. Part of it must have been that I didn't really understand divorce, which wasn't big in those days and in my family didn't yet exist. But the larger part must have been that since I'd never detected the slightest affection between my parents, a divorce, whatever it was, seemed a natural enough thing.

My concern was more practical. "What's happening to the house?" I asked, thinking of the secret room, "and Queenie?"

"Your father's taking care of Queenie. We'll be moving into a new house and Queenie will come back."

Now it was getting interesting. "Where's the new house?"

"Burnie's looking for a house to buy. We'll stay in Playa del Rey."

Sixteen years with Dad, and she never owned a house; not yet married to Burnie Adams, and they were already shopping for a house.

"What about Carol?" I asked

"Carol knows all about it. I'm taking her to New York next week to enroll in a new school. You'll be starting school here next month."

Now that was news. I'd never gone to school in Sewickley.

"You'll be going to the Sewickley Academy, a wonderful school."

I was horrified. The Sewickley Academy, just across Beaver Road from the Edgeworth Club, looked suspiciously like a military school. I could not let this happen.

"I won't go to the Sewickley Academy," I said, defiantly.

"Of course you will. Carol is going to a wonderful school in New York, called The Masters, and you're going to the Sewickley Academy. I've made up my mind."

"I'm going to El Segundo."

"Don't make trouble. Not now. I won't stand for it. You're going to the Sewickley Academy just like Uncle Jim did. You love Uncle Jim, don't you?"

She was good at planting guilt like that. I knew Uncle Jim had gone to the Academy, just like all my Oliver and Shields cousins went there, but I'd vowed after military school never to set foot in another private school. I had to take a stand. "If Burnie finds a house I can still go to El Segundo," I tried.

"It takes time to find a house. I have to go to Reno for the divorce."

"What about Billy?"

"Billy's coming with me."

"I won't go to the Sewickley Academy," I repeated.

"Yes you will. It's settled."

For Mother, things were often "settled" that in fact were settled nowhere but in her mind. But indeed, this might have been settled if Grandpa at that moment hadn't come out of his den, rattled a cane from the stand by the front door and walked into the drawing room looking for me. He was dressed in tie, vest and hat, but I'd learned to distinguish his walking tie, vest and hat from his going-to-Pittsburgh tie, vest and hat.

"Ready?" he asked, smiling.

"Grandpa," I pleaded, "Mother says I have to go to the Sewickley Academy. I don't want to go to there."

He looked from Mother to me and back again. He knew about it, I could tell. Everyone knew about everything except me. I heard the sound of his cane gently tapping on the carpet.

"Caroline. . . if the boy doesn't want to go to the Academy. . ."

"Daddy!" Mother practically shrieked, "We've already discussed this."

"Look at your son, Caroline. He clearly doesn't want to go to the Academy, and there is the perfectly good Edgeworth school right down Beaver Road."

"Daddy, you agreed. . ."

"I said talk to Jimmy. . ."

I was like a slave at an auction silently witnessing the bidding over his future and knowing enough to stay silent. Grandpa held the cards, and it was a question of whether he was serious or just bluffing.

"It's none of your business," Mother said.

That's what did it. If Grandpa was just putting on a good show, knowing that school decisions are for parents, not grandparents, but wanting to show he was on my side, Mother had overplayed her hand.

"None of my business!" he sputtered. "This boy will be staying in my house, living with your mother and me, eating at our table while you're two thousand miles away for months. You've asked me to pay his tuition at the Academy just as you've asked me to pay for your lodgings in Reno. If he's miserable at school, we in this house, not you in Reno, will also be miserable. And you say it's none of my business! Bosh! Public schools were good enough for me. Private schools didn't do a thing for you. I say let him go where he wants."

With that, Mother stood and left the room, and Grandpa and I took our walk.

Looking back on it, what strikes me is that Grandpa said nothing to me about the divorce. It was the first one in the family, and though he had no particular affection for Dad, it's odd he didn't let his feelings out at some point. I think he just put it out of his mind. Both Grandpa and Granny would come to like Burnie Adams, a solid, sociable guy it was impossible not to like, but they hadn't met him yet. Mother would have told them about him—or at least told Grandpa for she rarely spoke to Granny—but I doubt that made it an easy pill for this old-fashioned couple to swallow. Mother would have already brought Bunny Warren into the story. You needed grounds for divorce in those days.

The Edgeworth School, I have to say, was the right decision. During the fall semester of the eighth grade, I made some good friends, which was new for me in Sewickley where most of my friends were grown-ups. Granny fussed about wanting to have Stewart drive me to school in the Buick, but Edgeworth was close enough to walk and I wasn't about to be dropped off by a uniformed chauffeur in front of a public school. Grandpa took my side in that matter, too. In a shop course, I made a bedside lamp in the shape of a rabbit for Granny, who cried when I gave it to her. Amateurish as it was, she put it on her bedside table, and it worked.

In Nevada, you could get a divorce in six weeks only if it was uncontested. Dad must have been shocked when he received the papers, opening the mail alone with Queenie on Montreal Street surrounded by the Oliver furniture that had followed us from Pittsburgh to New York, Connecticut, Wichita and Playa del Rey. The first thing he did was contact Tom Morris who advised him to contest the divorce. I learned about that later that fall when Grandpa informed me Mother would be staying in Reno longer than expected, and I would not be going home until Christmas, which was fine with me.

Sad to say, Dad fought the divorce not for principle but for money. Getting money out of Grandpa would have been the ultimate revenge for Ramsa, but at the end of three months, the Nevada courts dismissed his case. By then, Dad had already started selling off the household belongings. He didn't get much for anything except the Oliver silver, which brought him enough for the down payment on a little ocean-front house in Manhattan Beach, just down the strand from Bunny Warren's. He didn't find the Shields 1785 silver tea set, which Mother must have hidden somewhere he didn't look—maybe even in the secret room—but he got most everything else.

Ramsa died that summer. Grandpa harrumphed when I asked him about it, and Dad never wrote or called while I was at *Sucasa*, but sometime that summer the partners realized that for lack of funds they couldn't operate an airline to Mexico. They couldn't compete with the scheduled airlines. They ran a few charters out of Burbank to Campeche and Mérida, but those rough jungle cities lacked the tourist appeal of seaside resorts such as Acapulco and Mazatlán. Dad was right about the potential of Quintana Roo and Cancún, but his timing was wrong. When the Mexicans finally realized the possibilities for white sand beaches so close to the Mayan ruins, they developed them themselves, just like they finished Grandpa's railroad, *El Chepe*, finally connecting the Midwest to the Mexican Pacific—but too late to do U.S. farmers any good.

Mother married Burnie Adams in Reno, and I returned to Playa del Rey at the Christmas school break on the Super Chief, in my own compartment, getting off at each station and making it back to the train each time with no complaints from conductors or porters. The four of us—Carol stayed at the Masters School in New York—settled into a pink, rambling, three-story, Spanish-style hacienda with a tower in the middle and large pepper tree in the front patio at the south end of Playa del Rey, bigger than the Montreal Street house and closer to the ocean. Mother seemed content with Burnie, a big, horny guy who'd apparently discovered at age forty-nine that girls weren't as available as before. When I came upon his stash of naked beauties hidden behind the upstairs bar, some of the reasons for this easy-going bachelor's decision to take on a woman ten years his junior with three children and a Dexedrine habit became clearer.

Burnie had a degree in aeronautical engineering from Yale—where he'd taken classes in Leet Oliver Memorial Hall—and was working for Lear Aircraft in Santa Monica. Santa Monica was still a small world in those days: Dad had kept his Ramsa plane at Clover Field only a stone's throw from where Burnie designed the Lear jets that would fly out of Clover Field, soon to be known as Santa Monica airport. But Burnie quit his job at Lear—Oliver money had a way of doing that—so he and Mother could throw themselves into ballroom dancing at the dance studio on Wilshire, across the street from Dad's E. F. Hutton office.

Billy and I had normal enough lives in the pink house on Rindge Avenue (the whole hill would be wiped out ten years later by the Los Angeles Airport), at least normal for us. Burnie became the father Billy never had, and if at thirteen I was too old for a new father, Burnie and I got along just fine. He was a quiet sort of guy, I was a quiet sort of kid and so dinners at seven turned mostly into show-time for Mother, whose Dexedrine habit made her more erratic than usual. One day I came home from school to find she'd cut off all her hair, shaved it down to the scalp, like a prisoner. She'd had the ultimate bad hair day and solved the problem by lopping it off. This was a period when she and I avoided each other whenever possible, and when not possible, like at dinner, I went silent and she got bossy.

Finding other people's weaknesses made her feel better about herself, for Mother had always been a bundle of insecurities. Dad couldn't take it, but big, silent Burnie knew how to roll with the punches. With me, she couldn't be mean the way she was with Carol because boys were foreign to her while she knew all the sensitive girl spots, but that didn't keep her from trying. I'd learned an early age to clam up about my personal life. There was a Miranda rule in our house even before Miranda because anything said would be used against you, normally in front of others to cause maximum pain and bring Mother maximum attention. Men were central to Mother's universe, but boys were a nuisance. We were pointless, a bother, a useless interference in her life who didn't even have the redeeming quality, as girls did, of being easy prey.

The family trips to *Sucasa* each summer stopped. Mother took Burnie back to meet the grandparents the following summer, leaving Billy and me in the hands of Mrs. Little, the housekeeper. Carol graduated from the Masters' School and flew out to Playa del Rey the following summer, followed by two Sewickley boys, including Sam Adams, who lived in the house across the street from Shields Presbyterian and was heir to some kind of industrial fortune—bathroom fixtures, I think. I was almost fourteen by then, ten years younger than Sam, who impressed me as the coolest guy I'd ever known. He had a journalism degree, was an actor, played the piano, did flips off the high board at Westport and, best of all, let me drive Mother's Chevy station wagon, though I was too young for a license. When I drove it into a gas pump at the station on Manchester and Pershing, he took the blame. At the end of summer, after we drove Carol to the growing L.A. Airport on Sepulveda to fly back to Pittsburgh, Sam told me he was going to marry my sister.

Burnie, not Dad, gave Carol away the following June, which was 1953, and she whispered in his ear coming down the aisle at Shield's Church, "I don't want to do this." But she went through with it, which she probably shouldn't have done. It's too bad she couldn't ask Dad to give her away, but he wouldn't have gone to Sewickley and would have been drunk if he had. Still in school, I missed the wedding but have seen the pictures from the Allegheny Country Club reception many times.

Granny, Grandpa, Carol, Mother, and Burnie Adams, at Allegheny Country Club reception for Carol's wedding to Sam Adams, June 13, 1953.

Mother and Burnie made an impression on the Sewickley natives with the latest Arthur Murray moves.

Among the wedding pictures is one of Grandpa, age eighty-six, dancing with Granny, eighty, dressed in a flowing white gown with hugely bouffant sleeves. It's likely the last time they danced, for Grandpa died eighteen months later. Nearly blind by then, Granny had taken off her glasses to dance, and the look in her eyes is so dreamy and far away that she must have transported herself back to some other dance-floor lost in time, maybe the ballroom at *Sucasa*. Grandpa looks magnificent, a bit of a mug on his face for the camera, elegant in tuxedo and wing-tipped collar, holding Granny in the perfect waltz position, though he'd never been to Arthur Murray. Like the weddings of the Oliver sisters in 1904 and 1906 and Jim Crittenden in 1939, Carol's wedding kept to the same pattern: Shields Church followed by Allegheny Country Club.

It's what I loved most about our lives at *Sucasa*: the tradition. I planned to continue it when my turn came.

But fate has its surprises. About a year after Carol's wedding, Burnie came knocking on my bedroom door at the pink house one evening, his jowly, bloodhound face drooping more than usual. I was doing homework. Mother wanted to see me in the living room, he said. It was an unusual summons. Mother hadn't called me to a conference since the drawing room at *Sucasa* to announce her divorce from Dad.

Except at dinner, I didn't see a lot of Burnie. He'd seemed happier since his early retirement and spent mornings in the shop he'd built in one part of the three-car garage downstairs. They'd have lunch and a drink and a nap and then head to the dance studio in Santa Monica. They'd tried to have a baby. Mother was forty and driving me home from school one day when she asked what I thought about having a baby brother or sister. I suspect Burnie put her up to it for Mother was not big on soliciting other people's opinions. Their efforts came to naught. The Wichita abortion, I would learn from Carol, made her infertile.

Burnie loved Mother but sometimes seemed flummoxed by what he'd gotten himself into, keeping himself busy around the house with his engineer's skills. It was a big house, dating from the 1920s when Playa del Rey was still an exotic outpost for the movie crowd coming to work at MGM in Culver City, a few miles away. He spent hours each day in his shop working on home repairs and using any extra time to build cabinets and furniture and exotic inventions like a weathervane for the tower that relayed wind direction to an electrical display by his desk—though he had no possible reason to need to know the wind direction. Because of my distant relationship with Mother, Burnie had more trouble adjusting to me than I did to him. I think he was embarrassed because he, like Dad before him, was living off Oliver money. The home repairs were to prove he was still useful, and one day he showed me calculations on how much money he'd saved by doing all the work himself. His *amour-propre* needed that.

Mother was waiting on the living-room couch, Manhattan or Old-Fashioned in hand, I could never tell the difference. I dropped into the chair by the fireplace. Burnie lit a Herbert Tareyton. Mother wasn't one to beat around the bush—tact and diplomacy not belonging to her repertoire of social skills. Something on her mind, she sailed right in and damn the torpedoes.

"Your sister married a fairy," she said.

Burnie gulped. "Coco, I don't think that's the way to handle this."

"How would you know?" she insisted. "He's my son."

I wasn't sure what I'd just heard. I knew the word "fairy" of course. It was a solid member of the teenage male lexicon, but I'd never really thought about its precise definition. Whatever it meant, it was a useful word, like turd or fart, that boys used to ingratiate themselves with their peers.

"Do you know what a fairy is?" asked Mother.

I had no clue what she was talking about.

"Sam has been caught in Sewickley with a boy. He's in jail," said Mother.

"This isn't fun for any of us," said Burnie, stolidly, "Carol called your mother. It's in the papers back there. She's coming out here for a while."

"A fairy," said Mother, pursing her lips as she did when trying to be taken seriously, "does it with boys." She took a sip of her drink. "Do you know what 'it' is, Jimmy? Have you done 'it' yet?"

"Coco" said Burnie, "really."

As a matter of fact I hadn't, but she'd be the last to know.

"Sam's in jail?" I muttered. "What do you mean—caught with a boy?"

"Don't ever do it with a boy," said Mother, wagging her finger. "One in the family is enough."

Kids, to be perfectly honest, were a little unsophisticated in those days, not just me, but my friends as well. Mother's meaning was not entirely clear to me.

"Jimmy," said Burnie, "let's get to the point." He took a drag on his cigarette. "Your mother and I think you should stop picking up people in your car," he said. "Will you agree to do that?"

"Or just pick up girls," said Mother.

I'd made the mistake of telling them that coming home from high school after baseball practice or games I sometimes gave hitchhikers rides along Manchester Boulevard where no city buses ran. I'd just turned sixteen and had a license, but earlier had often hitchhiked along Manchester without anyone saying a word.

"Girls don't hitchhike," I said. "Anyway, they're just kids. I know most of them from school."

"How about if you just give rides to the kids you know?" offered Burnie.

I wanted out of there. I was confused about what they were saying, and needed fresh air. It was time for a walk on the beach.

"That's fine," I said, knowing they had no idea whom I knew and whom I didn't.

But Mother wasn't done. She gulped her drink and stared me down.

Remember this," she said. "A woman is a gadget you screw on the bed to get the housework done." Burnie winced. "You're about the age. Just make sure the gadget is a woman."

It was brutal for Carol. When the news hit the Pittsburgh papers, Granny took to her room. Mother once told Carol that Granny would fall to her knees to "pray for Caroline"—even with company present—when she'd started going out, and now she was probably praying for Carol. Shades of the baby books. Grandpa knew the Edgeworth cops who cruised the estate nights and sent them checks each Christmas. They were sympathetic to the family, but had their job to do. There would be a trial. It was rough on everyone, and Carol came to Playa del Rey to think things through. She told me what happened, and I told her about Mother's lecture on fairies.

Mother never let her forget it. She had hammered her as a girl and now hammered her about her husband. "Carol married a fairy, Carol married a fairy," she chanted one night over drinks at Jim's house when they were all visiting Sewickley. This enlightened repartee took place just up the path from where Granny had taken offense at Harry Thaw's mere stares sixty years earlier at the Oliver house.

Despite the histrionics, I don't think Mother had a thing against Sam's or anyone else's sexual habits. How could she? Sex was as natural for her as putting on lipstick. When Billy brought Susan, his wife-to-be, to the pink house a decade later, Mother confronted her in the upstairs hallway stark naked. She wanted to explain, she said, that though Burnie was sleeping in a separate bedroom since his prostate operation, they still had sex once a week. Susan, who'd been on the way to brush her teeth, stood listening, not knowing where to look. She'd

Jim Crittenden's house, 1965.

never even seen her own mother naked. Mother helpfully assured her that though men's bodies changed with age, their penises did not.

Susan married Billy anyway.

For all of her sexual naturalism, Mother had hang-ups that showed themselves in strange ways. Christmas of 1958, while I was on leave from the Army, Mother, Burnie, Billy and I flew back to visit Granny. I didn't know it at the time, but it was the last time I would set foot in *Sucasa*. Grandpa had died three years earlier, and Granny would die the next summer. I was stationed for basic training at Fort Ord, near Monterey, and had a ten-day leave. Sam Adams was going straight by then, so to speak, and he and Carol, who were living in Pasadena with their two small children as Sam pursued an acting career, didn't join us at *Sucasa*. It was the first trip for any of us on the new transcontinental jets, which came into service that year and, non-stop, cut L.A.–Pittsburgh flight time in half.

Jan Crittenden, always a beautiful woman, had a twin sister named Adele—Dell for short—just as beautiful. Though Jan had been a surrogate mother for me as much as Jim was a surrogate father, I'd only met Dell once or twice as a small boy. The Lyon twins were Pittsburgh girls from Shadyside, but until Jim and Jan married at Shields Presbyterian in 1939 neither had any connection to Sewickley. As much as I'd seen Jan around *Sucasa*, I'd never seen Dell there. I'd just turned twenty-two that Christmas, an age of male fearlessness, a good age for soldiers. Dell was eighteen years older than I, in the prime of womanhood, petite, brunette and sexy. She was staying for the holidays with Jim and Jan, while the rest of us put up on the other side of the estate with Granny at *Sucasa*.

Jim and Jan gave a Christmas party, and Dell and I, the only unattached out-of-towners, did some dancing and drinking and ended up in a window alcove behind the Christmas tree, schmoozing and watching the yard outside fill up with beautiful new snow. Given the situation, the rest was inevitable. Despite the family connection, we weren't blood related, had had a few drinks, were physically attracted and as for the age thing, it didn't enter my mind and probably not Dell's either. We were just a guy and a girl making out at Christmas under the mistletoe, as discreetly as possible. I was a soldier with a few days leave left before shipping out to God knows where, and Dell was doing what any red-blooded, female American patriot would do.

At some point Mother had spotted us, for the morning of my departure for California, she confronted me at *Sucasa*. Both of us hung-over and sleeping in (I in Grandpa's bedroom; she in her childhood bedroom across the hall) we ended up, strictly by chance, *a due* at the breakfast table, or not entirely *a due*, for we had Bobby and Dicky for company—though, not knowing the life spans of canaries, I'm not sure they were the original birds.

We exchanged good mornings. I spotted the *Post-Gazette* propped on the brass newsstand by Grandpa's place, which now was mine, and ageless Edith popped in to take our orders. Outside, the great lawns were blanketed in pristine snow, and the evergreens groaned under the weight of fresh powder. I took it all in, for in a few hours I'd be back under the palms. Mother was unusually quiet, waiting for the moment. After Edith delivered our breakfasts and the door to the pantry swung closed, she let loose the throat-clearing that meant something big was coming.

She'd seen Dell and me at the party.

"She's Jan's age, you know."

I looked up from the newspaper. "They're identical twins."

She missed the sarcasm. "What did you have in mind?"

I could have laughed, but Mother never made me laugh, which is too bad. If I could have laughed at her everything would have been different, and a question like that was definitely funny. There was a long silence as I considered my options, as I always did with her, trying to remember if we'd ever had breakfast alone before at *Sucasa*. I was sure it had never happened. We were too careful.

"What do you mean?" I asked.

"You embarrassed everybody."

"What do you mean?" I repeated.

"Jan must be mortified."

"*What do you mean?*"

At this point in my life I still knew nothing of the cowboy, of her elopement with Dad or with her summer trysting in Sewickley with old boyfriends. I knew nothing, and she knew I knew nothing or she wouldn't have dared bring up a few innocent Christmas smooches with the sister of her sister-in-law.

"Dell and Jan have no secrets from each other," she said. "Dell will have told her everything."

"There's nothing to tell."

She looked very smug. "It's a good thing you're leaving. What would your grandmother say?"

"Say about what? That I kissed Dell?"

"She's my age," she said. "What could you have been thinking?"

It was my turn to be snotty. "She's not your age. She's ten years younger."

"Eight years."

It was a weird scene. For years, Mother had pried—or tried to pry—into my romantic life, yet here she was denouncing me for the most innocent of brief encounters. Dell's family connection was part of it, but it was really the age thing. I suspect Mother was annoyed that Dell appealed to someone her son's age while she was married to turn-of-the-century Burnie Adams—a gentleman yes, but also flabby, boring and bald.

For Mother, there was no such thing as innocent relationships. It was either hot sex or nothing. Tenderness, affection, hugs, hand-holding, emotional rather than physical needs, all that was alien stuff in her universe. Dell and I would never see each other again, though we did exchange a few letters, ones that went beyond her patriotic duty. She eventually married an older man and settled down in East Liberty. Jan never said a thing to me about it. I suspect it rather pleased her.

§

Bunny Warren was an attractive, working woman with a grown son and a wide circle of Manhattan Beach friends, and despite their matching red hair it was only a matter of time before she tired of Dad's ways. He'd become pretty much of a slob, able to pull himself together from time to time if forced into some kind of appearance but spending most of his time at the tracks and the bars. Bunny was through with him, he shrugged it off over a few drinks as he shrugged everything off, sold his Manhattan Beach house and moved on. Having lost the income from Mother's trust funds, his only steady revenue was from Millie Oliver's wedding present, enough to keep his gambling and drinking going. He doubled his money on his little red house, selling it for $12,000, but had he held onto it longer he could have had $50,000. Today all those beach-front lots are worth millions. Dad was afflicted all his life by bad timing, fatal flaw for a gambler.

He moved into various hotels and apartments, going from Hermosa, to La Cienega, to downtown, to Hollywood and finally back to Manhattan Beach, not far from where his house had been. I saw most of his rooms over the years, including his last one, which was in Pittsburgh, and they got progressively worse. When I got out of the Army in October, 1960, I met him at Pancho's in Manhattan Beach—where he'd first run into Bunny back in better times—to watch the first of the Kennedy-Nixon debates. He'd moved to a room in Manhattan Beach to be near Carol and her second husband, who were trying to get rid of him. Carol's kids called him "Grandpa who drinks gin." His room was squalid.

One thing about Dad: He was always at home on a barstool, and I'd seen him on a few over the years. As a young man, I used to join him here and there around Los Angeles, often at a piano bar for there was some good talent around in those days—guys like Jess Stacy, Bobby Troup, Matt Dennis, Pete Jolly, Page Cavanaugh—and between sets we'd talk politics, horses, money, the usual things. He'd often arrive with a few drinks in him already, but for a couple of hours would be good company. If we had dinner, he'd want to go on drinking afterward, which is when I left. Thinking back on it, I wish I'd looked out for him more, but it would have been hard. He was a difficult man to get close to, and not the sort to admit any need for help.

When his Manhattan Beach landlord eventually evicted him, Carol tried to get him to move back to Pittsburgh, but he brushed her off. He hadn't set foot in Pittsburgh in a quarter century and hadn't talked to his parents in almost as long. I didn't yet understand his estrangement from his own family—his parents, brother and sister-in-law and niece. Just as he needed a job but would never admit it, he needed a family but would never admit it. When things went wrong for him, shame took over, and the social drinking that started during Prohibition became a necessary habit, cutting him off from everyone. When Carol finally got him on a train for Pittsburgh he got off in Las Vegas and after gambling for a few days was back on her doorstep. By that time I had my first newspaper job in San Francisco and didn't see him at all.

Peripeteia

Deaths, Sucasa *faces its future, travels abroad and a last tango at Allegheny.*

Nollie, me, and mother at the Rindge Avenue pink house, 1967.

After three newspaper jobs in the States, I moved to Berlin in early 1964. A few months before his murder, President Kennedy had made his *Ich bin ein Berliner* speech, and that's where I wanted to be. I had two friends in Berlin, an American I'd met in San Francisco where I worked on *The Examiner* and a German I'd met in Hawaii where I worked on *The Honolulu Advertiser*. Ignorant of foreign countries, peoples and cultures, it was time to educate myself. Though his accomplishments were meager because he had so little time, Kennedy had inspired us all. I flew to Europe to learn something about the world and didn't come home again to live for fifteen years.

I found a dumpy room on Niebuhrstrasse, off the Kurfürstendamm, where the iron grinding of the elevated Strassenbahn grated constantly in my ears, and the landlady had a strong, un-Germanlike aversion to cleaning up. I enrolled in the Goethe Institut in the Grünewald and set out to learn the language. Within a few months I found homier surroundings with a room in Frau Emmy Lohmann's apartment at 11 Xantenerstrasse. One evening, after I'd been a Berliner for about six months, she came knocking on my door with news of an *Anruf aus den Vereinigten Staten*. The only phone was in her room, and I took the call sitting on her bed.

I rarely went into Frau Lohmann's room, which was smaller than mine for she lived off the rent—130 marks a month ($32.50)—that roomers like me paid, plus her small pension. Most evenings we spent in my room sitting near the huge ceramic *Heizung* that gave off warmth from bricks of coal she placed inside each icy Berlin morning. When that wasn't enough, she brought in a bottle of Weinbrandt to warm us inside out. We'd sit together at my table and she would tell stories, just like Granny. When it was warmer, we'd sit on my sunny little balcony overlooking the street.

She'd had a life, this woman, as any Berlinerin who'd outlived four husbands—"a Hungarian, a good German, a bad German and a Red"—and survived two wars must have had. She was heavy with fat legs and moved slowly, but with her bright blue eyes, coquettish ways and the kind of rosebud mouth men like, it was easy to see she'd been a belle. I listened to her for the stories and for the language, which I already loved, especially her Berliner accent, easy to understand with its sharp "k" sounds—saying *Ick* instead of *Ich*. Separated by forty years in age, Frau Lohmann and I were friends from the first. She loved racy talk, and I loved to listen. When the East Germans finally opened a crack in the wall to allow the elderly to come west, we traveled to East Berlin together on the Strassenbahn to pick up her ninety-two-year-old mother. Emmy's legs were too heavy to make the climb down and back up the stairs at Bahnhof Friedrichstrasse, so I brought up Mutti by myself. She'd been born in 1872, the same year as Granny. Bismarck was chancellor at the time.

I took the phone from Emmy's bedside table and heard Jim Crittenden on the other end. He didn't beat around the bush: Dad had taken a fall outside the Pittsburgh rooming house where he lived. He was dead. His body was in the morgue.

"Do you want an autopsy?" Jim asked in his matter-of-fact medical way.

Stunned, I didn't say much during that conversation. Jim didn't know how the accident had happened, whether Dad had fallen on the steps outside the house or fallen off the curb and been hit by a car. His body was found crumpled on the sidewalk with head injuries. His mother was notified and called Jim, who worked nearby at the University of Pittsburgh Medical Center. Jim had not seen Dad since the trip we'd all taken together to Rosarito Beach, in 1947, seventeen years earlier, when I was ten.

I knew that rooming house. On my way to Berlin I'd stayed a few wintery days with Jim and Jan on the estate and called Granny Goldsborough to ask about Dad, who'd returned to Pittsburgh some months earlier. Carol had put him back on the train in Los Angeles, only this time put him on our old friend the Super Chief, not the Desert Wind that went through Las Vegas. His only chance for escape was Albuquerque—my favorite station—and in those days the tribes didn't have casinos. I can only imagine the mental state he was in to return to Pittsburgh, a city he'd not set foot in for thirty years. It was the penultimate defeat in a lifetime of defeats.

"You don't want to see your father," Granny had said on the phone.

"I think I should."

Grandpa Goldsborough had died a few years earlier but Granny, the last of my grandparents, was still living in the same Hampton Hall apartments on Dithridge Street, next to the University of Pittsburgh campus, where they'd lived all my life. Dad's room was on Craig Street, one street down. I hadn't seen him since the night at Pancho's in Manhattan Beach when we'd watched the Kennedy-Nixon debate four years earlier. I told Granny I was leaving for Europe and had no idea when I'd be back. I had to see him, I said.

"No, Jimmy," said Granny, never one to mince words. "I've seen him only once since he came back. That was enough."

Her voice was matter-of-fact, no remorse, no chagrin, no tears, just stolid Welsh pragmatism. Her son lived around the corner and she never saw him. That's how it was.

Why had he returned? Why be a drunk in the neighborhood where you grew up rather than out in sunny California where, drunk or not, you can scrape up enough *sous* to pay your way into the track and get a few wagers down? It would be the ultimate torture to find yourself staggering around the same streets where as a boy you'd been full of the promise of youth—Pittsburgh's next Andrew Carnegie, Thomas Mellon or Henry Oliver setting out to make his fortune. He would have passed ghosts on every corner. And if he'd somehow been drawn back to Pittsburgh because of his mother, for I could think of no other reason, why hadn't he cleaned himself up?

Despite Granny's advice, I went anyway, stopping first by Dithridge Street to see her. The Hampton Hall is unchanged, the same majestic old graystone rising behind sculpted hedges and long green, regal awning it had been when I was a boy. I used to set up a little stand and do magic tricks for the residents as they came in from walks on summer evenings. Nothing has changed about Hampton Hall or will anytime soon. Like so many WPA buildings built during the Depression, Hampton Hall has been designated an historic site, an immutable monument to Pittsburgh permanence.

She'd made tea, and I sat on the daybed in the living room where I'd slept as a boy. Elsie was her name, Elsie Cadwallader, and it was from her that most of our Welsh blood came. She was a handsome woman and stayed that way until the end, cheerful and direct, sprucing herself up for weekly bus rides down Fifth Avenue to meet the ladies for lunch at the Duquesne Club. We hugged and sat down to talk about Dad, but she couldn't do it. She tried, but she couldn't. She was wiping him from her memory as a means of survival. A mother's chagrin. They never talked. What she had to say went back to the period before disintegration.

"Sewickley," she said, "it ruined him."

"But he never set foot in Sewickley," I said.

"He felt he could use it, you know."

He had been wrong about that.

I walked up to Fifth Avenue and stood on the corner between Saint Paul's Cathedral and the old Webster Hall Hotel, where Grandpa sent me for newspapers. It was a blustery February afternoon with clumps of dirty snow frozen on the sidewalk and the few people out and about bundled up and moving fast. Around the corner on Craig Street I found Dad's rooming house, a half block down from the cathedral. It was run down, but no worse than some of the places he'd had in Los Angeles, just older. I walked up the half dozen steps to the porch and pushed open the front door. Inside a radiator was cracking. A hallway ran down one side, and in front of me were stairs leading to the second floor. Dad's room was number twelve, which was upstairs.

It was at the end of a dingy corridor, and as I walked along creaky floorboards covered by a threadbare strip of carpet, I felt jumpy. I had no idea what I'd find and how either of us would take it. I'd seen my father in bad shape many times, but never truly down and out. Bad as each day might be, he'd been resilient, and the next day, like the next race, might be the one to get well again. This looked like the last race, and after coming this close I wasn't sure I wanted to go on. Stopping outside number twelve, I heard a door open down the hall, but when I turned, no one was there. I knocked, and the sound pounded through the building. I knocked again, softer this time, and still no answer. I turned around where I'd heard the door open, and saw it quickly close.

I opened an unlocked door and knew immediately it was his room. I knew his smell. The window was closed with shade down and radiator on, and the room reeked of dirty sheets and booze, the sweet-acrid odor I remembered from other rooms in other places. The bed was unmade and there were *Saturday Evening Posts* strewn about the floor. I let up the shade and looked out on a fenced-in backyard of dirty snow and trash. Beyond that was Hampton Hall, where Granny sat alone nursing the last of her tea.

Was it only fifteen years since I'd dashed down the sand paths with Queenie in Playa del Rey to pick up the latest *Post* for him? He'd give me a quarter for one of those giant Hershey bars with nuts, and we'd all feast on it. He could still do two dozen leg lifts on the backyard fence and ride the breakers for an hour. In that short time, I had graduated from college, served in the Army, started law school in Berkeley, worked on three newspapers and was on my way to Europe. In that time, my father, still a young man by any chronological reckoning, had destroyed himself with booze. He was committing suicide. Women use anorexia, men prefer booze.

Thank God he wasn't there. Granny was right. Obliteration was the only way. Standing there, unable to move, my mind reeled from scene to scene like a drowning man—driving to the bootlegger's in Wichita; waiting outside the Ocean Park movie theater; riding to the E. F. Hutton office on Wilshire, top down, Queenie howling madly in the ocean breezes; driving with him to Las Vegas in my first car, the beat-up green Ford I got when I turned sixteen. I stood there alone in that dumpy room, frozen in time, the time it takes to drown. What if he'd come down the hall, staggering, reeking, unshaven? Would he even recognize me? I went out, shut the door and leaned against the wall to compose myself.

The phone line crackled. "Do you want an autopsy?" Jim repeated.

I had no idea. "What do you think?"

Sensing bad news, Frau Lohmann handed me a snifter of Weinbrandt.

"I saw him," Jim said. "He had damage to the head. . . maybe hit-and-run."

"So why do an autopsy?"

"I believe in autopsies," he said. "You might learn something. He was fifty-five. You're the eldest son. . . heart disease, for example."

"I doubt my heart's anything like his," I said. "Physically, I mean."

"Right," said Jim.

§

With a cold wind blowing out of Poland and snow flurries falling on the city, I bundled up, caught the Strassenbahn at Charlottenburg station and headed for East Berlin. It was the day after Jim's call, Frau Lohmann was out, I'd slept badly, skipped my classes and needed to be alone with my thoughts. East Berlin was good for things like that.

The Strassenbahn passed through Zoo Station and clunked along on the high tracks over the River Spree, past the ruined Reichstag, over the Berlin wall where you could almost reach down and touch the broken glass cemented on top to rip the hands and legs of any Ostie intrepid enough to try it, finally pulling into Friedrichstrasse, where all foreigners exited.

A frequent crosser, I knew the drill well. The Grepos would study my passport as though it were some undecipherable scroll, make me show how much money I had, eventually clear me without bothering to hide their contempt for both me and the passport and I would be free to roam the barren streets of the German Communist capital. I hurried out of the stuffy station into the wintry blasts outside, heading for the river.

Rivers calm me, all of them—Ohio, Spree, Hudson, East, Thames, Seine. When I've lived near rivers, that's where you could find me. Arriving on the banks of the Spree, with only a few desolate souls and their dogs for company, I felt alone, depressed and guilty, so far from home, wherever home was. The timelessness of the German river, unchanged in millennia, seeped into me, calmed me as I walked, its permanence offering perspective. I tried to focus on my father's wasted life, so pointless, so totally insignificant. Not just insignificant in terms of achievement—how many people achieve something special? But insignificant even in terms of effort.

"*Wer immer strebend, sich bemüht,*" God says to the devil in *Faust*, "*den können wir erlösen.*"

In short, it's the striving that counts, not the achieving. Dad measured everything in money, but money without striving is meaningless. It seems so simple.

"I did strive, damn you," he would have said. "I only threw in the towel at the end. Before that I had more ideas in a week than you'll have in a lifetime."

That's how he saw things. Maybe he was right.

His life was so different from Mother's, yet similar. Like so many in Sewickley, Mother, born into wealth and luxury, believed it her natural right to spend and live as she wanted; to squander her life away frivolously. Wealth, family and opportunity conferred only privileges, no responsibilities beyond keeping up appearances. Some people are born rich and some poor; some to make money and some to spend it. You play with the hand you're dealt. Why agonize?

Desolate, needing human contact, I nodded to an amiable-looking gent in captain's hat and slicker out in the snow walking a frisky dog. "*Tag*," he said. He knew I was foreign, though how he knew I couldn't tell, for I was dressed like him. My face, I suppose. I look American. I nodded back, complimented his ugly dog, wondered briefly if he wanted to chat, but dog was in a hurry. Anyway, how I would explain Mother's philosophy of wealth in the German Communist capital?

With Dad it was different. He came from a comfortable home, nothing more, bourgeois, they'd call it here. He went to Exeter, the best of the boys' schools and might have finished Princeton if the Depression hadn't come along. It was only after he married into Oliver money that things started to come apart. He saw his newfound wealth not as a right—how could he?—not even as an opportunity. It was a windfall. It was as though he'd won the lottery, and all he had to do was figure out how to spend it.

He used his newfound wealth not to strive, but to avoid striving, not to work but to avoid work. As much as he took himself to be a bold investor and entrepreneur, he proved cautious and unsure at key moments of his life. The failure was fundamental. He missed the boat, he told me, and there's only one boat. He was wrong about that, but he believed it, and the idea wrecked him.

I began to understand why his relations with Grandpa collapsed. In a way, they had both started from similar situations, each marrying a wealthy Oliver woman. Grandpa took control of his wife's money, invested it, built a house, raised a family, increased the fortune, continued the tradition. Dad blamed Grandpa for not giving him control of Mother's inheritance, but what did Dad ever do to win Grandpa's trust and confidence? I can only guess what happened in the beginning for I wasn't there, but I was there at the end, at the collapse of Ramsa, and I saw what happened. Grandpa was ready to help, and Dad drove him away. In the end, he drove all of us away, even his own mother.

I walked the canals near Marx-Engels Platz, watching the bargemen work their boats, reminding me of my walks with Grandpa to Dashields locks. How strange to have these thoughts about the destructiveness of inherited wealth deep inside East Berlin, where there was no such thing as inherited wealth. Each society has its flaws and corrects them or pays the price. Even cut off behind the Berlin Wall, where private property did not exist, I was dragged back to Sewickley to reflect on the damage done by too much private property. Nearly two centuries after Major Daniel Leet was hunkered down in the snow at Valley Forge, I was standing in the snow flurries of East Berlin thinking about my father's wasted life. That, too, goes back to Sewickley. How would his life have been different without the windfall, had he been forced to work, to strive, like most of us?

As God tells the devil in *Faust*:

> *Solang' er auf der Erde lebt,*
> *Es irrt der Mensch, solang' er strebt.*

Which, less poetically, can be summed up as: We all screw up, but some screw-ups are worse than others.

§

I didn't make it to the Allegheny Country Club for my wedding, which took place at the Église de la Trinité in Paris, but did get there eventually with my wife. My initiation to the club came on New Year's Eve, 1973, which was also my wife's birthday. Nollie, short for Marie-Noëlle, was a young French woman I'd met my first year working for the *New York Herald Tribune* in Paris, where I'd gone after Berlin. In '73, we were living in New York with our two young children while I spent a year at the Council on Foreign Relations. The four of us were invited to Jim Crittenden's for the Christmas holidays, and Mother, a widow since Burnie Adams' stroke in '68, was flying in from Los Angeles. I drove to the Pittsburgh airport, an easy trip across the Sewickley Bridge into the hills above the Ohio, to pick her up. It was good to be back in Sewickley, where we hadn't been together in fourteen years—since that other Christmas when she'd caught me with Jan's twin. *Sucasa* had been sold by this time, and the estate was beginning to be carved up.

There was to be a New Year's Eve ball at the Allegheny Country Club. Jan made the reservations, cleverly omitting the fact that I would be escorting Mother and Nollie alone while she and Jim spent a comfy New Year's Eve over pasta and beer with friends in Leetsdale. I didn't mind. I'd heard about parties at the country club but never been to one. Unlike with most young women, Mother was always on good behavior around Nollie, not taking the usual liberties. Being French, Nollie was a bit too exotic for Mother to confront naked in the hallway or offer instructions on the use of diaphragms at lunchtime. Raised in the strictest of Parisian Catholic bourgeois households, she would have thought her mad.

Mother was excited. It wasn't just anticipation of dancing, showing off the latest Arthur Murray moves to Sewickley's uninitiated, but some of these people she wouldn't have seen in a quarter or even half a century. They would have known her parents, known about the cowboy and some would be lovers and cousins. I would know few of these people and Nollie none, but for Mother it was different. It was a homecoming, and she was giddy.

I have a love-hate affair with country clubs. The love is the easy part. They are as stuffy as I am. Places like the Allegheny were built for America's best and brightest and brought to our shores the best English tradition of clubby gentility. To hobnob at country clubs is to know you are superior. Even boorish, type-A personalities learn the code of civilized behavior practiced inside the walls. To play golf at a place like Allegheny, especially when your great grandfather was a charter member, is a refined experience, free of the grubby insolence of public courses.

The hate part is more sinister: These places make me feel guilty. The façades are splendid, but I know what lies underneath. I know that if I knew any of these people better, really knew them outside the constraints of their codes of conduct, I wouldn't like them and they wouldn't like me. For years, these clubs were bastions of Republican WASPism, sexism and racism, and many have been slow to change. I suspect Grandpa, a Democrat surrounded by Republicans, felt the same way, which is why he seldom went to the Allegheny. He'd been there, of course, not just for Carol's wedding reception, but for his own, a half-century earlier. But he didn't hang out there. Maybe he once played golf there, for he had clubs in his den closet, but I never saw him at the Allegheny.

Lester Lanin was made for all-nighters. The quick two-step is designed to get the pores going, forcing alcohol out of the system almost as fast as the bartenders pour it in. As I stepped from the car after a snowy ride up to Sewickley Heights, I heard the strains of *Night and Day* and watched as a valet helped the women up the front steps. Mother and Nollie floated down the hall corridor together, and the music carried us into the handsome living room, where we checked coats by a tall Christmas tree and made our way through a sea of people toward the dining room and bandstand.

Mother, Nollie, Alex and Kelly at Rees Street, 1972

It took time to wade through the crowd, Mother pausing to introduce us to friends and cousins amidst a din of music and chattering voices. I saw many Sewickley eyes glued to Nollie's clingy Pucci gown, a gift from Mother who'd bought it for a dance contest and decided she didn't dare. We eventually reached our table, fortunately far enough from the bandstand so we could hear each other.

"Get me a martini, will you?"

"I thought I'd get Champagne."

"Champagne for you, Jimmy. I want a martini."

"You had one at Jim's. You'll never make it to midnight with martinis."

"Oh, get off it. Get me a drink. Nollie and I want to talk."

I pushed across the dining room toward the veranda, where several bars had been set up. In summer the veranda is a terrace opening onto lawn tennis courts. The snow on the lighted lawns outside glistened under the tall firs. Only a horse and sleigh were missing, though club stables were just down the path. The horses were smart to stay home on a night like this. 'Whose woods these are I think I know.' Stuffily, I wondered how dangerous it would be driving home full of Champagne down icy roads. It's easy to get lost on the Heights and end up in a black wilderness where the woodsmen haven't changed since Iroquois days. *Deliverance* country, my daughter Kelly calls it. A few miles away live mountain people who've never heard of Lester Lanin or the two-step or even the Allegheny Country Club.

I entered a bar line and surveyed the room, brightly lit and festive with balloons and crepe. Bubbling talk from thirty tables competed with a Latin medley from the bandstand. The women, all ages and dressed in a multitude of fashions and colors, were in contrast to the men, mostly middle-aged to elderly, whose variety of appearance ranged from white dinner jacket to black, with an occasional daring cummerbund.

A woman approached as I waited.

"Hello Jimmy," she said, smiling, holding out her hand. "I knew your father."

I snapped to attention. I'd never heard that phrase in Sewickley before. My father was a stranger in Sewickley.

"How is he?" she asked.

She was elegant, *très comme il faut*, about Mother's age. I noticed a single strand of pearls and pearl earrings barely hidden by bouffant gray hair. Trim and athletic in a mint green chiffon gown, she belonged at the Allegheny. I could see her on the golf course and tennis courts outside, or bounding along the woodsy paths on a dappled mare. She'd known Dad? Didn't she know he'd died? But how would she know? Should I tell her? I wasn't going to depress her on New Year's Eve.

"How do you know me?" I asked.

"Well, certainly not from Red," she laughed. "You don't look at all like him. I saw Coco."

Gray-green eyes, she'd have been a society knockout. Who was she? What could she tell me?

"You know Mother?"

"Mmmm. . . not really," she said.

I was sizing this up. "Dad's not here," I said rather pointlessly. "I don't think he likes Sewickley."

She laughed. "He never did. He always wanted to leave Pittsburgh. We met in Shadyside after he came back from Princeton. He was a sport." She paused. "He's all right?"

"Uh. . . actually, I haven't seen him in a while."

"Oh. . ." She decided not to pursue that. "Your wife is lovely."

"Thank you." That sounded dumb. "Would you like to come over?"

"Oh, no, no. Heavens no. I'm here with my family." She pointed across the room to a large and boisterous table. "But I couldn't resist. I came here once to a dance with Red ages ago. I thought you might like to know." She smiled. "It wasn't New Year's but except for all the years it's the same." She laughed. "I think Lester Lanin played that night too, if that's possible."

"What did you say your name was?"

Actually, she hadn't said.

"My name's Catherine, but it doesn't matter. . . your father wouldn't remember me. Probably better off that he left. Judging from you, I'm sure he did well for himself. Happy New Year, Jimmy."

As quickly as she'd come up, she was gone. Maybe I could look her up later. I got the martini, ordered the Champagne and went over to the window where I could look out at the snow and get a grip. Then I returned to the table, where Mother tossed it down and instructed Nollie to order another when the Champagne came.

"Let's dance," she said. "You're going to be busy tonight."

I danced a medley with Mother, mentioning Catherine, but she was too busy complaining about my dance steps to pay attention. I danced with Nollie, and when we returned to the table Mother was gone.

Nollie and I had our own language games. We spoke French and English interchangeably and went off into German and Spanish for fun and to keep our conversations private. When we played Scrabble together, we allowed words in all our languages, even Italian.

"You know," she said, "I think you're wrong about Coco."

"What's she been telling you?"

"It's what I've been observing. You're all so critical of her and maybe you're all wrong."

"What's she been whispering in your ear?"

"No, no, listen to me. You all think she was irresponsible and blame her for this and that, but look at you children, the three of you, Carol, Billy and you. You're perfectly happy, normal people. Do you know that? Do you know how rare that is in one family—that all the children are perfectly happy, normal people? Don't you think she deserves some credit?"

Nollie was radiant that night, more beautiful than ever.

"I've told you. We reacted to her and to Dad. We saw what they were and did the opposite. Being a lousy mother motivated us."

"*Voila`*. You see, I'm right. You owe it all to her. *Si elle était une sainte, vous seriez tous des diables*. Look at it this way: She left you alone. She left you alone to become whatever you wanted."

I looked closely at Nollie in the low-cut gown that was attracting too much attention at staid old Allegheny. Exactly one year later, we would be divorcing in Paris as the seven-year old contradictions of an age-old culture clash overcame both of us. The coming year would be dreadful, but this was the end of a very good year. I checked my watch. Nollie would turn thirty in a little over two hours.

"You know, I met a woman at the bar who knew my father. Early 1930s it would have been. She said he was a sport. Now agree with me that something ruined his life."

She shook her head. "That's Coco's fault, too? There's no predestination, you know. People become what they want. Coco became what she wanted, and you don't like that. But give her credit for leaving you alone to become what you wanted."

How could Nollie, with her loving, doting parents, possibly understand? She liked Mother, unusual for a woman, and I'd already decided I liked that. And maybe she was right. Brought up in an attentive, controlled household, she envied the freedom we'd had in Playa del Rey—just as I envied the structure given her by her very loving parents. Children are always wishing they had different parents. What parents manage to get everything exactly right?

After midnight and final dances, we drove back down from the Heights, listening to the musical crunch of chains on fresh snow, peering into the darkness spookily illuminated by headlights and wondering if the car would slide off at the next turn, disappearing into the woods below. Jim and Jan were still up with their friends when we got home, drinking Champagne and waiting for us. It was a grand night, one that kept going until we tottered off to bed at three, and Nollie and I made love. It was the greatest of all New Years' Eves. For Mother and me, it was the culmination of our lives in Sewickley. Jim and Jan were already thinking of moving to California to be close to Jamie and the granddaughters.

Mother would never return to Sewickley, and I would return only years later when I decided to confront the ghosts that had been chasing me for so long.

§

Sometime around that Christmas of 1973—maybe a little earlier, maybe a little later—a strange thing started to happen. Or maybe it's not so strange: Mother and son began to grow closer.

As a widow, Mother had come to visit us in Paris several times, putting up at the elegant Bristol Hotel on the Faubourg Saint-Honoré, but stopping by to visit each day, taking the children out alone on afternoons when Nollie and I had work to do. She couldn't have been more correct, more grandmotherly, so different from how she'd been as a mother when she couldn't wait to be rid of us. The children loved her company.

Divorced, I brought the children to live in New York in 1979 when I joined the Carnegie Endowment, and she came back each Christmas, settling in at the old Gotham Hotel on Fifth and 55th and spending her days along Fifth Avenue. She'd loved New York from her days at Spence—loved it especially at Christmas with the snow, the hotels, the bustle, shopping for clothes at Saks and toys at FAO Schwarz. My office was in Rockefeller Center, and she'd come by to watch the ice skating and then come up to the 54th floor to meet me for lunch. One day she reported chatting on the way up with David Rockefeller, whose office was one floor up from mine. They'd been alone in the roomy express elevator, she'd remarked that he looked familiar and he introduced himself. They were in his house, so to speak. She'd always talked to strangers easily.

Her arrival was always a good excuse for festivities, and one year I co-hosted a Christmas party with a friend at her place on Central Park West. Many luminaries were there, friends of mine and of my friend, who worked in finance. At one point I spotted Mother and McGeorge Bundy, my friend's uncle, standing alone together, talking, laughing, tossing down martinis that I, as bartender, was mixing. I was fascinated. Mac Bundy talking to Mother. People stopped by to chat with them and drifted away, but Mother and Mac stayed glued to each other. Even Mary, Mac's wife, didn't interrupt.

Mother and Mac Bundy. . . ?

Kelly and and McGeorge Bundy during our visit to the Bundy house, Manchester, Massachusetts, 1980.

What could the New England Brahmin and the Playa del Rey ballroom dancer possibly have in common, the former national security advisor and the ex-Sewickley socialite? What were they having such a good time about? What were they talking about—Arthur Murray dance steps? How to make a good martini? Missile throw weights? I'd had some chats with Mac Bundy over the years, but never as much fun as Mother was having with him. And never had I had such a conversation with Mother.

They came back for refills and, ignoring me, went back to their tête-a-tête. I can still see them, Mac in rimless glasses swallowed up under those high cheekbones and Mother in a long purple dress and fur collar looking very high Episcopalian as she charmed one more man in her life. Did she even know who he was? But she wouldn't care. Mac was just one more man paying her court.

The next summer, visiting the Bundys with my children at their home in Manchester, Massachusetts, I found myself alone with Mac one morning in the kitchen. I meant, of course, to ask him about his Christmas party conversation with Mother. I'd asked Mother about it, but she didn't remember a thing. So there we were, Mac and I, munching bread and sipping coffee across the Bundy family kitchen, everything primed for an answer to the question that had been tantalizing me.

I never said a word about it. We got onto Vietnam and never got off.

LOOKING FOR LOST TIME

A return to Sewickley and Shields shows that some things are immutable; others however, are unrecognizable.

Sewickley Village, 1952. Courtesy Sewickley Valley Historical Society.

Three decades after the 1973 trip to the Pittsburgh airport to pick up Mother for the Christmas holidays, it's past midnight and I'm in a rental car picked up at what is now Pittsburgh International Airport and heading for Sewickley and the Edgeworth Club. At least I thought I was heading for the Edgeworth Club. Pittsburgh's airport not only has a new name but is in a new place, near enough to the old one that I thought I knew the way, but it's clear I'm hopelessly lost. The sleepy rental car agent carefully marked on a map the highway to take, the turn at a place called Moon Township, and it was to be straight down the hill to the Ohio River, the Sewickley Bridge and the Edgeworth Club, where I'd booked a room for the week. I only-half paid attention to him, nodding impatiently as he marked the route in red ink. It was nearly midnight, a late and dark weekday night in a somnolent airport, and of course I knew the way.

I never saw Moon and took off on a wild ride on freeways with no exits because there are no towns to exit to. Nothing in California or Europe compares to being lost in the wilds of Western Pennsylvania, unchanged since Indian days. Take a wrong turn and you won't get off at the next cloverleaf and turn around. There are no clover leafs. There were no cars, no lights, no signs, no people, no exits, only dark woods on both sides as I plunged deeper into the night going, I was certain, the wrong way.

Angry, I still could laugh, breaking the eerie silence. What a fitting way to return to Shields, searching for the past and lost an hour after I arrive. It should be a lesson. Seeking to unlock memories buried deep in the hippocampus, undecipherable flickers of light popping into my brain like a broken newsreel, I am lost in an unfathomable sea of dark forests. Major Daniel Leet trod these paths during his surveying, but what am I doing two centuries later lost in Indian country with only beams from the car to navigate by? A road sign said Carnegie. Up ahead Mount Oliver. The names were familiar but not the places.

The USAir flight, delayed in San Diego, had arrived in Pittsburgh at 11:30 p.m. With only a carry-on bag, I figured to be at the Edgeworth Club for a late snack and a long drink by midnight, only 9 p.m. California time. The Pirates were playing in Los Angeles so I would have television entertainment until bedtime. Now it was 12:30, I had missed someplace called Moon and was nearing someplace called Carnegie. This was an interstate highway, why were there no other cars? I pulled to the shoulder to examine the rental agency map again. Alone in this dark place, the lights of my car shone out into the blackness like from a lone ship lost in the vasty seas. Carnegie was nearly in Pittsburgh. I was heading upriver when I wanted to go down.

I got off at Carnegie, but found no town and no people. It was closing on 1 a.m. If I turned around, according to the map, I could find Interstate 79, but, retracing my steps, I missed the dark turnoff and had to drive across the center divider, where my car, some kind of red Jeep, got stuck. I had visions of spending the night lost on a center divider somewhere deep in Western Pennsylvania forests, the howls of wolves in my ears, but the car spun free, and I was heading back to 79. A sign said Erie to the north, Canonsburg to the south, two places I didn't know. Remembering that Sewickley was north of Pittsburgh—the Ohio River, oddly, flowing north at its inception—Erie seemed the better option. By 1:30 I was standing under the red brick porte cochère of the Edgeworth Club, ringing for the night porter.

B. G. Shields, former editor of the *Sewickley Herald*, curator of the Sewickley Valley Historical Society and a Shields and cousin by marriage, met me for lunch at the club the next day with Jay Brooks, another Shields and owner of *Newington*, the first Shields house, built in 1821. Thus began my week of investigation, retracing steps I'd first taken in these parts fifty years earlier. Awakening at 9 o'clock, I'd gone down to the club pool, long blue slit etched in the green of these former Iroquois woods, pausing a moment at the table where Jane Shape watched me dive while tending Jamie in his pram. It couldn't have been the same table, but was in the same place. The gray flagstone terrace overlooking the pool area was unchanged, and except for the missing high board, the pool was the same, its long lanes shimmering in the morning sunlight. Everything came rushing back.

"Insurance," said one of girls vacuuming the pool when I asked about the removal of the high board, and I remembered the stories of Carol's now-divorced first husband, Sam Adams, and his buddies coming drunk out of the club bar to practice high dives late at night. That's when they weren't jumping off the Sewickley Bridge, which killed one of them and caused Sam's friends to serve jail time for negligence. How many drinks would it take to jump off the Sewickley Bridge? Maybe one of them had missed the pool off the high dive as well. I told the girl I was taking my first Edgeworth Club swim in fifty years, observed the puzzled look of a sixteen-year-old contemplating a fifty-year gap between laps, did a half mile to drown out the jet-lag, showered and climbed into the Jeep to drive to *Sucasa*, or what was left of it.

I was exhilarated, as I always was on these leafy streets home to so many memories, but also anxious, for this was the first time no one would be waiting; the first time I would be a stranger in the place I had the presumption to feel I knew better than anyone except maybe Major Daniel Leet himself.

Before Shields, I had to see Sewickley. I headed up Beaver Road, parked the car in front of the Penguin Book Store with its familiar black-and-white sign, and poked into a few shops. Isely's Ice Cream, Knapp's Drugs, Hegner's Hardware, Thomas Jewelry, Murphy's five and dime, Carroll's Music, the shops of my youth, were gone, replaced by new ones, but the buildings were the same. The facade of the Sewickley Theater, where I'd seen *National Velvet* and *The Wizard of Oz*, looked the same, but the theater itself had been turned into a kind of indoor *souk*, which I avoided. I introduced myself to the owner of the Penguin, Margaret Marshall, former photographer on B. G. Shields' *Sewickley Herald*, informing her I'd hung out there as a ten-year old. Around the corner on Broad Street, the barber shop was still operating, and I stopped in to greet a pleasant gent who'd been there a mere twenty-five years and so couldn't have remembered my last haircut there, on the way to Europe in '64.

Back in the car, I headed up Broad, the same street Leet Oliver and Will Crittenden took to chug their way up Blackburn to the Allegheny Country Club in Leet's new 1905 Cadillac. The Sewickley Valley Memorial Hospital, where Jim Crittenden practiced, now stands at the foot of Blackburn. I took Centennial back to Academy Avenue, named for the dreaded Sewickley Academy, and continued to Woodland Road, passing Chestnut, the road that brought us home from the country club that snowy New Year's Eve filled with too much gin and Champagne. Except for houses here and there where vacant lots had been, nothing along Woodland Road had changed.

For a Californian, the immutability of Sewickley Valley is astonishing. I still remembered the houses along Woodland by the families that had lived in them—Semple, Oliver, Brooks, Foster, Doyle, Shields, cousins everywhere. At the end of Woodland, just before it turns sharp right at the lily pond to go down to Little Sewickley Creek, stand the brown

B.G. Shields, 2001.

stone pillars that mark the beginning of the Oliver estate, though who would know that now? In its day, the estate stretched high into the hills beyond the farm to Backbone Road, near the Allegheny Country Club, miles away. Outside the pillars, on the hills where the cows pastured, a house stands where Grandpa and I had picked our way through cow pies to the farm. But there is only one house; in California, there would be ten. Across the way, where the Shields homestead stood for a century and a half, looms a half-finished giant monstrosity. I look once and quickly look away

Creeping past the pillars, I edge the Jeep up to where the path to the lily pond splits off from the road. Leaving the car to inspect, I find the path obliterated. To descend, I'd have to cut through the poison ivy, risking spending the rest of my week bathed in calamine lotion at the Edgeworth Club. I stare down through the trees toward the ruins of the footbridge over the creek, but can see no further. What's left of the pagoda, I wonder? What's left of the lily ponds themselves, created by the great Olmsteds?

Back in the car, farther on, I pass the carriage house where Leet had briefly kept his new Cadillac and where I'd learned to play craps with the men who worked the estate. The carriage house has become a ranch-style home with a pool. Ranch-style in Shields? Did they know the history of this place? Should I knock and tell them? On the right, Jim's old house, where I'd smooched with Dell and stayed with Mother, Nollie and the kids on my last Christmas here, stands weather-beaten but unbowed.

Then it gets bad. Down the road, where the Oliver and Shields houses and the Japanese playhouse stood, I catch another view of the monstrosity. The new property owner—a dot-com millionaire, I learn—knocked everything down in preparation for his house, which has all the architectural charm of a hospital building. I sense generations of Shields turning over in the mausoleum. Money still won't buy taste. Cruising past Jim's, I receive another shock: Next to *Sucasa's* former red-brick, slate-roofed garage, over which Stewart and Douglas, the chauffeurs, lived, stands a new house, crammed into space where only trees and chicken and duck pens had been before. It occupies the exact spot where Mother and I stood in the only picture of us alone together, me at attention, she at ease. The new house doesn't belong, but I decide not to knock and express my outrage. The owners probably like their house.

I glance down the long gravel driveway toward the former *Sucasa*, and memories come flooding back. I know every bush, every tree, every path, every stone in this place. The round rock by the little grassy mound where I would sit to watch goings-on at the garage still occupies its space. Houses and habitants come and go; nature is immutable. I cast my eyes into the distance toward the cinnamon fern whose delicate frond graces the first page of the *Sucasa* album. I can't quite see. It must still be there. Ferns are immutable, indestructible. Slowly my gaze turns to the house, or what's left of it. I already know what happened to *Sucasa*, but only now does the full impact hit me.

Following Granny's death in 1959, *Sucasa* stood unoccupied for a time. Mother and Carol returned from California and along with Aunt Jan went through the house picking out things they wanted. I was in the Army, and Burnie Adams, my step-father, wrote me that "your mother (red), sister (green) and aunt (blue) went around with rolls of colored stickers and tagged about half the stuff. Following this a lot of relatives and close friends were invited in and sold leftovers at appraised prices plus thirty-three to fifty percent. We are getting the complete dining room set and a lot of tables etc. Also silver, linens, some books, a lot of

Thomas Leet Shields homestead, 1854-2002.

fine China and countless odd items. I don't know where the hell we are going to put the stuff when it gets here."

I'd read Burnie's letter from the top bunk of a Fort Sill barracks, staring at the ceiling's drab beams and slats and day-dreaming of each room at *Sucasa*. It was true; I could remember every room and piece of furniture. Grandpa's den was my favorite: the tufted leather chaise longue where he napped under a wall crammed with Crittenden pictures—mother, father, brothers, cousins. No Olivers or Shields on that wall. Next came three leather chairs facing the fireplace and the Philco floor radio in front of which Granny and I played double solitaire or fish while Grandpa read his newspapers and we listened to the evening programs. The den was where I first took an interest in the news; learned about things from broadcasters like H. V. Kaltenborn, Gabriel Heater, Fulton Lewis Jr., Walter Winchell—radio names that live on.

Over the den mantel hung a large portrait of Grandpa's father, the governor, and, at the room's end, by the window looking out on the fountain and my favorite beech tree, a smaller portrait of his father-in-law, James Oliver, the man whose death made his marriage possible. Next to the Oliver portrait stood Grandpa's desk, its nooks and crannies bulging with papers. On the mantel under the governor's portrait stood my favorite object of all: a cast-iron sculpture of a hunter pointing his rifle at a tree stump about eight inches away. Grandpa would cock the spring of the rifle, lay a penny on its flat top and shoot it into a hole in the log. I lay on my Fort Sill bunk and wondered whether a red, green or blue tag got the hunter.

How many things I might have saved! I'd have put my tag on just about everything in the den, plus the rattan furniture in my bedroom, the velvet rocker in the drawing room (my legs could finally reach the ground), the carving table and portrait of Henry Crittenden with the curls in the dining room. I'd have gotten the brass cages from the breakfast room to become homes for new canaries named Bobby and Dicky, the Chinese gong from the hallway to announce dinner and the ancient Shields bed warmer in Granny's bedroom. Years later, thanks to B. G. Shields, I did recover, from an old house in Leetsdale, a touring trunk someone had bought at the final *Sucasa* sale. It bore the initials CCG—initials of both my mother and sister—and now belongs to my daughter. Now she can pass it on.

Sucasa was less than a half century old when Granny died, but like so many of the moguls' mansions built soon after the turn of the century—*Franklin Farm* of B. F. Jones, *Farmhill* of Edith Oliver Rae, *Ridgeview* of Joseph Horne, *As You Like it* of Mrs. William W. Thaw, to name but four—was so big that potential buyers were limited. How many families need thirty-five rooms, a separate maid's floor and a ballroom in the basement? A Catholic order made an offer to turn the house and grounds into a convent, but Jim turned it down.

The next offer came from Oliver Kauffman, the Pittsburgh department store magnate and rival of Joseph Horne. Ollie Kauffman was the younger brother of Edgar Kauffman, for whom Frank Lloyd Wright had built his most famous house, Fallingwater, at Bear Run outside Pittsburgh. Jim assumed Ollie shared his brother's love of buildings and would preserve the pride and joy of *Sucasa* architect Frederick Russell, but Ollie lacked his brother's taste. *Sucasa* was guillotined, decapitated of its second and third stories, robbed of porticos, pillars, porches, gables, dormers and several of its chimneys. It was transformed into a red brick blockhouse, missing only gun slits. The first time I saw it in 1964 on my way to Berlin, I decided never to look again. But I suppose it can be taken as a tribute that *Sucasa* wasn't razed to the ground, the fate of most of the great mansions.

So now I am back, and this time my intention is to go inside. I shall bear witness. Whatever is left, I think, is worth seeing. Leaving the Jeep thing outside the former garage, I walk down the winding brick path toward the kitchen. The red beech tree, where I perched to keep an unseen eye on the adults as they came out for strolls after lunch, still towers overhead. The fish pond, in the shade of the beech tree directly under my second-floor bedroom window, is gone, as is, of course, my former bedroom. As I approach the house a huge Labrador dog barks and bounds from the back porch. He looks aggressive and obviously is there for a purpose, but suddenly backs off, sensing I have as much right to be there as he. Maybe he detects my scent on the kitchen doorway, through which I passed hundreds of times. Dogs know things like that.

Rather than continue barking or do something worse, dog, curious, circles and decides to shadow me, staying respectfully behind by about ten yards. Peering through the screen door into the kitchen, I detect no sign of life and start walking around the house, trailing my canine shadow. I peek into the breakfast room where Grandpa and I took our eggs together. Dog doesn't approve and starts barking again. I am about to protest when I understand his concern: the breakfast room is now a bedroom. I want to enter immediately, denounce the crimes, but first must make contact with the new owners, who bought it from the Kauffman estate.

I continue down the brick path toward where the Oliver house stood, pass under the trellised grape arbor where early family photos were taken, cross the driveway past the old playhouse site and climb the knoll above which the Shields homestead sat. B.G. Shields lost title to the homestead when her husband—the third or fourth Daniel Leet Shields, one loses count—died in 2001, and the house was sold by Mellon Bank to the dot-com millionaire who tore it down before the preservationists even knew it had been sold. Any California building dating to 1854 would automatically be a historical monument, but in Shields that's apparently not old enough to qualify. Where was the zoning commission; where was the historical society? A few articles B.G. sent me from the *Post-Gazette* lamented the homestead's passing, but by then it was too late for anything but tears.

That evening, in a lingering, sultry, late August heat that soon would bring out the fireflies, I drive to the Sewickley Valley Cemetery. The Crittenden plot is at the cemetery's highest point, a grassy corner under a canopy of trees in the hills overlooking the lush Ohio River Valley below. One's eye follows the Sewickley Bridge across the river, into the woods beyond, where Washington camped on his trip downriver to meet with the tribes. Grandpa, who died in 1955, might have been buried in the Shields mausoleum, but their stillborn baby, the first Caroline, had been buried in the cemetery in 1908, two years before Mother was born, and so Grandpa, eighty-eight, naturally followed her there. Granny, eighty-seven, died at Sewickley Valley hospital July 23, 1959, with Dr. Jim Crittenden in attendance.

Granny and Grandpa were only a few months apart in age at their respective deaths, unusual in our family, in which women tend to outlive men by decades. Two days before Granny died I received in my Fort Sill barracks a box of cookies she'd had baked for me at *Sucasa* by Viola, the cook from Ambridge. What more touching sign of love than to receive cookies from your grandmother ordered from her death bed.

§

How odd that the only child buried with Granny and Grandpa is the one who didn't live. Jim died in Playa del Rey in 1992, and there was an awkward funeral for him at a nearby Westchester church in which he'd never set foot with a pastor who'd never heard of him or of Sewickley. Mother died in 1999 in a nursing home in Palm Desert, still cursing Carol and me for having moved her away from her dance studio. We passed on a church ceremony for her. The many Sunday mornings spent in the little white chapel and Shields Presbyterian listening to the sermons of the Reverend Dr. Browne didn't take for either of the *Sucasa* siblings.

The ashes of both Jim and Mother were interred in Inglewood Cemetery near Los Angeles, which makes sense for Mother who had no love for Sewickley and wanted to be buried next to Burnie Adams, her second or third husband depending on whether the cowboy counts. Carol, Billy and I were at graveside with a handful of grandchildren and in-laws and had our words to say. Carol wrote a limerick that started, "there was an old lady of eighty / who never pondered a subject too weighty." Billy called her a woman who dedicated her life to "fun."

I'd pondered for some time what to say. Her life had been so frivolous, so ordinary given all its advantages. But I couldn't say that.

As for our relationship, it had been brittle for so long—two people separated by a gulf so wide that any attempt to bridge it seemed forced. But I couldn't say that.

Yes, things had improved at the end, but a few holidays in Paris and New York didn't erase a lifetime of unease. But I couldn't say that.

As the eldest son, the chronicler of the family, I could not stay silent while the others spoke, but what was I to say? I could neither speak the truth nor avoid it.

My mistake, I knew, was to have viewed her through my own prism, to have judged her by my own values, distorting the essence of what she was. I was like a bad novelist, one whose characters take on aspects of his own personality, are limited by his own perceptions, fail to take on a life of their own as the best characters must do, improvising in ways their creator never anticipated. To be true to her I had to understand her story, examine her life as she would have done, if she could have done such a thing.

When my turn came I praised her as a woman of her era, an era in which women were judged less by their achievements than by their children. Their children were their achievements. Yes, Mother might have been ahead of her time—some Sewickley women managed that—but she wasn't. Yes, she might have used her advantages to do more than dropping out of schools, eloping twice and becoming an aging ballroom dancer—some in Sewickley achieved more than that—but she didn't. Too much money had a lot to do with it.

But if there was failure, it was failure in my terms, not hers. It wasn't in her to make more of her life any more than it was in Dad. I wish it had been, but it wasn't. It's hard to reproach people for something they just didn't have. If I examined her life through her eyes, I saw that the only thing she expected of herself, the only thing really expected of girls of her era, was to raise a family. And that she had done... and done it by overcoming a hefty obstacle: Dad. She overcame it and left behind a good family, three children, all thriving. Maybe it was accident; maybe not.

It was, I suppose, more eulogy to us than to her, but I think she would have liked it. I think she would have liked all the family eulogies. There were no others. No one from Arthur Murray, the "only family she had," showed up for the funeral.

§

The next day B. G. Shields took me to *Newington*, where Jay Brooks, descendent of David Shields, has restored the house built by Eliza and husband David in 1823. Jay, who keeps the keys both to Shields Presbyterian and Shields Mausoleum, across the way from *Newington*, shows me the church restoration under way, thanks to the Episcopalians. Shields Presbyterian has become Shields Episcopalian, and I can feel Eliza protesting from her residence next door. Why Episcopalians now outnumber Presbyterians in these lands settled by Scotch-Irish immigrants fleeing Anglican persecution is something not even B. G. Shields can answer. I wonder if Dr. Browne, whose plaque hangs in the church to remind me of our teas together, could answer it. But who cares today whether bishops or elders are in charge, whether the church features a pulpit or an altar? Eliza and Granny might care, and Eliza would hate the organ, but those battles belong to other times. The mausoleum, if not the church, is unchanged from the day Granny took me through it, telling me its stones were as solid as those of our family.

The next day we go to Ridge Avenue, where the moguls lived before moving to Sewickley, giving Ridge its reputation as "Pittsburgh's Park Avenue." I close my eyes to imagine the avenue a century earlier, its great houses marching up the hill from the grassy park at the bottom, ladies strolling under parasols to protect them from soot, not the invisible sun; carriages rolling by. Both the James B. and Henry Oliver houses are gone, but the Benjamin Jones house, now a college, still stands. The Thaws had a house on Lincoln Avenue, not far away, and I see Granny and Harry Thaw, the murderer who weaseled out of jail, strolling under the shade trees.

The James B. Oliver address, 701 Ridge, where Granny was reared, where Grandpa settled when returned from Mexico and where Mother and Uncle Jim were born, is now a commercial building. I come across the following paragraphs about Ridge Avenue in an 1888 book about Pittsburgh women, *The Social Mirror*, (newly published thanks to the Sewickley Valley Historical Society), in a chapter entitled, "Women of Wealth:"

> *The Oliver mansion is beautifully situated on the hill side of Ridge Avenue, and is handsomely fitted up. Their horses and turnouts are stylish and well kept. Mrs. Oliver is quite fond of society and entertains frequently and handsomely.*

Each paragraph in this strange little book, authored by Adelaide M. Nevin, concerns a different woman of the era. Miss Nevin was society editor of the *Pittsburgh Leader* at the turn of the century (her cousin,

Newington, 2006.

the composer Ethelbert Nevin, *Sucasa*'s Beaver Road neighbor, wrote the lullaby *Mighty Lak a Rose* that later became a Dixieland classic). The following entries give the tone of Miss Nevin's book. After "Oliver" comes "Painter":

> *Mrs. Park Painter, nee Guthrie, of Ridge Avenue, is the wife of another millionaire, having besides a very comfortable little fortune in her own name.*

Then "Park":

> *Mrs. W. G. Park of Ridge Avenue, has a charming house, fine clothes, stylish equipages and entertains and goes into society all the time. Mrs. Park, as Miss Betty Sweitzer, was one of the most beautiful girls in Allegheny. Mr. Park's share of his father's estate will exceed half a million.*

Then "Patrick":

> *Mrs. Wallace W. Patrick, the accomplished wife of the banker, has a beautiful home, charmingly fitted up, on Ridge Avenue.*

She is an ideal hostess and entertains frequently. Mrs. Patrick is tall and elegant looking, with white hair and a good deal of color. Her husband is worth at least half a million. Her daughter, Miss Margaret Patrick, makes her debut in society this season.

It is an extraordinary tome, totally politically incorrect by today's standards with references to women's plumpness, garrulousness and attractiveness in "the Hebrew style." It has an obscene obsession with wealth ("It is quietly whispered among their friends that Judge and Mrs. Mellon, of Negley Avenue, are not worth more than six or eight millions."). It is, however, a faithful glimpse of 1888 Pittsburgh bluenose society.

Mother was born a generation after Miss Nevin's Ridge Avenue ladies, at a time when more opportunities were open to women, but she was as much a product of that environment as they. If she managed to move from elegant Ridge Avenue and stately Shields to the bohemian climes of Playa del Rey; if she was able to exchange the ballroom at *Sucasa* for a dance studio on Wilshire; if she managed to take the girl out of Ridge Avenue and out of Shields, she never quite managed to take Ridge Avenue and Shields—and the Pittsburgh money that went with them—out of the girl.

§

After Ridge Avenue, B. G. points her car up the Allegheny River past the old Heinz ketchup works ("red ripe tomatoes, distilled vinegar, corn syrup, salt, spices, onion powder") toward the immense Allegheny Cemetery. A funeral cortege arrives at the same time we do, and the archivist is busy with it, but an attendant offers a map that he says will help if the graves we seek belong to "famous people," those whose tombs are marked by name on the map.

We soon find the name we're looking for—Oliver—dead center, section twenty, up the path from Thaw, Jones and Mellon, Pittsburgh's great industrialists, center stage, neighbors to the end. Beside the James B. Oliver sarcophagus, across from the granite obelisk of Henry Oliver, sits the tomb of David Leet Oliver, Granny's little brother, whose death changed so many lives. Without the nail that flatted his tire and turned his car, I would not be standing in that spot. Next to Leet lies his mother, Amelia Neville Shields Oliver, "Millie," who by uniting Leets and Shields with Olivers in 1870, changed the history of the Sewickley Valley. The lairds of land united to the titans of industry. Millie's largesse helped

Former Sucasa, 2006.

Dad avoid the decisions that might have made his life a success. As I stand pondering these baroque monuments, I think of Dad, wondering where he is buried, perhaps somewhere in this very cemetery, in an unmarked common grave, a fitting end to a wasted life. I should have asked Uncle Jim about that, but now he's gone, too.

The next day it's time to search for Mother's contemporaries. Is anyone left? Becky (Oliver) Doyle, who was with her when she was expelled from Westover and who married the land-holding California Hollisters, had died a few years before in Santa Barbara, but I find her sister, Nancy Doyle Chalfant, in the house in Sewickley Heights where she has lived since the war.

"Coco was wild," says Nancy, ninety, called Nanky, three years younger than Mother and Becky. "She climbed out of windows at night." There is no disapproval in her voice. Nanky would have loved to "escape" Sewickley as Mother had done, but events thwarted her. "Sewickley was so snobbish, so confined," she says. In a monograph for her daughter, Verlinda, a retarded child who died young, she writes of "a useless round of parties, singing lessons, volunteer work, bridge, golf. After graduating, I wanted to go to college. My parents looked into the idea but decided against it for fear that girls were allowed too much freedom at college."

"Too much freedom at college"—the phrase sticks in my mind. Might Caroline Crittenden, like Nanky Doyle, have considered college? Rosie Richardson, Mother's best friend, would know, but to my great disappointment, I learn that Rosie has just died. Later I walk up to the Richardson house, in the Edgeworth hills above Chestnut Road. Same house, but nobody knows what I'm talking about. Still, my question answers itself: Mother was expelled from Westover, never finished Spence, never showed the slightest inclination for reading or learning of any kind. In my life I never saw her with a book, never saw a book in her house. Granny and Grandpa could not possibly have objected. College is better than cowboys. Forget it, Mother would have said.

There remains one task before leaving Sewickley:

What Oliver Kauffman did to *Sucasa* is an atrocity. It's too bad Jim didn't sell to the Catholic convent after Granny died for they would have kept the house and lands intact. Whatever sectarian battles Catholics and Protestants may still be waging in Northern Ireland, they're long behind us in America. The Presbyterian Shields, Olivers and Crittendens would have accepted a Catholic convent on their lands for the sake of keeping them intact. And *Sucasa* would have been saved: Convents need rooms and space. The nuns would give me a tour of the house and grounds. We would sit and have tea and I would tell them secrets only I know. They would blush but be avid for more.

The new owners, Peter and Suzanne Friday, whom I have phoned, greet me in a friendly way, knowing I can tell them more than they can tell me. I am the first one to visit them who knows the history of their house. Unlike Ollie Kauffman, whose architectural surgery nearly killed the patient, they've sought, as much as possible, to bring the house back to life. They've restored the drawing room and Grandpa's den to something resembling the original states, preserved most of the kitchen, made the basement ballroom functional again—not for balls but for offices—even added a second story over the kitchen wing for their children, where the nursery had been. I creep up the stairs. Their children now sleep where Mother and Jim slept as infants nearly a century before, and Carol, Billy and I as babies a generation later. I peek in the room. The beds are unmade. Where are Mabel and Rose, the upstairs maids? Why isn't Jane Shape here, rocking baby Jamie in his crib?

Above all, the new owners have kept what remains of the land intact, refusing to subdivide the great lawn leading toward Beaver Road into a separate plot. If Grandpa were still here, he'd grab his cane and we'd be off down the driveway to Beaver Road, up Church Lane, past church, mausoleum and the parsonage, all the way to the river, just like before, with tea awaiting us on the way back. The owners escort me courteously through their house, probing me every step of the way. I promise to send them pictures of the house as it was, for they have no idea of its history or its original structure.

Is that the smell of Grandpa's cigars I detect in the den? Is it possible? The green shutters to the windows are unchanged, still opened and shut from inside with hand cranks, a chore I did as a boy. In the drawing room I pause to recreate the Venetian sofa where Granny sat as she poured tea afternoons at four. I loved taking tea with her, sometimes just the two of us, little old lady and little boy, milk or lemon? The thin tapestry that adorned the wall above the sofa reappears, and there is Granny reaching for the secret buzzer to summon Edith with more tea sandwiches, chicken salad and cream cheese, cut into tiny squares, crusts surgically removed. There is Mother, motionless on the sofa, telling me about divorcing Dad as I rock in the velvet rocker, my legs finally reaching the floor.

The house is changed but the real *Sucasa* will never change. Not for me. Reality exists in the mind only, said Plato. The second story is still there, I can feel it above me—Jimmy's room in rattan, the grandfather clock ticking on the landing and Granny fusting about with her bibelots on the sun porch. Across the hall, Grandpa is coming out of the den to select a cane for our walk to the river or perhaps the lily pond, and down the hallway in the breakfast room I hear Bobby and Dicky chirping away. I smell the shepherd's pie Viola is preparing in the kitchen from yesterday's roast, and see Edith setting the table for lunch. Jane Shape is still nineteen—finally I am old enough for her.

I know all the rooms in this house by heart, even the closets. What does it matter if they are physically gone? I can see them. I can smell them: the upstairs linen closet of lavender and rose; the downstairs ladies' powder room of lilac; grandpa's den of leather. This was my first house. No one forgets his first house, not one like this.

Beyond the windows, the great lawn stretches to the woods leading down the hill toward the river. Shields Church prepares to abandon its

Sucasa with Granny, Mother and Jim, circa 1915.

Presbyterian past and be consecrated Episcopalian. I feel the ghosts of the family. I can't tell this to *Sucasa*'s new owners, who would think me mad, but I feel the family everywhere. Out the window, a chipmunk scoots across the grass heading for the sycamores. As a boy I tried to catch one like it for a pet. Put salt on its tail, said Granny. Perhaps this chipmunk is a descendant of that one. A great, great, great. . . but wait, I don't know how long chipmunks live. I must look it up. Beyond the grass are the trees, beyond the trees the river, beyond the river the woods. Granny and Grandpa, who told me the stories, now live up on the hill.

I must write it all down before I forget.

Photo by Sam Hodgson.

James Oliver Goldsborough is an award-winning journalist who has written on national and foreign affairs for four decades from the United States and Europe, where he reported for the *New York Herald Tribune, International Herald Tribune, Toronto Star* and *Newsweek* magazine. He is a former Edward R. Murrow Fellow at the Council on Foreign Relations and senior associate at the Carnegie Endowment. His previous book, *Rebel Europe: Living with a Changing Continent*, was praised by Charles Champlin of *The Los Angeles Times* as "the most important book I have read in years."

Goldsborough has been a reporter, editor and columnist for the *San Francisco Examiner, Honolulu Advertiser, Arizona Republic, San Jose Mercury-News* and *San Diego Union Tribune.* He is a contributor to the *New York Times Magazine, Fortune, Foreign Affairs, Foreign Policy*, the *Readers' Digest* and *Politique Étrangere.* A graduate of UCLA, he attended UC Berkeley Law School and later served in the U.S. Army, attached to Special Services. He currently writes for the on-line newspaper *Voice of San Diego.* He resides in San Diego.

I N D E X

The author's immediate family members (Amelia Oliver and William Jackson Crittenden; Caroline Jackson Crittenden Goldsborough Adams, William W. "Red" Goldsborough, Jr., and siblings Caroline "Carol" Goldsborough Adams MacGregor and William W. "Billy" Goldsborough III) are deeply imbedded throughout the story and are therefore not indexed separately except where they appear in images and on the family genealogy on pages 4-5. The extended family home in the Sewickley Valley, *Sucasa*, is treated likewise. Page references in italic indicate images.

CHECK YOUR LOCAL BOOKSELLER FOR COPIES OF

Misfortunes of Wealth
by *JAMES OLIVER GOLDSBOROUGH*

ISBN 978-0-9770429-9-9

from THE LOCAL HISTORY COMPANY
Publishers of History and Heritage

www.TheLocalHistoryCompany.com
sales@TheLocalHistoryCompany.com

If your local bookseller is not able to provide you a copy of this title,
visit our website above, or contact us at:

The Local History Company
112 NORTH Woodland Road
Pittsburgh, PA 15232-2849

Or—Call 412-362-2294
Fax 412-362-8192

QUANTITY ORDERS INVITED

This and other titles from The Local History Company *are available at special quantity discounts for bulk purchases or sales promotions, premiums, fund raising, or educational use by corporations, institutions, and other organizations. Special imprints, messages, and excerpts can also be produced to meet your specific needs. For details, please write to us at the address above, or telephone 412-362-2294.*